AIR ACCIDENT INVESTIGATION

NEW EDITION

DAVID OWEN

Patrick Stephens Limited
AN IMPRINT OF HAYNES PUBLISHING

First published in 1998

This new edition first published in 2001

British Library Cataloguing in Publication Data
A catalogue record for this book is available from the British Library

ISBN 1 85260 607 X

Patrick Stephens Limited is an imprint of
Haynes Publishing, Sparkford,
Nr Yeovil, Somerset, BA22 7JJ

Tel: 01963 440635   Fax: 01963 440001
Int. Tel: +44 1963 440635   Fax: +44 1963 440001

E-mail: sales@haynes-manuals.co.uk
Web site: http://www.haynes.com

Typeset by J.H. Haynes & Co. Ltd.
Printed and bound in Great Britain by
J.H. Haynes & Co. Ltd, Sparkford.

Contents

Introduction

Why yet another book on the safety of flying in today's airliners? Flying safety – particularly airline flying safety – is one of those subjects which has produced a seemingly endless supply of books over several decades. The factors which stimulate this apparently unceasing interest are complex, and I can only speak for my own reasons in writing this particular book. Statisticians tell us that flying is one of the safest modes of travel we have, and that by far the riskiest part of any flight is the drive to and from the airport. Nevertheless, we remain all too aware of the terrible consequences of any major breakdown of the aircraft itself, or of the control system designed to manage countless conflicting aircraft movements in close proximity to one another.

Three reasons probably account for this perception that flying is inherently dangerous, compared with say driving down a busy motorway. One is the contrast between the cosy normality within the passenger cabin, with meals and drinks and duty-free bargains and in-flight movies, and what we can see on the other side of a thin transparent window-pane. Out there the atmosphere is too thin to support life, the temperature is way below freezing, the airstream is moving past at hundreds of miles per hour and the hard and unforgiving earth lies miles below.

Secondly, we know that so long as the system works properly, we will reach our destination with nothing worse than a degree of travel sickness, a slight hangover or a frustrating delay. But if something goes wrong seriously enough to bring that aircraft down, or break it up in mid-air, we know the consequences are almost certain to be terrible and final. The newspaper photographs of tangles of wreckage, totally unrecognisable as the remains of a sleek and powerful airliner, are all too familiar. That terrible transformation happens in an instant's impact, and the lives of hundreds of people can be terminated in that same agonising moment.

The third reason arises out of the first two. If we are travelling down a motorway, we can see the first signs of fog, or spot traffic building up and slowing down ahead, and take action accordingly. We know that if a major mechanical fault arose in the vehicle in which we are travelling, we can stop on the hard shoulder, and wait for help. Of course we can still fall prey to the unexpected, and people do still die in motorway pile-ups. But the numbers in any incident are still comfortingly small, and we can draw consolation from the fact that in most cases, potential dangers can usually be seen and avoided. The world is still under our control.

Not so with airline travel. Not only are we unaware of most of the potential dangers which could affect our chances of surviving a particular flight, but when we take our seats and wait for take-off, we are all having to put our absolute trust in a wide variety of people to carry out their duties with total professionalism and expertise. Not merely pilots and air traffic controllers, but also maintenance engineers, baggage handlers, people operating the security checks on passengers and baggage, those who designed and built the aircraft, those who regulate the airways and air traffic control systems, those who manufacture the millions of spare parts for the aircraft and its engines, and those who check, inspect and fit those parts – the list is potentially endless.

This is the core of the problem. In flying we have to depend on numberless individuals whom we shall never know and, in most cases, never see. The factors which determine whether ours will be one of the vast majority of flights which are relatively uneventful and totally routine in their outcome, or one of the minuscule minority of catastrophes, we will neither understand nor appreciate. We may not know whether flying is growing safer or more dangerous with every passing year, or whether it is as safe as it can be, or should be. We feel starved of information, which would help us understand the real nature of the challenge we undertake when we arrive to check in for our flight.

Which brings us to the reason for this particular book. The fact that flying is such a statistically safe activity is literally no accident. If there is any compensation for the awful human and material costs of an air crash, it lies in the work of one particular group of people, who investigate and analyse the accidents which *do* occur. If the factors involved in causing a particular accident can be analysed, then the system can be changed to provide defences against those factors, and we are all safer as a result. Changes to aircraft design, to maintenance procedures, to air traffic control routines and to pilot training all help to make future accidents less likely. It is this ultimately inspiring and encouraging story which is the subject of this book.

The accidents reviewed in these pages have all been chosen to show how a hitherto unexpected threat became revealed through a careful and infinitely painstaking process of detection, every bit as remarkable and demanding as anything practised by the likes of Sherlock Holmes. Not only identified, but neutralised through improvements intended to ensure the threat can never cause a repetition of the disaster which first brought it to light.

In reading the story, prospective passengers can take comfort from three more points. The first is that any individual would have to spend several entire lifetimes flying to stand the remotest statistical chance of being involved in a serious accident. The second is that the accidents reviewed in this book represent the tiniest of fractions of the thousands of flights completed successfully every day. The third is that, because of the investigations described in these pages, almost all the accidents described are even less likely ever to occur again. They represent the rungs of a ladder, by which airline flying is climbing nearer to the absolute goal of perfect safety.

David Owen

Acknowledgements

Any book, particularly on a subject as complex as this, must depend on the help of a wide band of specialists, from librarians to picture researchers, and it's impossible to name them all, since many gave their help anonymously. Instead, I'd like to thank all those who came to the aid of the project at the Chester, Liverpool and Manchester Reference Libraries, and at the picture library desks of Associated Press, Popperfoto, Wide World Photos and the Adrian Meredith Library.

However, some individuals gave so freely of their time and expertise that the only repayment I can make is to thank them here. Frank Taylor of the Department of Air Transport at Cranfield University, the faculty which trains the air accident investigators of tomorrow, gave invaluable help on the areas which the book should examine and advice on sources of information and illustrations. Dick Skinner of DRA Farnborough was especially helpful in tracing early investigation material relating to the original Comet crashes and the more recent Lockerbie investigation. Ted Lopatkiewicz of the National Transportation Safety Board in Washington DC, also gave vital help in tracking down information on several US aircraft accidents and T. A. B. Horvath of ICAO in Montreal allowed the reproduction of specialist photographic material.

Finally, Squadron Leader Frank Lovejoy, officer commanding the NDT Squadron at RAF St Athan, supplied essential information on state-of-the-art fatigue and corrosion detection capabilities for the final chapter of the book. To them, and to all who helped in so many different ways, my sincere thanks and my equally sincere apologies for any errors they may spot in the finished work, which are entirely my responsibility.

1

In the beginning

A Boeing 747 taking off.

Even the most blasé and experienced airline passenger would admit, when pressed, that there is something not quite natural about flying. On the tarmac, a modern airliner like a Boeing 747 or an Airbus looks as big, as heavy and as immobile as a block of flats. Even when the engines are running, and the ponderous beast charges down the runway to attain flying speed, the idea that the curved wing section causes the air above it to speed up relative to the air below it, generating a partial vacuum above the wing's upper surface, seems little more than a scientific curiosity. Certainly, any force this deliberate imbalance might create seems scarcely capable of lifting almost 400 tons of aircraft with all its fuel, cargo and occupants into the air, and keeping them there while it crosses half the world.

The technology that makes this possible is awesome in its complexity. Exotic alloys and composite materials provide a lot of strength for very little weight, and it is just as well they do. A present-day airliner spends more hours in the air in a single year than its pre-war predecessor covered in a working lifetime, and over a far wider range of operating conditions. On each and every flight it has to be pressurised to enable its crew and passengers to survive in the thin air of the stratosphere, miles above the earth. Every square metre of the fuselage skin carries a load of more than six tonnes when the aircraft reaches its cruising altitude. On every sector of every flight that load is imposed, maintained for several hours at a stretch and then relaxed.

If that were not enough on its own, the temperature changes impose a different kind of load on the aircraft structure. A hot day at a tropical airport can warm the aircraft to a temperature of more than 50 degrees Celsius, but within less than an hour that same plane can be chilled to 75 degrees Celsius below freezing as it reaches the top of its climb. So engineers have to design every component to very careful and precise limits, without the comfort of the safety margin common in almost every other vehicle.

The uncomfortable truth is that every scrap of unnecessary weight uses up more fuel and increases operating costs. Yet one microgramme of additional strength could make the difference between flying in perfect safety, and a catastrophic failure. No wonder that pilots say the three most useless things in the world are the part of the runway behind you, the atmosphere above you, and the fuel left in the refuelling truck. A fourth could be added – the weight saved by paring the strength of the aircraft a whisker too far.

To cope with these demanding requirements, production methods have become highly sophisticated. The majority of the loads imposed on an aeroplane are carried by the skin, and the tiniest variations in skin thickness can result in huge changes in strength and weight. Wing skin panels are placed in baths of acid, and eaten away to a controlled thickness in a process called chemical milling, more accurate and consistent than traditional methods of physically paring away unnecessary layers of metal. The result is a precisely shaped panel with a tapering thickness and localised strengthening which contributes to the overall toughness and flexibility of the wing: tough enough to carry the loads, and flexible enough to cope with the shocks of turbulence in flight.

The engines too have a demanding job to do. Each one compresses the air entering at the front of the engine nacelle, then heats it by passing it through a spray of burning fuel to increase the pressure still further, then directs it out at the rear in a white-hot stream of propulsive gas to push the aircraft along. Simple in principle and reliable in practice, this nevertheless involves complex assemblies of turbine blades spinning at hundreds of revolutions per second. Because of the stresses they undergo, which impose loads several thousand times that of gravity, these small components have to go through as many as 50 different production processes in their manufacture.

With this powerful combination of high speeds, high stresses, high temperatures and highly inflammable fuel close to a highly pressurised cabin, flying may seem even more unnatural and potentially dangerous an activity than before. Yet so careful are the engineers and so clever the technology that it remains by

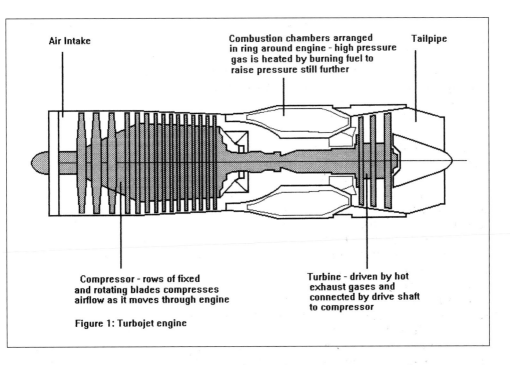

Air Intake

Combustion chambers arranged in ring around engine - high pressure gas is heated by burning fuel to raise pressure still further

Tailpipe

Compressor - rows of fixed and rotating blades compresses airflow as it moves through engine

Turbine - driven by hot exhaust gases and connected by drive shaft to compressor

Figure 1: Turbojet engine

far the safest way to cover long distances open to us. In crossing to the other side of the world, the most dangerous part of the trip remains the totally earth-bound drive to and from the airport. Insurance underwriters regard driving a car as being 25 times more likely to end in a fatal accident than flying in an airliner.

The reason for this is that safety is, in every sense, no accident. Because the consequences of aircraft failure are so catastrophic, nothing is left to chance. Modern aircraft have vital systems duplicated and even triplicated wherever possible. Structures are built to ensure that a partial failure still leaves the aircraft with enough integrity to survive, and leave the pilot enough control to bring it back to earth. Navigational systems position the aircraft precisely without the need for radio communications in areas where signals are poor, weather radar warns pilots of thunderstorms or turbulence, air traffic control guides them to their destination and separates them from other en-route traffic, and automatic landing systems can place them at the runway threshold after an approach through darkness, rain, snow or fog.

Yet perfect safety remains an unattainable ideal, and accidents continue to happen. The most careful design can never guarantee that some unpredictable combination of circumstances may not outflank the defences. All that engineers and administrators can do is try to meet two requirements. In the first place, to ensure that accidents occur as rarely as possible, by the application of the utmost human ingenuity and care. Secondly, that when they *do* happen, they are investigated as diligently and effectively as possible. The causal factors must be found, so that that particular window of misfortune can be firmly closed for the future, by revising the engineering, the operating methods, the back-up systems or the training of those involved.

Back in the first dawn of passenger flying, safety seemed a much simpler objective. At the end of the First World War, a huge surplus of wartime aircraft offered a new way for the adventurous and the well-off to travel in search of business, pleasure and escape. Conditions were spartan in the extreme. When the first international service began between Hounslow and Paris in July 1919, the flight took 2¾ hours and the converted de Havilland D.H.9 light bomber had space for just one passenger, sharing the open cockpit with the pilot.

But the pace of development was quickening, with new aircraft offering more space for more passengers, and a modicum of comfort. By the standards of the time, the D.H.16 was positively palatial, with room for four people in a cabin with a sliding roof, which could be closed before take-off to shut out the weather. Even the massive Handley Page 0/400 heavy bomber carried two passengers, swathed in fur-lined coats, helmets and goggles in what had been the open gunner's cockpit in the nose of the plane, in addition to twelve in the main cabin.

Within three years, passengers had the choice of flying 'inside or outside', though usually, the pilots preferred the open cockpits they had grown up with. Navigation was simple, as the planes stayed firmly beneath the cloud-base, and in most cases they merely followed the trunk roads or main-line railways, looking out for landmarks such as lakes or woods to confirm they were on course. When traffic increased, pilots arranged to fly to the left of the road or railway line they were following, so that planes travelling in opposite directions could avoid colliding with one another.

Sometimes flying seemed surprisingly similar to driving in other ways too. If an engine overheated, the pilot would try to put down in a field near to a house, where he could borrow a jug of water to top up the cooling system. Breakdowns were simply dealt with and engine failures meant landing in the nearest large field and trying to undertake repairs. All crews carried chewing gum and insulating tape to plug leaks in oil or coolant pipes. If all else failed, they carried English and French money to transfer passengers to the nearest train.

This was all very well when the weather was good, but there was no reliable forecasting system to warn when it might be bad. To find out what lay ahead, pilots had to take off and look for themselves. Lowering cloud bases and poor visibility turned the excitement of flying into real danger, and it was essential for the captain to put down before his visibility disappeared. In the winter there was icing to worry about, and on the cross-Channel routes to Paris and Brussels, the additional danger that an engine failure meant a ditching in the sea.

In America, passenger flying got off to a slower start for a variety of reasons. Early aircraft had little real speed advantage over the express train on the short journeys their limited range allowed. The real reason for the popularity of the London to Paris service was that it avoided the tedious delays of transferring from train to boat for crossing the Channel and then back to another train on the opposite side. But faced with the long distances and the luxurious trains of North America, passenger flying held few attractions at first. Instead, commercial flying in America began by carrying the US mail, which generated income for the new airlines which they were able to put to developing routes and services for the future.

A Handley Page H.P. 42 biplane airliner being serviced at Imperial Airways' maintenance hangar. Slow, stately and reliable, this was pre-war flying at its most luxurious. (Adrian Meredith Photo Library)

By the early 1930s, Imperial Airways operated a fleet of four-engined Handley Page biplanes, the H.P.42, which carried 38 passengers on the London to Paris service. They were large and slow, cruising at an unambitious 110 mph, but were also comfortable and reliable, and modified 24-seat versions with larger fuel tanks were used on the African and Indian routes. The interior was like a Pullman carriage in the European version, with deep padded armchairs, replaced by wicker seats and rush sunblinds on the tropical aircraft. Passengers enjoyed a hot lunch en route of up to six courses. The journey to India, with overnight stops in hotels, took a full week, but was still considerably faster than the P&O Line.

The H.P.42s had an excellent safety record. In nearly ten years of operation, not one of them suffered a serious or fatal accident. Yet this low-key state of affairs could not last for long. At the time of their introduction, the spectacular increase in passenger flying in America had begun. Slow and noisy aircraft like the Ford Tri-Motor, whose passengers had to wear earplugs to prevent being deafened, and where the vibration shook spectacles off the nose, were replaced by the first of a family of aircraft which would change the face of commercial flying for ever.

The Douglas DC-1 was a twin-engined, all-metal monoplane which could fly twice as fast as the H.P.42. Its production version, the DC-2, was succeeded by the immortal DC-3, known variously as the 'Gooney Bird' and the Dakota. With enough power to fly on one engine, with cabin heating and effective sound proofing, it was a highly attractive proposition, and more than 11,000 were built in a decade, making it perhaps the most successful single airliner design of all time.

Yet safety was becoming an increasing problem. With more and more scheduled services flying over remote areas, the consequences of an engine failure were considerably more serious. The old option of putting down in a handy field was not much use in crossing the Atlantic. Increased distances meant flying higher to ride above bad weather, and that meant having to accept the difficulties and hazards of blind flying. In cold or wet conditions at altitude, icing was a new problem, with layers of ice coating the wings and control surfaces, reducing lift and impairing the pilot's ability to make the aircraft do what was needed.

Some improvements seemed to compound the problem. More instruments gave pilots more information, but increased their workload, so it was easy for the most careful and experienced of aviators to make a mistake under pressure. With the areas around major airports becoming more crowded with increased incoming and outgoing flights, the collision risk became steadily greater, and safety margins grew tighter. The process of analysing accidents and mishaps to see what contributed to their cause was responsible for a whole series of improvements to aircraft design, air traffic control systems, airport layouts and other operational matters. Fortunately, as the numbers of passengers and their journeys climbed to new heights, the accident rate did not keep pace.

As aircraft themselves grew more capable and more sophisticated, so have the techniques for finding why they failed to perform as they should. An engine failure on a Handley Page biplane airliner was a clearly visible problem, and the aircraft flew so slowly that even an emergency crash-landing was survivable, so it was easy to trace what had happened from the statements of witnesses or participants. But where a modern, pressurised jet airliner crashes as a result of encountering a microburst, or suffers catastrophic structural failure several miles above the earth, the resulting heap of scattered wreckage may seem to the layman to defy all analysis or explanation.

Only by the most careful and detailed scrutiny by specialist inspectors, and the most painstaking sifting of evidence can the combination of factors which conspired to overcome the safety systems be traced and identified. Only when such factors have been tracked down can action be taken to ensure they are eliminated in the future. When a classic investigation of a crash involving a military aircraft flown by a skilled test pilot was eventually traced to the presence of a metallic particle approximately the size of a grain of salt in one of the fuel feed valves, the immensity of the inspectors' task can be clearly understood.

What kind of things can an accident investigator learn from a crash site? The first priority is to collect and preserve evidence that may be perishable. This might include signs of icing, either on the wings and control surfaces, or within the engine. It might include taking samples of the fuel, where this has leaked on to the ground, so that fuel contamination can be examined as a possible causal factor. It might even include the settings of instruments, controls and switches, since these might be moved by other investigators at the site.

Reconstructing the aircraft's last moments of flight means deciding on the speed and angle of its impact with the ground. Even where it dives steeply into the ground at high speed, in what is sometimes called a 'smoking hole impact', investigators can still draw some conclusions from the wreckage. Usually this is a tangled mass of metal in a deep crater, with the dirt which originally filled the crater piled up in a rim around it. If the aircraft crashed vertically into the ground, which happens very rarely, the rim of dirt would be the same all the way around the crater. Where that isn't the case, the highest area appears on the side of the crater to show the direction the plane was heading, and often the bulk of the wreckage appears on this side too.

In other cases, the aircraft hits the ground in a shallower, less violent impact. Here the wreckage tends to spread in a fan-shaped pattern radiating from the actual point of impact, with the heaviest items found furthest away. Usually these are the engines, or any major piece of wreckage with one or more engines attached, and these too show the direction in which the plane was travelling when it crashed. In cases where a crosswind was blowing at the time, some of the lighter pieces of wreckage will be affected by the wind, distorting the pattern of the wreckage. The length of the scar made in the

Signs on the ground showing the aircraft's flight path prior to the crash. (Reproduced by permission of ICAO)

Damage to trees showing the aircraft's angle of approach. (Reproduced by permission of ICAO)

ground by the crash can yield useful information on the angle and speed at which the plane crashed. The damage seen on major parts of the wreckage can also reveal the angle of impact, and in terms of the speed, any source of information is useful. In some cases, cine film or videotape shot by eyewitnesses can give very accurate information on the aircraft speed. In others, recordings of the radar traces at air traffic control centres can be used to show the aircraft's course and speed, at least up to the point where its descent took it below radar cover. Finally, the air speed indicator in the cockpit is a geared instrument which may preserve the last reading at the instant of impact.

Usually, investigators draw up a wreckage diagram. This is a plan of the ground, showing the impact point and the aircraft heading, and indicating the position of the main items of wreckage, together with any patches of fuel, or burned areas. An example is shown in Figure 2, though in most cases a grid would have to be used to transfer measured distances on the ground into accurate equivalents on the plan.

Aircraft wreckage surrounded by tall trees, showing the impact occurred with little or no forward velocity. (Reproduced by permission of ICAO)

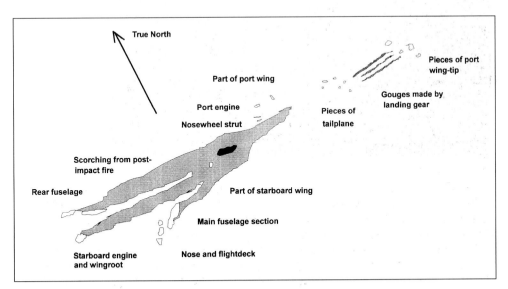

Fig 2 Diagram of a wreckage trail.

Very often, there are signs of fire in the wreckage, and the most difficult question for the investigator to answer is whether fire in the air helped to bring the aircraft down, or whether the fire was caused by fuel being spilled in the impact. Here too, there are tell-tale clues. Fires which start while the aircraft is still airborne and which burn through the aircraft skin, are fanned by the slip-stream, and the soot, scorching and melted metalwork form a pattern along the direction of the airflow across the structure of the aircraft. They also tend to burn at a much higher temperature (1,400°C upwards) than fires which break out on the ground after a crash due to spilled fuel, (800–1,100°C) and this is reflected in the way different materials melt.

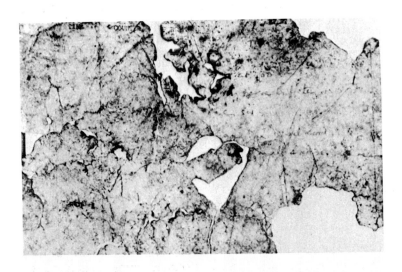

NORMAL PHOTOGRAPH OF SOILED DOCUMENT

INFRA-RED PHOTOGRAPH OF SOILED DOCUMENT

Scorched documents before and after infrared treatment. (Reproduced by permission of ICAO)

If an inflight fire doesn't burn through to the outside airstream, the clues may be more difficult to spot. Any reference to fire on the radio messages between the aircraft and ground control, or any of the crew found wearing smoke hoods, would mean an in-flight fire. Any fragment of wreckage with fire damage on the inside or outside surface is examined very carefully. A badly crumpled section of aircraft skin panelling, for example, will only show fire damage inside the tightest folds if the fire was burning in flight, or after a ground fire intense enough to burn through the crumpled metal.

Parts of the aircraft structure which have broken apart on impact can reveal other clues, if fire damage is present on both parts. If the damage follows the same pattern across the break, but the edges of the break are clean, then the fire was burning before the aircraft crashed. Similarly, any fragments buried in the impact crater which are seen to have fire damage when they are dug out, were burning before the crash. Finally, post-impact fires which melt the metalwork of the aircraft structure always tend to show the metal flowing downwards towards the ground in the position in which the wreckage is lying. In-flight fires show molten metal following the direction of the slipstream.

Similar signs can help identify the work of the terrorist in causing an aircraft crash. Damage caused by a bomb on board is usually omni-directional, spreading outwards in all directions from the location of the explosives. Moreover, the signs of damage show forces acting from the inside of the aircraft towards the outside, as opposed to impact damage which usually acts in the reverse direction, inwards from the outside.

Other signs of bomb damage may be more difficult to spot. One of them may be bending of major aircraft structures like the wing spar or parts of the fuselage framework, in a way which would not be consistent with the shock of the crash. Close to the site of the explosion, metal may be forced to behave abnormally by the force of the detonation. Metal which normally bends under stress may become brittle and snap or shatter into pieces. The metal fragments of the

Elevator control and elongated slot showing the direction of the impact forces.
(Reproduced by permission of ICAO)

bomb casing itself will be driven at high speed into the adjacent parts of the aircraft. Putting these components under a scanning electron microscope will reveal signs of pitting and erosion, and the changes in the grain of the metal where bomb fragments have impacted against it.

Fortunately, terrorist-induced accidents are still relatively rare, even among the small number of serious accidents which *do* occur. Much more common as a causal factor is a break-up of the aircraft's structure, either due to weather loads, abnormal control inputs or fatigue failures of crucial components. The difficulty lies in deciding whether a particular failure happened first, and helped to cause the crash, or whether it was an inherent weakness which failed under the impact shock of the crash itself, which was caused in the first place by other factors.

This is why air crash investigators try to establish the location of all the major parts of the aircraft on the ground. If something caused the aircraft to break up in flight, then major parts of it will probably be found some distance away from the main wreckage. Working with a diagram of the aircraft, they mark on it all the major structural assemblies which make up the complete aircraft, as they trace them among the scattered wreckage. If any large areas are missing, then structural failure at height could be part of the story.

American crash investigators sometimes use the mnemonic TESTED to help ensure no major parts of the aircraft are overlooked. The initial T stands for the tips of the wings and tail. If these are found at the crash site, they are usually fairly easy to identify, and if they *are* present, then the rest of the wings and the tail assembly are likely to be there too. The first letter E stands for the engines, together with the propellers and all their blades, for non-jet aircraft. The letter S stands for primary and secondary control surfaces like rudder, elevators, ailerons, flaps and trim tabs. The second letter T stands for the entire tail assembly, while the second letter E reminds them to check for external devices like landing gear, and wingtip fuel tanks. Finally the letter D stands for doors, which includes hatches, canopies and windscreens.

Where large parts of the aircraft seem to be missing, the evidence points strongly to in-flight break-up. The reasons for that break-up may involve searching for the missing wreckage by back-tracking along the aircraft's ground track to locate them, a task which may involve the most exhaustive and wide-ranging searches. In the case of a DC-10 which was crippled by the break-up of a turbine disc in one of its engines, the crucial engine parts were found in a field some 80 miles back from its crash-landing at Sioux City Airport, a similar distance to the widest spread of wreckage from the Pan American Boeing 747 which exploded over Lockerbie.

Nevertheless, not all failures result in separation of the components involved. Stresses are particularly high in the wings outboard of an engine nacelle, and if a spar gives way the wing can be bent sharply. For the investigator the crucial question is, did this happen in flight and help cause the crash, or was it caused when the aircraft struck the ground? Here, as in many other questions of what happened when (and in what order) the answers may be revealed by the patterns of surface scratches caused when the aircraft hit the ground. If these scars are not continuous around the bend in the wing, the failure probably occurred when the aircraft was in the air.

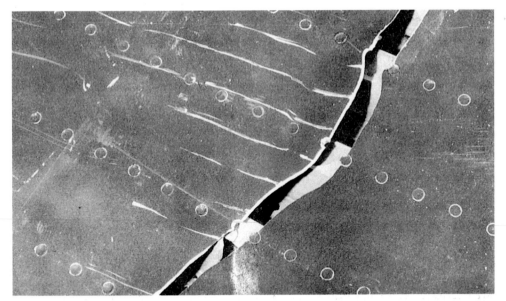

Score marks which do not continue over a fracture in the wreckage, showing the impact which caused the scoring happened after the breakage. (Reproduced by permission of ICAO)

In a crash where the wreckage is badly scattered, inspectors are sometimes able to learn a great deal more about the sequence in which the break-up occurred by putting the pieces together in their proper places so that scratch marks and other signs of impact damage can be compared to adjacent parts of the structure. In some cases, this means laying out the wreckage on the floor of an aircraft hangar, for example, in a two-dimensional reconstruction. This effectively displays the aircraft pieces as a flat plan, as might be obtained if the original fuselage was slit along the centre-line at the top and laid out flat.

In other cases, investigators may build up a wooden frame of the size and shape of the aircraft, which is then covered with a 'skin' of wire netting so that the different pieces of wreckage can each be hung in the appropriate place. Once the whole laborious process of collecting, transporting, identifying and reassembling the wreckage has been completed, the resulting reconstruction can reveal valuable information of how the original structure broke up, or the sequence in which different parts became detached.

The pattern in which the wreckage is scattered can also show at what stage the different pieces became separated from the main structure of the aircraft. As each piece breaks off, it slows down quite quickly and then falls vertically through the air. Unfortunately this means it will be carried on the prevailing wind for a distance governed by the amount of time it takes to fall to the ground. By plotting the whereabouts of each piece on the ground and, using the strength and direction of the wind at the time, investigators can plot their trajectories in reverse to produce a reasonable picture of the break-up sequence.

Some pieces may show paint particles left by other parts striking them. Scratches may be caused by other fragments flying off before impact, and the

Not to scale

RIGHT WING PLANK LAYOUT

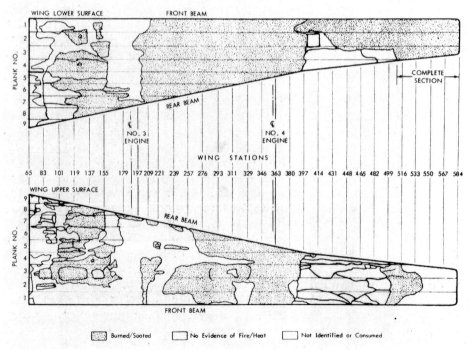

Reconstruction of the wing structure of a crashed aircraft. (Reproduced by permission of ICAO)

Cabin reconstruction. (Reproduced by permission of ICAO)

extent of those scratches helps to show which other parts had or had not become detached before that damage occurred. If skin wrinkles or other features like scratches are continuous across adjacent pieces of wreckage, then the damage which caused those wrinkles or scratches happened before the fragments broke apart. On the other hand, if they are not continuous, then the fragments broke apart first.

Individual panels or pieces of the framework of the aircraft can also reveal the stresses imposed on them before or during the crash itself. If an aircraft flies into severe weather, for example, very fierce gusts of wind or severe updraughts can impose the same kind of positive-g loads as pulling out from a dive too quickly. The wings and tailplane tend to be bent upwards. The upper surfaces of both wing and tailplane will be compressed and will show unmistakable signs of buckling in a series of diamonds between the ribs and stringers which form the internal framework. Other types of stress where the wing or tailplane is twisted can cause buckling on both surfaces, but the direction of the buckles can show which way the structure was twisted.

Engines too can contain valuable clues, and pose important questions. Were they running normally at the time of the crash, or was engine failure a factor in bringing down the aircraft? Propeller driven aircraft show more information from the state of the blades. If they were not turning at the time of the crash, the blades will be bent backwards in the direction of impact. This shows they may have been feathered because of an engine problem encountered earlier, or the engine itself may have seized because of internal damage.

In most other cases, the blades will be bent opposite to the normal direction of rotation of the propeller, with scratches running crosswise on the blade

Propeller with damage showing it had been windmilling at impact. (Reproduced by permission of ICAO)

Propeller with damage showing it had been under power at impact. (Reproduced by permission of ICAO)

surfaces, dents in the leading edge of the blades and other signs of damage. This at least shows the blades were turning, though this may simply mean the propeller was windmilling at reasonably high speed without the engine delivering any power at all. Careful checking of the engine systems may show which is the right answer in an individual case.

Sometimes the scars made by the blades on the ground in the seconds before impact can indicate either the speed of the aircraft at impact if the engine rpm is known, or the rpm of the engine if the aircraft speed is already known. Since many aircraft have constant speed propellers, with the pitch being varied with changes in power settings to keep the engine working at optimum speed, this can reveal useful information.

Jet engine with signs of damage showing it was under power at impact.
(Reproduced by permission of ICAO)

Jet engine with signs of damage showing it was not under power at impact.
(Reproduced by permission of ICAO)

Jet engines show different kinds of signs to those who know what to look for. Because a turbine rotates with much less metal to metal contact than the reciprocating engine, where pistons rub up and down in the cylinders on each and every revolution, its insides are a much cleaner surface on which to read evidence of impact damage or other factors. For example, any foreign body sucked into the engine will show as damage to the first stage compressor blades. Holes in the engine casing may mean engine components flying off at speed. Sharper edges than normal to the compressor blades may mean the rotor shaft has been knocked out of alignment at impact, letting the two sets of blades rub against each other, to create a sharpening action if the engine was turning at the time.

Investigators will also check the cockpit instruments for any signs of what they were reading at the time of the crash. Damaged instruments may have jammed in position with their readings 'frozen'. Sometimes the glass of the instrument shatters and the needle may be lost, but its position can be revealed by the areas of the inner face which are. not damaged by glass fragments. Other instruments like air speed indicators and rate of climb and descent meters are driven by trains of gears which often lock under impact shocks, so their readings are preserved.

Other clues come from the various warning lights in the cockpit display. If a bulb is off, then the filament will be cold, so that it usually breaks under the impact shock. If a bulb is lit, then the hot tungsten filament tends to stretch, which can offer a vital clue if certain warnings were shown to be displayed at the time the aircraft crashed.

In many cases though, a crash may well be due to a whole sequence of events which, when added together, made it impossible for the aircraft to continue flying. One consequence of the efficiency and reliability of modern airliners, particularly those working on short to medium-distance routes, is that they fly a large number of sectors in a very short time. The constantly changing loads of landings and take-offs, climbs and descents, pressurisation and depressurisation, not to mention the more unusual stresses imposed by storms or turbulence, alternately stretch and relax the structure, over and over again. This is the classic recipe for metal fatigue.

Although today's passenger aircraft are constantly checked using sophisticated X-ray and ultrasonic crack detectors, and though designs are drawn up to allow fatigue to be contained wherever possible, at least to the point where it can be seen and rectified, accidents

Aircraft power lead which has been cut by propeller blade. (Reproduced by permission of ICAO)

Warning light bulb from aircraft instrument panel, with stretched filament showing the warning light was illuminated at the moment of impact. (Reproduced by permission of ICAO)

have occurred in the past where the most apparently trivial defect can provide an escape route for fatigue to spread and overcome the whole aircraft.

The weaknesses which can allow this to happen form a long and complex list. The root of the problem is that fatigue can start wherever stresses in a component are more concentrated than they should be. For example, if a hole is drilled in a part during manufacture, and the drill bit is not as sharp as it should be, or the hole is not cleaned out properly after drilling, burrs or notches can be left in the hole which result in stress concentrations. Tool marks left in the surface of components after they have been machined to fit a particular location can also cause stress concentrations as can badly fitting bolts or botched repairs that were meant to stop fatigue cracks which were already detected, from spreading further.

Finally, some accidents – as we shall see – have nothing at all to do with any failure of the aircraft, or any of its operating systems. If the crew make a mistake over their position on a descent to an airport at night or in bad weather, then a perfectly serviceable aircraft can crash by simply flying into high ground. If a highly stressed and inadequately supervised air traffic control system fails to prevent two aircraft on conflicting courses from entering the same area of sky at the same moment, they may collide. In all these cases, investigators will have to look beyond the remains of the aircraft themselves to find the factors which helped to cause the accident.

More and more evidence, in any kind of passenger aircraft accident, is being brought to light through the operation of different types of recorder. The so-called 'black box' flight data recorders (FDRs) are designed to be robust enough to survive crashes, and are actually brightly coloured to make them easier to spot at the crash site. The earliest versions used steel or aluminium tape, with a moving stylus which scratched a trace on the tape surface to record the altitude of the aircraft, the indicated air speed, the compass heading and the rate of climb or descent.

More recently, these analogue FDRs have been replaced by much more sophisticated digital recorders which can collect an almost unlimited amount of information, depending on their design and software. In addition to the basic data preserved on the analogue recorders, they usually log the aircraft's attitude in pitch (nose up or nose down) or roll (banking to the left or right), the power settings on each engine, whether or not flaps were lowered or thrust reversers selected, the hydraulic pressure in the aircraft systems for operating control surfaces or landing gear, the outside air temperature (which is important where icing is suspected as a causal factor) and the position of the controls.

Other information which may be recorded, depending on the version of FDR used, includes the wind speed and direction, the aircraft's position in latitude and longitude, the position of the throttles and the fuel flow, the performance of the navigation aids and whether the landing gear was up or down. Increasingly this information is now capable of being played back through a computer linked to a flight-simulator program so that the aircraft's movements can be re-created using the data recorded in the FDR.

Another invaluable aid to determining the sequence of events through the eyes and ears of the flight-deck crew is provided by the cockpit voice-recorder, or CVR. This information is usually only released to help in the investigation of specific accidents. In the United States, CVR information is held by the National Transportation Safety Board for at least 60 days after an accident, and cannot be used in civil damages cases. The only parts of the transcript of

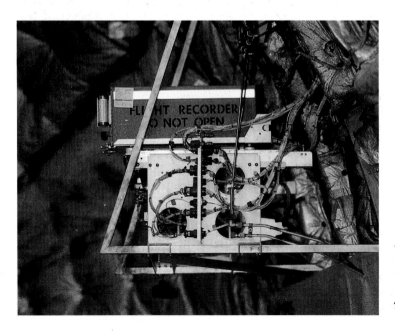

A modern flight data recorder on a Boeing 777 – the investigator's greatest ally. (Mark Wagner)

the recording which are ever made public are those which are relevant to the enquiry. In Britain, the CVR can only be examined under the supervision of the Aircraft Accidents Investigation Branch, and the actual contents are only rarely released to the public.

Nevertheless, the CVR recording does give valuable additional information to the investigators. The flight data recorder may show the crew initiated an unexpected turn on the initial approach to a difficult airfield in bad weather, but only the CVR can provide an explanation, from their conversation, as to *why* they did it. Useful information can also be provided by the background sounds on the recording too. When these are analysed, they can sometimes suggest the detonation of explosives or the operation of a particular control at a specific stage in the flight.

Other recordings which can be used to help to analyse the causes of an accident include the information from digital air traffic control (ATC) radar systems. For example, the Federal Aviation Agency in the United States keeps all ATC radar data for at least 15 days. If an accident should happen in an area covered by this type of radar display, investigators can usually check the aircraft's course, track over the ground, heading and speed during the prelude to the impact. Unfortunately, the radar trace usually disappears as the aircraft drops below radar cover (which is why military pilots spend so much time training to fly at extremely low level to avoid enemy radar surveillance) but the lead-up to that disappearance can add a great deal to the overall picture.

All this information adds up to a complex and apparently overwhelming mass of data which must be sifted through to find the vital factors which helped to cause the accident. To the lay observer, the most surprising fact about air accident enquiries is that in the vast majority of cases, even when faced by a pile of apparently unidentifiable wreckage, the investigators manage to isolate the reasons why it happened. In addition, this vital knowledge makes it possible for them to suggest changes in the design of the aircraft, the operating procedures, the air traffic control network or the navigation aids, to ensure as far as possible, that this particular type of accident never happens again.

In many cases, as the later chapters will show, revealing the truth involves a slow, painstaking and logical process of deduction. One brief example from more than 50 years ago can show how inspectors approach their task in practice. In the demanding and dangerous days of wartime flying, accidents on training flights were all too common, but it was still seen as essential to determine their causes as far as possible. If a particular accident was seen to be connected with a flaw in a particular aircraft, or dangers caused by a particular manoeuvre, trainee pilots could be warned accordingly, and the toll in valuable machines and even more valuable aircrew could be minimised.

Would-be bomber crews in training had to practise the violent evasive action which might save their lives if spotted by enemy searchlights or night-fighters. One autumn night in 1943 a Lancaster from a training unit was crossing southwest England at more than 15,000 feet on a searchlight co-operation and fighter affiliation exercise. As planned, the bomber was caught in the beams of several searchlights on the outskirts of Exeter. The pilot threw the heavy bomber into a series of steep turns to throw the searchlight operators off their aim, but suddenly and without warning the Lancaster went into a long steep dive, from which it never recovered.

When the bomber hit the ground it was upside down. The crew was killed, and the aircraft caught fire after the crash. But some facts were clear enough. The wreckage trail was only a few hundred yards long, so the bomber had been virtually intact when it began its fatal dive. However, the pattern of the wreckage showed some parts of the aircraft *had* broken away in the final stages of its plunge. These were the elevators, fins and rudders, the starboard tailplane, the outer parts of both wings and the rear section of the fuselage with the port tailplane still attached to it.

What had happened to cause this disaster? The key to the sudden and final dive was the collapse of the Lancaster's tail structure. When the starboard tailplane was examined closely, rivets holding the metal skin in place had sheared, so its upper surface had become separated from the supporting framework. As the rows of sheared rivets extended across gaps where framework and skin had broken into separate pieces of wreckage, the skin separation had come before the break-up into different pieces.

When the pieces of skin panelling were assembled, the investigators could clearly see marks on the skin showing the starboard tail-fin had collapsed on to the tailplane *before* the tailplane had begun to break up. When they checked the fin, they found that one of the vertical posts forming its framework had sheared on its outboard side, level with the tailplane. A close inspection of the broken end showed the fracture had occurred in a section of the post which had holes drilled in it for the rivets fixing the fin skin panels to the post. One of the holes was slightly out of position, so the drill had removed enough of the material of the post to start fatigue cracks.

As the pilot had flung the bomber into a succession of steep turns to evade the searchlights, the load on the fin had increased to the point at which the post failed. The fin collapsed on to the tailplane, and the pilot lost control. The Lancaster fell over into an inverted dive, and without the full use of rudders and elevators, it was impossible to recover. During its long fall, the other parts had also become detached, but its fate had originally been sealed by one small rivet hole slightly out of position. Like so many of the causes revealed by the accident investigators, the kingdom was lost for the want of a horseshoe nail.

2

Under pressure

The dawn of the jet age brought a revolution to passenger flying. Jet engines have a number of very powerful advantages over piston engines to improve both comfort and safety. Because the gas turbine engine spins with none of the reciprocating motion of the piston engine, it avoids the incessant vibration from which all piston-engined aircraft suffer. Because engine stresses are lower, reliability is improved and engine failures are much rarer. And because jet engines are much more powerful than piston engines, passenger aircraft can fly much higher, above the layers of icing and bad weather, and at much greater speeds so that journey times are greatly reduced.

Unfortunately these radical changes carried a price of their own, although the bill was a long time being drawn up. When the British aircraft industry led the world with the introduction of the elegant and beautiful de Havilland Comet, it made every other passenger plane in the world look obsolete. Work had started on the design only a year after the ending of the Second World War, though de Havilland had already produced a single-seat, twin-boom jet fighter in the shape of the Vampire, which would join the Gloster Meteor as the RAF's front line defenders for the post-war world.

The Comet's design was radically different from its contemporaries, almost all of which were modified from wartime bombers or transports. It had a sleek, streamlined fuselage, and a graceful profile tapering back to an upswept tail. It was powered by a quartet of de Havilland Ghost engines, developed from the Goblin which powered the Vampire. Unlike later jet airliners with engines slung in pods below the wing, the Comet's engines were fared into the structure of the swept-back wings themselves.

Producing 5,000 pounds of thrust apiece, they gave the airliner enough power to cruise at just under 500 mph, considerably faster than the most powerful fighters of only a year or two earlier. It could fly at heights between 30,000 and 40,000 feet with a load of up to 36 passengers. Even when the prototype made its first flight in July 1949, much of the American aircraft industry was still working on piston-engine designs like the Stratocruiser, the Constellation and the Skymaster. For the time being, the Comet appeared to have no natural rivals.

The new airliner made its entry into service on 2 May 1952, when Comet 1 G-ALYP (called in the phonetic alphabet of the time 'Yoke Peter') inaugurated a regular BOAC service between London Heathrow and Johannesburg, for a fare of £315. This was an expensive service for those who could afford the best, and from the airline's point of view it had an extremely lucrative market all to itself.

Already the manufacturers had plans in progress for a Mark 2 version which would carry more passengers at higher speed over longer ranges. Within four months of the start of the Comet's service career, de Havilland announced the even more ambitious Comet 3 which could extend jet travel across the Atlantic for the first time. Not only were passengers queuing up to try the aircraft, but airlines all over the world were queuing up to place orders.

With such a jump in power and performance, it would have been extraordinary if the Comet had *not* suffered teething troubles. For example, its high speed was made possible by a very fine wing section which provided efficient lift with the minimum of drag. However, it had one important weakness. The symmetrical aerofoil had no leading-edge slats, and it was actually possible for the pilot to hold the nose high enough on take-off to stall the aircraft. The result was a huge increase in drag, so that it could accelerate down the longest of runways and never reach flying speed, and Comet 'Yoke Zebra' was lost for this reason when it failed to take off from Ciampino Airport at Rome on 26 October 1952.

Four months later the problem reappeared. The delivery flight of the first aircraft to be supplied to Canadian Pacific Airways was routed through Australia and across the Pacific, as a means of demonstrating it to the Australian airline Qantas during a brief stopover. On 3 March 1953, the aircraft CF-CUN *Empress of Hawaii*, made a refuelling stop in Karachi. Taking off in early morning darkness for Rangoon in Burma on the next sector of its journey, the Comet's nose tilted upwards for take-off, but the aircraft remained stubbornly on the ground.

After almost a mile and a half of runway and overrun, it had still failed to unstick when it crossed a drainage channel which smashed the undercarriage. The aircraft veered off course and crashed into a nearby canal bed, before bursting into flames, killing the crew together with half a dozen de Havilland engineers who had been on their way to work with Canadian Pacific to smooth the entry of the new airliner into service.

By the time the Comet had been in service with BOAC for exactly a year, the aircraft was also flying a regular service between London and Singapore. On the first anniversary of the inauguration of BOAC's first jetliner service, on 2 May 1953, Comet G-ALYV arrived at Dum Dum Airport in Calcutta from Rangoon on its way to London. It took off at 4.20 pm on the next sector of the flight to Delhi's Palam Airport. Five minutes after take-off, it was handed over by the Calcutta Area controllers to Delhi Control. The Comet's crew called Delhi, who immediately responded, but from then on nothing more was heard from the aircraft.

The wreckage was found just 24 miles north-west of the airfield. The nose and centre section of the fuselage, together with the inner portions of the wings and all four engines, were lying upside down in an irrigation channel, and the rear fuselage lay nearby in a paddy field. Careful checking for the remaining wreckage revealed a trail extending for more than five miles. When the position of the major components was logged, and their trajectories estimated, it became clear that the tailplane had separated from the aircraft at height, causing a total loss of control. The tailplane surfaces showed the structure had failed because of huge loads acting downwards, which had overstressed it beyond its design limits.

Eyewitnesses spoke of a very severe thunderstorm and seeing flames in the sky as it passed overhead, before wreckage began to rain down in the vicinity. The public enquiry into the crash concluded the Comet had met very severe gusts of wind inside the storm cells. The crew had applied a great deal of force to the fairly insensitive power-assisted controls to recover control, and had overloaded the tailplane and caused it to collapse. This would have caused the aircraft to pitch forwards sharply into a dive, tearing off the wings at the area of maximum stress just outboard of the engines, and causing the pressurised fuselage to burst open as it plunged to earth. In the end, the major part of the blame was applied to the unusually fierce weather conditions, and the Comet was given a clean bill of health. The scheduled flights continued, and all went well for another eight months, until 10 January 1954, when the same Comet, G-ALYP 'Yoke Peter', which had started the London to Johannesburg service in May 1952, was homeward bound from Singapore. At 10.30 am GMT, the aircraft took off from Ciampino Airport in Rome on its way to London, carrying a crew of six and a total of 29 passengers.

The weather was calm, and the Comet climbed quickly through thin cloud layers towards its cruising altitude. It crossed over the Ostia non-directional navigational beacon on the coast, then turned north-west, still climbing. By the time it passed over Orbetello, on the Argentario peninsula, 20 minutes and 100 miles after take-off, it had reached 26,000 feet and was heading to cross the island of Elba, just over 40 miles ahead. At 10.51 am GMT Captain Alan Gibson DFC called up his opposite number, Captain Johnson, who had taken off just ahead of him in a London-bound BOAC Argonaut. 'Did you get my...' said Captain Gibson, but the sentence was never completed. The radio remained silent, and nothing more was heard from 'Yoke Peter'.

An Italian trawler skipper, fishing south of Elba, heard a series of explosions high overhead. He looked up and saw pieces of aircraft, some of them on fire and streaming smoke, fluttering down into the sea approximately halfway between Elba and the tiny island of Montecristo, 20 miles to the south. More and more vessels made for the area to search for survivors, but all they found was a selection of floating wreckage, including seat cushions, clothes, children's toys and several badly mutilated bodies.

Initial suggestions were made of a bomb on board the aircraft. However, post-mortems on the victims showed no signs of the metal fragments which would have confirmed the detonation of a bomb. What they *did* have were injuries which hinted at a sudden and very violent decompression. In other words, the aircraft *had* exploded, not from a terrorist bomb but from the pressure inside the fuselage as it climbed through the thinning air to its cruising height.

Metal fatigue was always a possibility, but de Havilland had carefully tested each section of the aircraft to twice the intended operating pressure, and their experiments had shown that the fuselage should stand up to this kind of pressurising and depressurising loads for at least 18,000 flights. Since 'Yoke Peter'

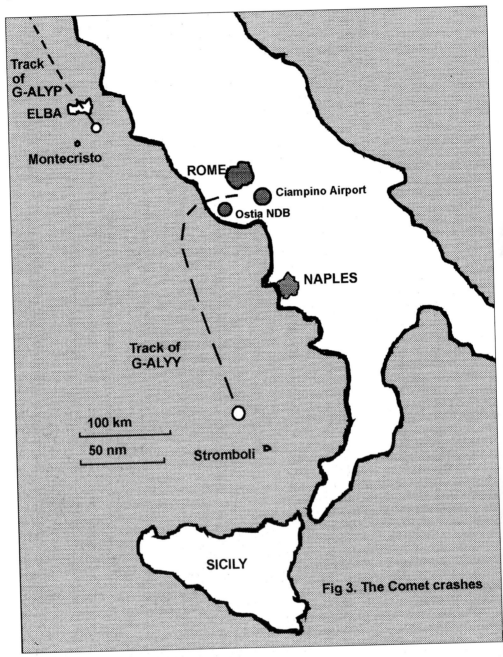

Fig 3. The Comet crashes

had only made around 1/15th of this total, there was nothing to explain this sudden and catastrophic failure. Moreover, the only evidence which could solve the riddle lay at the bottom of more than 600 feet of salt water.

When news of the accident reached the airline, all Comets were grounded until the results of the accident enquiry were released. The Royal Navy's Malta-based

Mediterranean Fleet salvage organisation had been reinforced by a squadron of local trawlers, to start searching for the wreckage on the seabed. To investigate the fatigue possibilities further, another BOAC Comet, G-ALYU 'Yoke Uncle', was taken to the Royal Aircraft Establishment at Farnborough, where its fuselage was immersed in a giant water tank, with its wings projecting out through the sides.

The water pressure was increased and decreased to reproduce the effects of pressurisation and depressurisation on a typical flight sector, and other rigs carried out the loads equivalent to the weight of the aircraft being transferred from the undercarriage to the wings and back again. By this means, the aircraft could be put through the stress equivalent of a three-hour flight in just ten minutes. The rig began working on a non-stop basis but it would still take weeks to reproduce the whole of 'Yoke Peter''s flying career.

In the absence of anything precise, the enquiry suspected in-flight fire, particularly since some of the bodies had shown burn injuries. Another possibility had been a turbine blade being shed by one of the engines and penetrating the fuselage skin to cause the explosive decompression. Instructions were issued to fix a layer of thick plating around the inside of the engine nacelles to guard against this possibility.

After two and a half months with no new evidence, when delays had caused BOAC an estimated half a million pounds, there seemed to be no practical alternative to letting the Comets fly again. Services were resumed on 23 March, though the tank testing of 'Yoke Uncle' continued without interruption, as did the

Water tank pressurisation test on Comet G-ALYU. (Reproduced courtesy of DRA – Crown copyright)

underwater search off Elba. The fears of BOAC and de Havilland began to recede. Perhaps 'Yoke Peter' had been a one-off after all. Until just two weeks later, when Comet G-ALYY 'Yoke Yoke', on loan to South African Airways, also took off from Ciampino Airport in Rome.

This time it was southbound, en route for Cairo and eventually Johannesburg, with a crew of seven and 14 passengers. The Comet lifted off the runway at 7.32 pm. Fifteen minutes later it was cleared to climb to its cruising altitude of 35,000 feet, and eight minutes after that it called Cairo to inform air traffic control of its predicted arrival time. That was the last contact with 'Yoke Yoke'. No more messages were received, and the aircraft and its passengers disappeared.

Once again, a search for any wreckage or remains was mounted. Under 'Yoke Yoke''s flight path, the fleet carrier HMS *Eagle*, escorted by the destroyer HMS *Daring* was sailing from her base at Malta for a goodwill visit to Naples. The carrier's Avenger torpedo bombers were launched the following morning to patrol the area from which the Comet's last messages had been received. After hours of staring down at empty blue water, one of the crews spotted floating wreckage near the volcanic island of Stromboli, 40 miles NNW of the Straits of Messina between Sicily and the Italian mainland. When the ships reached the vicinity, they picked up more poignant floating debris, including aircraft seats and cushions and five battered bodies. Another body was washed up on the coast a few days later, but with the sea at this point almost half a mile deep, there would be nothing more in the way of clues to the disaster.

Clearly there was something terribly wrong with the Comet, and the authorities had no option but to cancel the aircraft's Certificate of Airworthiness, effectively admitting the airliner was unsafe and grounding it indefinitely. Everything depended on what the Royal Navy and the Italian trawlermen were able to bring up from the seabed off Elba. Unfortunately, witnesses differed so much in their recollections over where they had seen the wreckage falling into the sea, that it was almost impossible to decide where to start the search. Only when they traced a photograph taken from a survey aircraft high above the sea, which showed the first boats on the scene picking up the floating debris on the day of the crash together with, in a corner of the frame, an identifiable part of the Elban coastline, did they have a definite point of departure at last.

From there, the search was extended backwards along the airliner's flight path. The trawlers dragged their nets along the seabed, hoping to sweep up items of wreckage as a catch. The Navy used more sophisticated equipment, searching the seabed with sonar, and whenever an echo was received, they dropped a marker buoy. Each marked site was then checked by underwater television cameras and a deep sea diving chamber, so that a view of whatever had caused the echo could be seen.

Piece by piece, the fragments of the Comet were recovered, examined, identified, photographed and then flown back to the Royal Aircraft Establishment at Farnborough, where 'Yoke Peter' was being painstakingly reassembled on a wood and wire netting framework. Because of the time taken to locate and then lift each piece of the wreckage from the seabed, this was bound to be a slow and painful process. But almost from the beginning, clues were emerging to show the investigators how the aircraft had broken up at the start of its plunge to the sea.

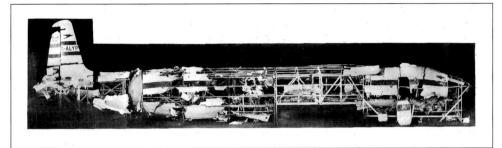

Post-crash reconstruction of de Havilland Comet G-ALYP, involved in the Elba disaster. (Reproduced courtesy of DRA – Crown Copyright)

The pattern of breakages in the fuselage skin and framework showed that the centre section had split apart before the front and rear sections had become detached. Panels on the port side of the rear fuselage and on the tail assembly were found to be scratched quite deeply by an object which had left traces of blue paint on the panels. When the paint was analysed, they found it was from the cabin seats, which showed that the fuselage must have blown apart while the tail was still in place.

To confirm this diagnosis, fibres from the cabin carpet were found trapped in cuts in the tail assembly. Other scratches along the surface of the port wing were found to contain traces of a different kind of blue paint. This was checked in turn, and found to be part of the airline's colour scheme applied to the side of the fuselage. For this to be scraped across the surface of the wing *before* the wing itself broke up, the fuselage must have been ripped open by a catastrophic explosion at the start of the disaster. As the reconstruction continued, they even found a piece of fuselage with paint and jagged edges which exactly matched the markings on the wing panels.

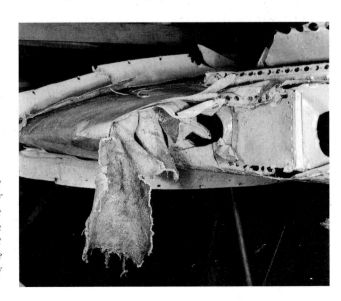

Pieces of cabin carpet trapped in cracks in the tailplane of Comet G-ALYP, showing that the explosive decompression caused the fuselage to burst before the tailplane broke away. (Reproduced courtesy of DRA – Crown copyright)

Within weeks of this discovery, while wreckage was still being traced, retrieved and added to the reconstruction, the long and so far disheartening water-tank test programme struck gold. The pressure inside the fuselage of 'Yoke Uncle' was increased to reproduce the stresses of a climb from sea level to cruising height, when the readings showing the pressure difference inside and outside the fuselage suddenly fell back to zero.

The fuselage was clearly leaking, a weakness which would have caused the aircraft to explode had it been several miles in the air instead of safely on the ground. The water was pumped out of the tank, and the breach was revealed as a huge tear on the port side of the centre section, starting from a fatigue crack at a rivet hole at the lower rearmost corner of the aperture for the over-wing emergency escape hatch. There were also other fatigue cracks already appearing around the cut-out for the ADF navigation aerial in the fuselage roof.

At first sight, this would explain the catastrophic explosion which had blown apart the fuselage of 'Yoke Peter', except for two discrepancies. None of the skin panels retrieved from the sea had shown any evidence of the initial fatigue crack which sparked off the disintegration. There was plenty of evidence of the break-up, but not of the initial split which caused it. Secondly, the tank test had produced this failure at the equivalent of two and a half times as much flying as 'Yoke Peter' had done at the time of the crash. The link was promising, but the proof was still missing, and the search was edging into deeper waters where only the trawlers could cope.

Fatigue failure beneath an escape hatch window in the fuselage of Comet G-ALYU during a water-tank pressurisation test. (Reproduced courtesy of DRA – Crown copyright)

The team at RAE Farnborough realised that a signpost was needed to help the trawlers find the remaining wreckage. They built a series of scale models of the Comet, in sections to represent the major parts of the aircraft after it had disintegrated. The sections were held in place by removable pins, each one tied to a thread of fixed length, so that when the models were launched from a balloon, the pins would be pulled in a timed sequence letting the different sections pull apart in exactly the same sequence as on the real Comet. The whole process, and the pattern in which the different pieces fell to the ground, were filmed with cine cameras, and then translated into a map which should reveal the whereabouts of the remaining wreckage.

It took more than five weeks of deepwater searching, but on 12 August 1954 one of the trawlers dragged up a section of the cabin roof which contained the cut-out for the ADF aerial. There, in the same place as the secondary cracks in the fuselage of G-ALYU in the test tank, was the fatal fatigue crack which had started the collapse of 'Yoke Peter''s whole structure. The cause was revealed at last, and now all that remained was to ensure it could not happen again.

The formal legal enquiry into both Comet crashes began two months later, and the report was published in February 1955. The remaining Comet 1s were permanently grounded, and de Havilland's engineering procedures checked. It was clear the company had done its best with the knowledge available at the time. What was needed was a radical rethink on designing fuselage structures, so fatigue cracks could be contained without explosive decompression.

Panels from the upper surface of the fuselage of Comet G-ALYP recovered from the seabed off Elba, showing the initial cracks which led to the explosive decompression. (Reproduced courtesy of DRA – Crown copyright)

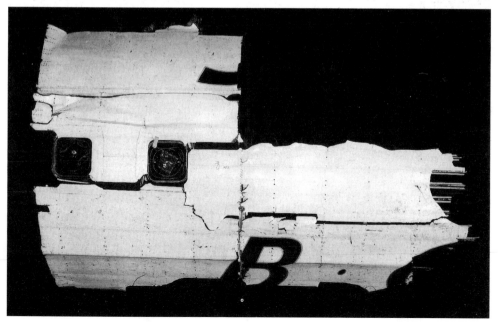

A combination of thicker skin and a closer structural framework, reinforced by additional cross-members would eliminate weak points if fatigue cracks did open up. Never again would an airliner fly apart as 'Yoke Peter' had done, from pressure-induced fatigue cracking and the resulting decompression. The only subsequent time a Comet would be blown to pieces over the Mediterranean would be due to a terrorist bomb, against which the most sophisticated aircraft engineering is powerless.

The second Comet crash remained beyond the reach of the investigators. Yet the evidence pointed to a general design fault which would have, sooner or later, shown itself in the remainder of the fleet. It therefore remained the most likely explanation for the second crash, confirmed by the post-mortem examinations on the six bodies recovered. These showed they had suffered the same pattern of injuries as the victims of the first crash, which was consistent with an explosive decompression.

For the Comet 1, this was the end of the line, as the remaining aircraft were permanently grounded. The Comet 2 was fitted with a redesigned and strengthened fuselage, for service as transports for the RAF, and a Comet 3 was used as a flying testbed for the Rolls-Royce Avon jet engines. By the time the larger and considerably more powerful Comet 4s entered airline service, four years after the 'Yoke Peter' tragedy, a new generation of competitors was already on the way, reaping the benefits of the Comet's hard-won experience to make them more reliable, more capacious, more efficient, and commercially infinitely more successful.

Yet fatigue remains a potential threat to the airliner, its operators and its passengers, and under special circumstances it can still turn a routine flight into a total disaster. One of the most successful airliners of all time, with a size and capacity unimaginable to the designers of the Comet, is the massive Boeing 747 Jumbo Jet. A familiar sight at airports all over the world in every conceivable livery, the 747 is able to fit into its enormous structure a massive choice of controls and operating systems to ensure a flight can continue in safety, even when suffering a series of failures or breakdowns.

It has two rudders, four elevators, four ailerons and duplicated hydraulic systems. Modern jet engines are so powerful that the plane can continue to fly even if three of the four power units should fail. Yet even an aircraft with this impressive battery of safety systems can be brought down by one tiny weakness in a vital place.

Most Boeing 747s are used on long-haul routes where carrying very large numbers of passengers on a single aircraft makes most sense. The Japanese market, however, uses special short-range variants of the 747 on internal routes like the Japan Air Lines service from Tokyo to Osaka. On 12 August 1985, Boeing 747 registration JA8119 was due to depart from Tokyo's Haneda Airport as flight No. JL123 at 6 pm local time. It carried a crew of 14 and a load of no less than 509 passengers, many of them families with children making the journey to celebrate a holiday weekend.

This holiday traffic caused delays, but the 747 finally lifted off from runway 15 Left at 6.12 pm. It was cleared to cross the island of Oshima to the south west of Tokyo, and to cruise at 24,000 feet for the flight of just under an hour to Osaka. Five minutes later the captain asked for a more direct route to his destination, which was approved within two minutes, and the aircraft continued to climb. As it reached its designated cruising height, the air traffic controller at Tokyo was surprised to see the transponder code next to the symbol for JL123 change to '7700'. This is the international emergency code, and within seconds a garbled message was received from the 747 asking for permission to return to Haneda Airport.

The controller approved, and told the pilots to make a right turn to follow a course of 090 degrees for Oshima island. The radar trace showed the 747 made an incomplete right turn to head north-west instead of the easterly course to bring them back to the airport. The height of the aircraft was also changing upwards and downwards by several hundred feet.

It was clear to the controllers that the crew of the 747 were in extreme difficulties, though they knew nothing of what had caused this disastrous situation. Messages were garbled and infrequent, and at one stage the aircraft's flight engineer hinted at a failure of one of the cabin doors. More disturbing was the fact that the crew had been unable to turn the aircraft on to a heading which would return them to Tokyo. Instead the 747 was following an erratic course away from the coast and into the mountains inland. First it turned north-west, then north, then north-east. By now it had descended to 22,000 feet, with its speed varying between 250 knots and 280 knots.

At just after 6.40 pm, less than half an hour after leaving Tokyo, the controllers were appalled to see the radar trace of JL123 suddenly begin a sharp turn to the right, with the height reading tumbling rapidly. The aircraft turned right round through a full circle and came out of the turn on approximately an easterly heading, having lost 5,000 feet of altitude. Three minutes later it turned back to the north, still descending until it levelled off at 6,800 feet, before starting to climb again.

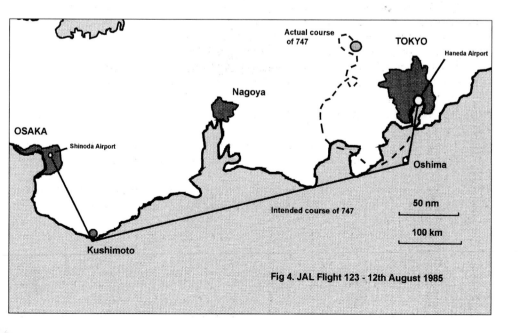

Fig 4. JAL Flight 123 - 12th August 1985

By 6.50 pm it was flying westwards, further into the mountains and still dangerously low and at a slow flying speed. Within two minutes it had shot up to 13,000 feet and two minutes later it had plunged back to 11,000 feet. Finally, at 6.56 pm, almost three-quarters of an hour after take-off, the trace on the screen showed another, much tighter right-hand turn, with the height reading unrolling fast, until at an indicated height of 8,400 feet the trace vanished and no more was heard from the aircraft. Only when a Japanese military aircraft reported seeing a blaze in the mountains was it clear that the crew's long struggle was over and the 747 had crashed.

No conceivable catastrophe should have overwhelmed a modern jet airliner with multiple safety systems so completely that the crew had clearly lost almost all control. By the time helicopters could be sent to the area it was already dark, and it was only the following morning that search parties could finally reach the wreckage. They found the aircraft had almost cleared a mountain ridge, but had brushed into trees which had torn away the tail and the port outboard engine before it collided with the ridge proper. The port wing had been torn away and the inner port engine had been thrown across the ridge into the opposite valley.

Amazingly, they found no less than four survivors lying in the wreckage of the rear fuselage. An off duty Japan Air Lines stewardess named Yumi Ochai had a broken arm and pelvis, a mother and daughter named Hiroko and Mikiko Yoshizaki had broken bones, but a 12 year-old schoolgirl called Keiko Kawakami had been thrown clear into the branches of a tree with no more than cuts and bruises.

Hillside and wreckage of the JAL Boeing 747. (Popperphoto)

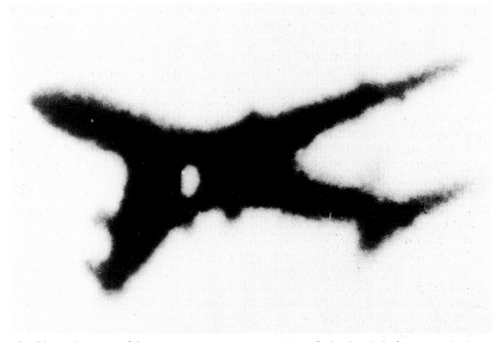

This blurred picture of the Japan Air Lines Boeing 747 in flight shortly before it crashed was taken by a bystander. Despite the lack of detail, it clearly shows the fin and rudder were missing. (Associated Press)

All the rest of the passengers and the crew of the 747 had died in the impact. From the viewpoint of the airline, the manufacturers and the whole air transport industry, the disaster posed a threat of frightening proportions. Was this the first proof of a fatal weakness in the 747, which would prove as fundamental as the fatigue cracking in the Comet? Until some explanation could be found which showed why this particular 747, out of all the hundreds built and apparently operating normally, should fall victim to such a total and inexplicable loss of control, then *all* 747s were potentially suspect.

At first, suspicion centred on the cabin door mentioned by the flight engineer in his communication with air traffic control. Fortunately for the investigators, the door in question was part of the wreckage least badly damaged, and it was in the closed and locked position. Telephone calls were received from people who claimed to represent terrorist organisations, saying that bombs had been planted aboard the aircraft, but in the absence of any other evidence, this too was discounted.

The first positive clue to the mystery came in the form of a photograph, taken by a witness on the ground as the stricken aircraft passed overhead. The print was blurred and the image small, but when it was enlarged there proved to be no sign of the vertical fin and rudder which was such a prominent feature of the 747. While this could have been due to a defect in the picture, this seemed a promising lead, though the loss of the rudder control should not have crippled the aircraft so completely.

Confirmation came within hours, when a Japanese naval destroyer sailing across Sagami Bay spotted pieces of floating wreckage. They hauled aboard a large section of a 747 tailfin, from approximately the spot where the aircraft had first reported an emergency. They started to search the surrounding area, and turned up a piece of rudder and part of the aircraft's auxiliary power unit, which was also housed in the tail assembly of the 747.

The off-duty stewardess survivor was a very valuable witness as she had been sitting in the tail of the aircraft, and would know more than the average passenger about what was, and was not, normal procedure. She denied there had been any explosion, but spoke of a sudden loud noise above and behind her, of the cabin filling with white mist, and of papers and light articles being blown backwards through the cabin. All this hinted at a decompression. She then described the aeroplane pitching slowly up and down and rolling gently first one way, and then the other, for the rest of its flight.

By this time, searchers had found the flight data recorder and the cockpit voice recorder, and these revealed still more information. A muffled thump could be heard on the cockpit recorder which was the sound of the decompression, after which the decompression warning alarm sounded. From the conversation of the flight crew, it soon became clear that hydraulic pressure in all systems was dropping, and finally an alarm sounded, to confirm that all hydraulic systems were lost.

This would mean the crew could not operate the ailerons, the elevators or the rudder, to steer the aircraft or control its height. All that remained to them were the throttles for the four engines, so that they tried to steer the aircraft by varying the thrust between the engines on one side and those on the other, and used the overall engine thrust to control the aircraft's climb and descent.

It was an appallingly difficult task, and in the end they were unsuccessful. Because of the impossibility of damping out the rolls from side to side and the undulating climbs and descents, their chances of achieving an emergency landing, even if they had managed to steer their way out of the mountains, was extremely slim. But it was still not clear what had caused all the hydraulic systems, and with them the main flight controls, to fail so suddenly and so completely.

After careful consideration, the only explanation for the cabin decompression and the loss of the fin and rudder appeared to be a weakness in the pressure bulkhead. This was a circular domed bulkhead at the rear end of the pressurised fuselage, shaped like an opened umbrella laid on its side. This was located beneath the fin and rudder, so a failure of this bulkhead could have directed the escaping air upwards into the fin and blown it apart from the inside. When investigators checked the bulkhead in the wreckage, it was found to be holed. But had this happened in flight, to cause the problems which led to the crash, or had it been caused by the impact itself?

By now, the Japanese accident investigators had been joined by representatives from Boeing, as manufacturers of the 747. The bulkhead was designed to last for a service life of at least 20 years, but it had to be checked. The actual fitting was in several pieces, but the edges were all saw-toothed from its being torn away from the rivets which held it in place. Only in one section

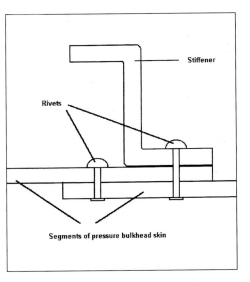

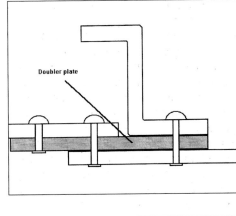

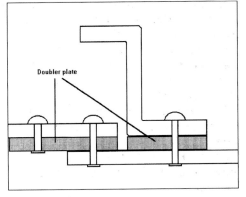

Fig 5 Above: Cross-section of pressure bulk-head of a Boeing 747.

Fig 6 Above right: Cross-section of correct repair to pressure bulkhead.

Fig 7 Below right: Cross-section of the incorrect repair to pressure bulkhead as involved in the JAL 747 crash.

was there a straight failure of one of the seams holding the different sections of the bulkhead together, at a point where a repair had been carried out some seven years before.

It emerged that the aircraft had made a heavy landing at Osaka in 1978, when the nose had been held so high that the tail of the 747 had made contact with the runway, tearing away some of the skin plating and cracking the rear pressure bulkhead. Repairs had been carried out by the airline, under supervision from Boeing engineers. Instead of replacing the whole bulkhead, they had replaced the lower half of it, splicing the two halves together with a doubler plate and three lines of rivets, one of which was used to hold a stiffening bar in place to keep the bulkhead in shape. Unfortunately in this case two separate doubler plates had been used, which meant that instead of the two rows of rivets holding the upper and lower halves together, there was effectively only one.

This error had two dramatic effects on the strength of the pressure bulkhead. Because one row of rivets was effectively redundant, the fatigue resistance of the bulkhead was only approximately one-third of its original value. However, the second result was even more important. The structure of the pressure bulkhead was designed so that, if a fatigue crack *did* appear, it could only extend for a limited distance before the stiffening straps forced it to change direction. As a result, any failure of the bulkhead would mean a small gap which would limit the release of air to a level which would not cause damage to the aircraft's tail structure.

In this case though, the faulty repair not only reduced the strength of the bulkhead, it also provided a route for the fatigue crack to run all the way along the seam joining the upper and lower bulkheads, so that when the bulkhead did fail, the huge outrush of cabin air was sufficient to blow the tail apart. From that moment, the fate of the aircraft, her crew, and the vast majority of passengers, was sealed.

Following this accident, changes were made to the tail design of 747s, including the fitting of a cover which would prevent air released from a failure of the rear pressure bulkhead from rushing into the fin assembly. The hydraulic circuits were changed to prevent all the fluid being lost in this type of incident, and to allow enough control to be retained to keep the aircraft flying safely.

Yet explosive decompressions are survivable, even in the most dramatic circumstances. Aloha Airlines, which serves the island group of Hawaii using short-haul Boeing 737s has a similar, but even more intense, pattern of flights to Japan Air Lines' internal route network. Sectors are short, and the timetable busy, so that each aircraft could average 15 sectors of around 20 minutes or so apiece, in a single day during the peak of the holiday season.

On 28 April 1988 one of Aloha's aircraft had already carried out eight of those sectors by lunchtime. It had flown from Honolulu to Hilo airport on Hawaii Island and back, followed by return trips to and from Maui and Kauai, two other islands in the Hawaiian chain. The aircraft, Boeing 737 registration N73711, then flew from Honolulu to Maui for the second time, followed by a sector from Maui on to Lyman Field on Hawaii island. Finally, at 1.35 pm local time, the aircraft took off once more, heading back to Honolulu as flight Aloha 243. It was cleared to fly at 24,000 feet for the short flight, and at 1.55 pm it reached its designated height.

Seconds later, the crew heard an explosion, followed by a scream and a loud rushing noise. The air rushed out of the flightdeck, wrenching off the door which communicated with the passenger cabin, and the captain was amazed to see open sky where the cabin roof would normally have blocked his view. The two pilots, together with an FAA air traffic controller occupying the jump seat pulled on their oxygen masks, and were relieved to find that the aircraft still seemed to be controllable, in spite of a tendency to roll slightly from one side to the other.

Normal procedure for decompression is to lose height as quickly as possible, and the captain reduced power and extended the speed brakes. The 737 began descending at 4,000 feet per minute, at a speed varying between 280 and 290 knots. The first officer set the emergency code '7700' on the transponder, and called Honolulu air traffic control to declare an emergency, and announce they were diverting to Kahului airport on Maui island, just over 40 miles ahead. The noise was deafening, and the first officer could not be sure her transmissions were being received. She switched to Maui Approach control and then to Maui Tower to inform the airfield they were coming in for an emergency landing.

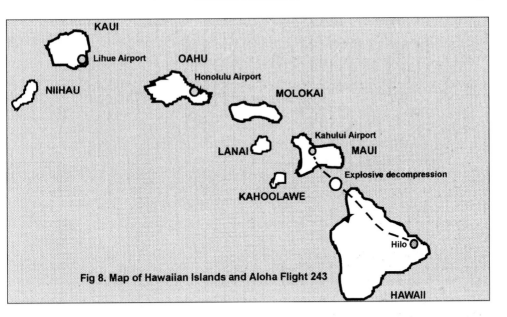

Fig 8. Map of Hawaiian Islands and Aloha Flight 243

As the 737 descended below 10,000 feet the pilots were able to remove their oxygen masks, and found they were able to communicate over the shrieking of the airstream by shouting at the tops of their voices. There was still no way they could tell the shocked passengers what was happening, or find out the state of affairs in the cabin behind them. All they could do was continue with as normal an approach as possible. They selected the flaps to increase lift and reduce speed, and lowered the landing gear.

Unfortunately, the panel light showing the nosewheel was down and locked failed to light. There was no way of checking whether this was a fault in the circuit or in the gear itself. At the same time, the pilots found that putting down more flap, or cutting the speed below 170 knots made the aircraft more difficult to control. Since there was a mile and a quarter of runway at the airfield, they decided to increase the approach speed to make the landing easier, but as the captain opened the throttles the port engine failed and the aircraft yawed sharply. With four miles left to run, there was time to take corrective action, and the 737 touched down smoothly and braked to a stop, with the nosewheel remaining firmly in position.

Only when they unfastened their harnesses and walked back into the passenger cabin did the pilots realise the damage done to the aircraft by the explosive decompression less than 15 minutes before. The whole of the roof and sides down to floor level in the First Class section had disappeared, torn away by the slipstream once the initial cracks opened up the fuselage skin. Miraculously, only one person had been killed, a stewardess who had been walking down the central aisle in the First Class section when the roof opened up, and who had been sucked out through the gap.

For the investigators of this incident, the chief problem was the fact that most of the fuselage skin which had torn away following the decompression has never been found. All they had to go on was the panelling left in position

The port side of the Aloha Air Lines Boeing 737 after a successful landing following the explosive decompression which blew the cabin roof away. (National Transportation Safety Board)

around the enormous hole in the fuselage, and the first significant sign they spotted was a row of rivets with fatigue cracks around them. Even more important, in the light of what happened, was the overlap joint between the panel with the rivet holes and the adjacent panel. This consisted of a cold-bonded adhesive strip, which was actually coming away from the panel, and showing signs of corrosion damage.

It was clear the operating life of the Aloha 737s was very punishing for any aircraft. Where a 737 might normally undergo one or two pressurisation and depressurisation cycles in a working day, the short flights between islands meant that the Aloha aircraft were undergoing this pattern of repeated stresses and relaxations six or seven times as often. Moreover, the combination of warm, humid, salt air around these tropical islands was the most corrosive atmosphere possible. Moisture was penetrating the joints between panels, and when this loosened the bonding, the entire stress of pressurisation and depressurisation was taken by the rivets fixing the panels together.

The investigators checked the rivets more closely, and found the holes were drilled with a bevelled profile so that the countersunk rivets could be fitted flush with the top panel for minimum aerodynamic drag. However, the problem was that the bevelled section extended all the way through the top layer of skin, leaving a sharp circular edge at the bottom of each hole. As the rivets were stressed and relaxed with each pressurisation – depressurisation cycle, these sharp edges provided perfect starting points for fatigue cracks at each rivet.

Normally, fatigue cracks are only able to extend for a short distance before they reach a reinforcing member designed to limit their travel. They can then only extend at right angles to their original direction, so that if the problem is

Damage to the starboard side of the roofless Aloha 737. (National Transportation Safety Board)

The Aloha Boeing 737 passenger cabin aft of the break which removed the roof. (National Transportation Safety Board)

uncorrected and a decompression occurs, a small flap opens up and the rush of air out through the hole will not damage the structure. In this case, it seemed as if fatigue cracks had appeared along a whole row of rivets, creating a fault line which crossed a whole succession of reinforcing members. As a result, when the cracks caused one section of panelling to fail, the failure was able to jump from one fuselage section to the next, until the whole forward cabin roof was torn away in the slipstream.

Amazingly enough, a Japanese passenger spotted what was almost certainly the initial crack when she boarded the plane. Because she was shorter than the average passenger, she saw a crack next to the cabin door which passengers with a higher eye-line would miss. The FAA inspectors contacted her, and asked her to show them on another 737 where the crack had appeared. The point she indicated was at almost exactly the same level as the tear where the panel had separated on the Aloha aircraft.

The inspectors checked the Aloha maintenance records. Though the airline carried out procedures by the book, the normal way of indicating test and maintenance procedures by the operating life of the aircraft expressed in flying hours, was not right for their operating patterns. Instead, they looked at the number of landings and take-offs. With as many as 16 sectors a day, the aircraft involved in the incident had already flown the astonishing total of 89,680 sectors. This was one of three 737s which had completed the highest number of landings and take-offs of any of its type anywhere in the world. The other two were also operated by Aloha!

Another worry was the fact that many of these aircraft were operating with a number of repairs to their fuselages, made necessary by corrosion damage and fatigue cracks. Because the aircraft were kept so busy, the only time for inspection and maintenance procedures was during the night, when it was more difficult to fit in the exhaustive checks which the aircraft really needed. Only by tightening up on maintenance procedures and limiting the amount of acceptable patches and repairs was it possible to ensure that such a potentially catastrophic decompression would never occur again.

The message of these incidents, for the industry and its passengers, is that metal fatigue is a problem which aircraft designers and operators have to live with. They can reduce the threat it presents by clever design. For example, the windows on the Comet 1 were larger than they need have been, and designed to give passengers as clear a view as possible. Their square shape with rounded corners produced high stress concentrations in the window corners, providing an ideal starting point for fatigue cracks. Now engineers design the bracing of the fuselage and its skin to ensure that where fatigue cracks start, they can only open up for a short distance before being stopped or turned, to minimise the damage caused by fatigue failure.

Yet the danger still poses as powerful a threat as ever, unless all the safety measures are in place and working properly. Maintenance procedures have to be rigidly followed, otherwise the routine repairs needed to keep an aircraft flying could turn into a fatal weakness which sets all the engineers' care at naught. Today's airlines spend very large sums on rigorous crack detection tests, using X-ray, ultrasonic and magnetic scanning equipment to reveal weaknesses which could escape the most searching of visual examinations. As the operating lifetimes of successful airliners last longer and longer, the potential problems of what airline operators call the 'geriatric jet' mean this kind of searching scrutiny will be even more essential in the decades to come.

3

Out of a
clear sky

The problem of metal fatigue only became important once aircraft had the power and performance to climb to very high altitudes, making it necessary to maintain cabin pressure at artificially high levels for the comfort and safety of crew and passengers. Another hazard, however, has been part of flying from the beginning. As the power of a typhoon can overwhelm the largest and strongest of ships, the violence of turbulence and thunderstorms remains as a potential hazard for even the most sophisticated modern airliner. Even before the crashes caused by metal fatigue, the original Comet disaster was the break-up of the Delhi-bound flight out of Calcutta on 2 May 1953 in the fury of a monsoon storm.

The crew were believed to have used too much force on the fairly insensitive power-assisted controls of the Comet, to compensate for the strong upcurrents and downdraughts. By the 1960s, however, controls were much more sensitive, and more was known about the right kind of action to take in storm cells. By slowing the aircraft's speed and reducing the control movements, the strain on the airframe could be lessened and survival prospects improved.

One advantage of the new jet airliners was that they could climb above much of the weather. Thunderclouds containing a potentially lethal combination of updraughts and downdraughts inside their cores presented little or no threat to aircraft flying far above them. By the time weather radar systems appeared on the flight-deck, pilots had the option of identifying individual storm cells, and changing course to avoid them.

Unfortunately that still left a more insidious threat. This was potentially even more dangerous because it could strike, quite literally, out of a clear blue sky. Where a towering, anvil-shaped cumulo-nimbus cloud mass left flyers in no doubt that this was extremely bad news, clear air carried no signposts. Without clouds to act as markers, the atmosphere ahead of an aircraft could be boiling with turbulence, without any danger signs at all.

When BOAC flight number 911 was due to leave Tokyo's Haneda Airport for its 3½ hour flight to Hong Kong on the afternoon of 5 March 1966, the weather was so fine and clear that the cone of Mount Fuji, 70 miles away, was unmistakable. The Boeing 707 was almost full, with 113 passengers and a crew of 11, and conditions seemed set for a perfect day. The only blemish was the sight of the blackened and smoking wreckage of a Canadian Pacific Douglas DC-8 which had crashed the previous evening on a trans-Pacific flight from Hong Kong to Vancouver.

Because of fog over the airport, the DC-8 was originally diverted to Taipei in Taiwan. Soon afterwards, conditions at Tokyo improved and the crew asked for clearance to return and try for a landing. On its final approach in darkness and fog, the DC-8 descended below the glide path, short of the runway thresh-old and struck a battery of approach lights and then the sea wall. The aircraft broke up and caught fire, and only eight of the 72 aboard survived.

Taxiing past this grim reminder of the hazards of flying, 'Foxtrot Echo' took off from runway 33L at 1.58 pm local time. The original clearance had been to fly under IFR (Instrument Flight Rules) on a heading to cross Oshima island 50 miles to the south, before climbing to 31,000 feet on the airway which paral-lels the south-eastern coast of the Japanese islands. However, by the time the 707 lifted off the runway, Captain Dobson had been allowed to change his clearance by air traffic control. Instead of flying direct to Oshima, he would be allowed to fly under Visual Flight Rules on an approximately south-western course towards Mount Fuji, before turning on to a more southerly heading to intercept his original airways clearance at Kushimoto, several hundred miles to the south-west.

After take-off, 'Foxtrot Echo' altered course to starboard, climbing over Yokohama and rolling out on a south-westerly heading to cross over the Chigasaki navigational beacon. By the time it passed over Gotemba the airliner had almost reached 17,000 feet. Then it banked to starboard, swinging on to a north-westerly course and starting a shallow descent, heading straight for the snow-covered cone of Fuji, standing out clearly from the surrounding landscape.

Minutes later, watchers on the ground saw a trail of white vapour coming from the aircraft. Within seconds, there were trails from both wing-tips, and then pieces were seen falling from the aircraft, followed by a puff of white, then black, vapour from the tail. The aircraft seemed to climb before falling into a flat spin. As it descended towards the ground, the witnesses could see the tail and the engines were missing. As the spin continued, first the outer part of the starboard wing and then the whole nose section broke away. Although the nose section caught fire on impact, the main part of the aircraft came down in a forest near the base of the mountain without any post-crash fire. All the crew and passengers were killed in the accident.

For the investigators, this was a most unusual problem. The weather was fine and clear, so at first sight there was nothing to account for the aircraft breaking up in such a violent manner. There had been no emergency radio calls, and the aircraft was not fitted with a cockpit voice recorder to record the crew's reactions to the disaster which had overtaken them. To make matters worse, the flight data recorder had been installed in the nose of the aircraft, where it was destroyed in the post-crash fire.

The only hint as to what had happened lay in the distribution of the wreck-age, scattered over an area ten miles long and more than a mile wide. The centre section of the fuselage with the port and inner starboard wings attached had impacted in a pattern which preserved the basic outline of the aircraft,

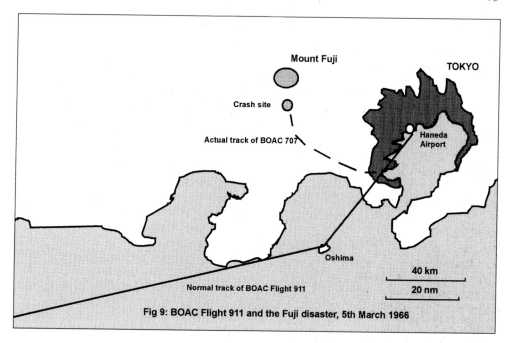

Fig 9: BOAC Flight 911 and the Fuji disaster, 5th March 1966

showing it had fallen in a flat attitude with very little forward speed. The other main assemblies were plotted on a map, and using the weather bureau's information on the strengths and directions of the wind at different heights below the disintegrating aircraft, the investigators were able to establish that the 707's fin, rudder and port tailplane had broken away first.

When they examined the individual pieces of wreckage, they found scratches and traces of paint on the port tailplane showing that the fin had collapsed across it as it tore away from the tail, tearing away the port tailplane as it did so. Because the tailplane was a single structure right across the rear end of the aircraft, this caused the starboard tailplane to break away too.

Closer examination of the fin showed the initial break had occurred at its starboard rear attachment points, where the upper bolt holes had failed under heavy tension stress. There were ominous signs of fatigue cracks around one of these bolt holes, but it was unlikely these could have started such a disastrous break-up of the structure without some strong external force.

Other pieces of wreckage contributed a little more detail. Examining the split between the outer part of the starboard wing and the main structure showed the outer part had been bent upwards before breaking away. The pylons supporting all four engines had been broken by a sideways force to the left which tore away all four power units from the wings. The nose section had been broken off to the left, but the cause of these violent forces was still obscure. The fire in the nose section had burned so fiercely that it was impossible to retrieve any instrument readings.

Fortunately for the investigation, one piece of wreckage proved much more eloquent in its testimony. Among the chaos of the main passenger cabin, searchers found an eight-millimetre cine camera with a partially exposed film.

When the film was processed, it showed images of the aircraft on the ground at Tokyo Airport, followed by two sequences showing the mountainous approaches to Fuji, taken through the starboard side cabin windows.

The first sequence showed a view of the Tanzawa Mountains, taken while the aircraft was still on a south-westerly heading and approaching Gotemba. The second sequence showed the distant Lake Yamanaka, after the 707 had turned on to the north-westerly course which would have taken it towards the summit of Fuji. During this sequence the camera suddenly skipped two frames of film and then showed out-of-focus images of the interior of the cabin before coming to a sudden stop.

The only logical explanation for this jump in the film was that the person holding the camera had received such a violent shock that the camera had been jerked violently and then dropped to the cabin floor. The timing, as revealed from the view seen through the cabin window, was close enough to coincide with the blow which had caused the start of the break-up of the aircraft. But the investigators were brought back to the original question. What had appeared out of a clear sky to strike the fatal blow?

Only the atmosphere itself could have produced that deadly power. The weather records showed that the depression which had brought the poor visibility which helped bring down the Canadian Pacific DC-8 the night before had moved away to the east of Japan. This left an area of high pressure to the west of Japan, over the mainland of Asia, creating a system of strong, dry winds blowing from the west and north-west. Instruments on the summit of Mount Fuji showed gusts of between 60 and 70 knots at the time.

Winds of this strength blowing across mountains cause enormous atmospheric disturbances in what is called a 'mountain wave'. In more temperate conditions, gliders are able to ride the updraughts over mountain ridges to gain precious height. With winds of this strength, though, the airflow can form what meteorologists call a 'standing rotor', rather like a huge whirlpool of air lying on its side along the lee side of the mountains and above the height of the summit.

In relatively moist conditions, this airstream produces a horizontal roll of cloud as a warning of the turbulence within. In these exceptionally clear conditions, the airstream was too dry for clouds to form, though weather satellite pictures showed roll clouds forming within the wave generated by winds blowing over the Suzuka Mountains 150 miles to the south-west.

In addition, a total of a hundred other aircraft flying between 27 and 80 miles of Fuji on that day reported moderate to severe turbulence. The closer they flew to the mountain the worse the conditions they met. One US Navy Skyhawk fighter searching for the 707's wreckage was battered so violently that the pilot was barely able to escape. When the aircraft returned, the instruments showed it had been subjected to upward loadings of nine times the force of gravity, and down loadings of almost half this intensity.

Measurements inside rotor clouds have shown vertical gusts reaching speeds of 70 mph or more, so this extreme turbulence has ample power to break up any aircraft straying into its influence. Almost certainly this was the fate of the BOAC 707 and its passengers and crew, on that brilliant afternoon over the mountains. Without any warning at all the aircraft reached the edge of the area of extreme turbulence and was swallowed up by forces its structure had never been designed to withstand. The first furious gust tore away the fin, slamming it down so violently that it carried away the tailplane as well. At the same moment, or very soon afterwards, all four engines were torn away from their mountings by these same powerful forces.

That catastrophe determined the course of the next few minutes. With the loss of the lift provided by the tailplane, the aircraft's nose pitched up and the speed fell away rapidly. As the 707 fell into an uncontrollable flat spin, the violent wind forces wrenched away the starboard wing, and finally the entire nose section of the fuselage during its long plunge to earth. The plumes of white and black smoke seen by the witnesses on the ground must have been caused by the almost full fuel tanks spilling their contents out into the atmosphere. The fate of the 707 had been a terrible lesson of the price of wandering into areas of catastrophically severe turbulence, but it had also provided a valuable warning. From this point onwards, the idea of CAT – Clear Air Turbulence – was rated as a much more serious threat, to be avoided at all costs wherever it may be encountered.

Mountain waves of the type existing over Mount Fuji on that day were fairly predictable, and easily avoided once the danger was appreciated. But CAT can occur in other situations where clear air appears to offer an escape route from even worse conditions. This was proven all too dramatically only months after the Fuji crash, on the other side of the world. Braniff Airlines' flight 250 was an evening and night-time service from New Orleans to Minneapolis, with several intermediate stops which included Tulsa, Kansas City and Omaha.

On the evening of 6 August 1966, the service was being operated by a twin-jet BAC-111, registered N1553, and the journey from New Orleans as far as Kansas City had been in clear moonlit conditions. On arrival at Kansas City though, the forecast for the next sector to Omaha was of a line of severe thunderstorms along an approaching cold front, and incoming pilots spoke with feeling of the intensity of the storms and the lack of any gaps between them.

Captain Pauly hoped to be able to avoid the storm line to the west, and the flight was cleared to Omaha at an altitude of 20,000 feet. Unfortunately, heavy incoming traffic meant the controller had to order him to take off and climb to just 5,000 feet, until the crew were advised it was safe to climb to their cruising altitude. Finally, when the BAC-111 was 12 miles north of the airport, the controllers cleared it to 20,000 feet. The crew replied that they would prefer to stay at 5,000 feet for the time being, but asked for clearance to divert further to the west. This was given soon after 11 o'clock local time.

Communications were then switched to air traffic controllers at Chicago, who mentioned that a southbound Braniff 111 was crossing the storm line as it climbed through 10,000 feet on its initial climb out of Omaha for Kansas City. The two crews compared notes, and it was clear that the southbound flight was encountering light to moderate turbulence at its much higher altitude, but the crew expected to leave it behind in ten more minutes or so. Captain Pauly, still flying at 5,000 feet and approaching the storm line, acknowledged the information at 11.8 pm. Nothing more was heard from the aircraft.

Witnesses on the ground saw the line of approaching thunderstorms six miles on the northern side of Falls City in Nebraska, when they saw the

BAC-111 appear through clear skies to the south-east four minutes after this last message. They thought the aircraft was trying to make for what appeared to be a clear spot between two masses of boiling thunderclouds, above a thin layer of low cloud. They saw it pass out of sight over the layer of cloud, and were horrified to see a ball of fire appear in the sky, followed by the blazing mass of the aircraft falling through the cloud layers to the ground. Some saw two large pieces of the aircraft fall more slowly to the earth, just before the storm front reached them and their view was blotted out by rain and a sudden increase in wind speed.

Once again, the investigators found the main part of the aircraft sitting in an attitude which showed it had crashed in a flat spin. Once again, the starboard wing had broken apart, and once again the tail had collapsed. In fact, these two large portions of the aircraft had clearly broken away before the crash, as they were found a long way from the main wreckage, and were completely untouched by the fire which had consumed the main part of the fuselage. Once again, to the disappointment of the investigators, the flight data recorder was too badly damaged to yield any useful information.

However, the 111 *was* fitted with a cockpit voice recorder, which revealed the two pilots had discussed the possibility of steering the aircraft through a hole in the line of approaching clouds. The Chicago controller advised them the front was 'pretty solid', and they then considered the possibility of diverting further to the west, towards Pawnee City. Finally, at 11.11 pm, a voice could be heard saying 'ease power back', and nine seconds later a rushing sound could be heard which persisted for another 26 seconds until the recording ended at the moment of impact. Test flights with recording apparatus in another BAC-111 showed that the initial background noise on the cockpit voice recording was consistent with the aircraft cruising at around 270 knots, which agreed with the tailplane trim settings in the cockpit, and with the speed which was recommended on encountering severe turbulence conditions.

The much louder rushing sound was more difficult to reproduce. In the end, the test pilots were forced to increase speed to more than 320 knots and also put the aircraft into a severe sideslip to re-create the sound heard on the recording. This showed that something must have happened to change the aircraft's speed and heading quite sharply, just 26 seconds before it smashed into the ground. Furthermore, the speed must have decayed very quickly during its plunge to earth, as the stall warning horn could be heard quite clearly in the last few seconds of the recording.

Once again, the investigators studied the positions and the condition of the main items of wreckage, to determine how the aircraft had broken up in mid-air. Reconstructing their trajectories from the much lower altitude of the 111 compared with the Fuji 707 proved more straightforward, and showed that just as in the Japanese disaster, the tail had failed first. This time the initial gust had torn away the rudder and elevators and broken the control cables. A second later, the aircraft had been flung upwards and to the left, with its nose pitching sharply downwards. Within two seconds the starboard wing had been bent downwards and broken away from the main structure by enormous stresses. The shattered wing tanks spilled fuel which caught fire, and caused the fireball seen by the watchers on the ground.

Calculations showed the intensity of gust needed to tear the control surfaces away from the tail involved a change in wind velocity of almost 100 mph in a fraction of a second. But how could this have happened in apparently clear air, more than five miles short of the main storm area? Meteorological experts from the University of Chicago explained that an advancing line of thunderstorms produces powerful updraughts of rising warm air within the storm cells, balanced by a flow of cold air downwards from high altitude which forms a mass of cold air ahead of the storm front.

As the storm front moves forward, this mass of cold air is pushed ahead of it, deflecting warm air at ground level ahead of the front upwards and over the top of the cold air. The differences in direction between the streams of cold air and warm air produce a sharp change in wind direction, in a phenomenon called 'windshear', which is described more fully in the next chapter.

However, there is worse to come. As the winds at higher altitudes drive the storm front forward, the mass of cold air ahead of the front becomes unstable, with its upper layers moving faster than the lower layers closer to ground level. This produces an overhang of cold air which traps the rising warm air ahead of the front and prevents it from escaping upwards. The result is a rolling mass of violent air at low altitude, similar in its pattern and its fury to the mountain wave which caused the Fuji disaster.

In one respect, this kind of turbulence ought to be expected in the vicinity of thunderstorms. But the effect shares another deadly factor with the mountain wave, in that it occurs *ahead* of the storm front, in what otherwise appears as clear and still air. By trying to steer through what was believed to be a clear gap in the storm front at an altitude of 5,000 feet, the crew of the Braniff

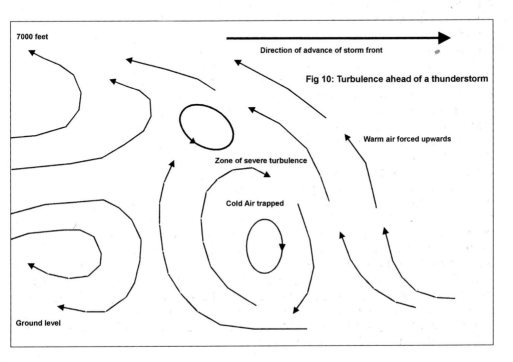

7000 feet

Direction of advance of storm front

Fig 10: Turbulence ahead of a thunderstorm

Warm air forced upwards

Zone of severe turbulence

Cold Air trapped

Ground level

BAC-111 was in fact heading for the most severe turbulence in the area, and a turbulence which was not shown on their weather radar. Only when the mechanisms underlying the formation and transmission of a storm front were better understood, could aircraft be directed clear of the threat which clear air turbulence presented. Had the flight climbed to its original clearance height, it would probably have crossed the storm front with no more danger or discomfort than its southbound opposite numbers.

If clear air turbulence remains one deadly form of unseen and only partly predictable hazard, one British Airways 747 encountered another on 24 June 1982, en route from Kuala Lumpur to Auckland in New Zealand on flight BA009, which had started from Heathrow the night before. After the 747, registered G-BDXH and named *City of Edinburgh*, had passed over Jakarta and was heading across the mountains of Java towards the southern coast of the island, the crew noticed a sequence of very strange symptoms indeed.

The first was a snowstorm of brilliant white particles blasting the front of the aircraft out of the darkness and glowing where they collided with the fuselage. Secondly, the stars were obscured, even though the weather radar indicated clear conditions. Thirdly, switching on the landing lights showed the aircraft was apparently flying through mist. Fourthly, the passenger cabins were slowly filling with acrid-smelling smoke. The cabin crew checked for any carelessly dropped cigarettes, but it soon became clear that the smoke was entering the cabin through the ventilation ducts.

The flight-deck crew were becoming increasingly perturbed by the intense sparks hitting the front of the aircraft, when they noticed the insides of the engines were lit up from within by brilliant white flares, and the leading edges of the wings were beginning to glow. Before long, violent electrical discharges were creating patterns of light on the wings and fuselage, and trails of brilliant light were emerging from the tailpipes of all four engines. More worryingly still, the engines were running roughly, with internal explosions at intervals.

Just two minutes after the pyrotechnics began, a warning lamp lit up on the flight-deck and the starboard outer engine failed. A minute later the port inner also failed, followed seconds later by the remaining two engines. With no power at all, the heavy 747 began to descend towards the sea seven miles below. The crew sent out a 'Mayday' call, but they had entered an area of heavy radio interference and found it difficult to describe their plight to ground control, until an Indonesian aircraft was able to relay messages backwards and forwards.

During the long glide towards the Pacific, the crew made a whole series of attempts to restart the engines, but without success. When the aircraft had descended to 30,000 feet, Captain Eric Moody decided to turn back northwards towards Jakarta, but the problem was that without engine power, the aircraft would find it difficult or impossible to cross the mountain ranges which lay between it and the airfield. Another problem was that the 747's two airspeed indicators were showing very different speeds, and engines could only be restarted successfully within a relatively narrow speed range. This meant the crew had to try several different speeds for engine relights, in case this was affecting the situation.

If these problems were not more than enough to cope with, the absence of engine power was causing pressure within the cabin to fall. The flight-deck crew were breathing oxygen, but the first officer's mask was not working properly, so the captain had to increase the rate of descent to prevent him suffering from oxygen starvation. As so often in a flying emergency, this reduced their options still further. Captain Moody decided that if the aircraft descended to 12,000 feet without any of the engines starting, they would have to turn away from the mountains and spend their last precious altitude trying to restart the engines, before the final expedient of ditching the aircraft off the coast. It was the stuff of which nightmares are made, with an inexorable plunge to the dark and pitiless sea waiting far below.

Fortunately, it never quite came to that. At 13,500 feet, their frantic efforts to restart the engines were rewarded with success when the starboard outer engine, which had been the first to fail 13 anxious minutes before, finally burst into life. To avoid overstraining the power unit, Moody decided to use the power to flatten the rate of descent rather than try to climb, while they redoubled their efforts to relight the other three engines. Two minutes later, they succeeded in restarting the starboard inner engine, and they were able to keep the aircraft in level flight, just above the safety height needed to cross the mountains to Jakarta.

Within minutes the other two engines had also been restarted and radio communications had improved, so that Jakarta was able to give the 747 clearance to cross the mountains at a safer altitude of 15,000 feet. As they climbed back to their cleared flight level, the crew were horrified to see the port inner engine showing the dreaded surging and jets of flames which had preceded the initial failure. Sure enough, it soon failed for the second time, and Moody told Jakarta control he was descending to 12,000 feet where the other three engines remained running smoothly.

Just over 20 minutes later, Captain Moody and his crew brought the 747 in to a safe landing at Jakarta airport. On the approach they noticed their view through the flight-deck windows was blurred and misty. Even the landing lights seemed ineffective, and it was only by peering through a narrow strip of clear glass at the edge of each window and comparing notes, that they managed to reach the runway. But it was only in the light of day next morning that they could see the damage the airliner had suffered.

The windows and the covers of the landing lights had been sandblasted until they were almost completely opaque. The interior of the passenger cabin was covered with a deposit of coarse black dust. The same ashy dust was found in the engines, and in the pitot heads which supplied the air pressure information to the two air speed indicator systems. But it was only when the local Rolls-Royce representative arrived to examine the engines and mentioned in passing that Mount Galunggung, an active volcano just to the east of their direct route to Australia and New Zealand, had suffered a massive eruption the previous day, that the cause of their terrifying experiences was revealed.

The British Airways 747 had flown right through the plume of ash and dust hurled into the atmosphere by the volcano. Because the debris was hot and dry, containing no appreciable moisture at all, it left no trace on the weather radar, though its effects could be seen all over the aircraft. The particles also carried a high electric charge, which was the reason for the spectacular lightning flashes on the skin of the wings and fuselage and the bursts of flame from the engines, augmented by the fuel fed into them during the succession of unsuccessful restart attempts.

It was only when the 747's long glide down towards the sea had taken it below the level of the ash cloud that those attempts were successful. Similarly, when the captain tried to use the restored engine power to climb to a safer altitude for crossing the Javanese mountains, the aircraft climbed back into the dust layers, and one of the engines immediately failed again. By descending back to a lower altitude, even without realising the nature of the cause of their problems, he saved his remaining engines from a similar fate, and made it possible to return to the airport.

The fate of *City of Edinburgh* high in the night sky over Java fortunately had a happy ending, both for the aircraft and its occupants, and for flying in general. Because the crew and passengers survived, and because the damage to the aircraft could be inspected on the ground, the dangers of flying into the ash cloud thrown out by a volcanic eruption could be understood all too well. There had been cases of aircraft experiencing problems when flying into more dispersed clouds well downwind of an eruption, but no other aircraft had flown so close to the heart of an eruption and survived.

Nor was this an isolated mishap with no long-term implications. Less than two weeks later another 747, this time a Singapore Airlines northbound flight from Melbourne to Singapore, itself lost the power of three of its four engines. Fortunately, the crew had read the reports of the earlier incident and had the advantage of knowing what the problem was. They descended to a safer altitude and diverted to Jakarta on their remaining engine, to find that the mountain had erupted again, and they had flown into the fall-out.

Here was another hazard which could not be predicted from any of the instruments carried on board the most modern aircraft. However, the huge plume of ash and dust hurled for miles into the sky showed up very clearly indeed on weather satellites, and volcanic eruptions were closely studied and reported, whenever and wherever they happened. By making sure crews were informed of hazards as and when they occurred, and flights re-routed to avoid ash clouds, it was possible to ensure that the nightmare which struck flight BA009 that August night in 1982 never appeared again. Indeed, if another aircraft should suffer the same fate, the crew will be well aware of the action they need to take to escape its grasp.

But nothing is certain in flying, except the workings of one particular variation of Murphy's Law ('If anything can go wrong, then sooner or later it will'). Even a relatively rare event like a volcanic eruption will eventually, over a long enough period, occur at exactly the right moment to escape triggering all the warning systems. Which is exactly what happened when a third 747, this time a KLM flight making an approach to Anchorage in Alaska on 15 December 1989 at 26,000 feet flew into an ash cloud thrown up by an erupting volcano called Mount Redoubt. Because the eruption had only occurred 1½ hours earlier, the crew had no warning, and once again, all four engines failed in quick succession.

Sectional drawing of Rolls-Royce RB211 engine, as fitted to the British Airways Boeing 747 involved in the Mount Galunggung emergency over Indonesia in 1982. (Rolls-Royce)

Particles of volcanic debris retrieved from different stages of one of the engines. (Rolls-Royce)

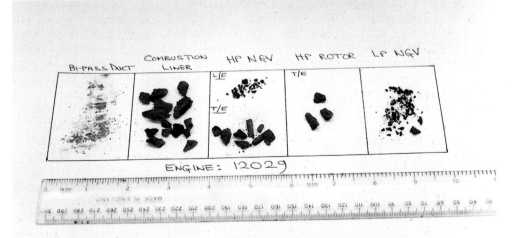

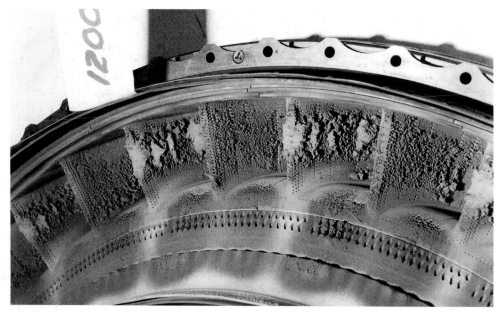

Damage to the guide vanes of one of the engines of the BA 747. (Rolls-Royce)

Damage to the compressor blades of one of the BA747's RB211 engines, caused by ingesting the harshly abrasive particles from the volcanic plume. In spite of this, the engines were restarted, and delivered enough power to carry the airliner over the mountains to a safe landing at Jakarta, providing ample testimony to the toughness and reliability of the modern jet engine. (Rolls-Royce)

By now though, the symptoms were well understood, and the causes were obvious in an area of known volcanic activity, and the crew carried out the same recovery drills as the British Airways team had done. By the time the 747 had descended to 13,000 feet they were able to restart all four engines and complete their flight. However, when the aircraft was safely on the ground, they found it had suffered the same comprehensive damage as *City of Edinburgh*, which eventually cost a total of 80 million dollars to put right. In future, the results of this particular type of apparently clear-air hazard seem likely to be increased costs, rather than increased casualties.

4

The winds of change

The performance of modern airliners and the increasing sophistication of weather reporting, weather predictions and weather radar on board individual aircraft, resulted in thunderstorms seeming to be less and less of a hazard. Because flights could be routed over the tops of many storm fronts, or diverted around an advancing weather system, many aircraft avoided the effects of the storms through which their predecessors would had to have battered their way. Even those which did encounter the fierce forces present in storm clouds were usually able to cope by reducing speed and riding with the updraughts and downdraughts to avoid overstressing the aircraft.

With this in mind, and with increasing traffic, controllers began to allow aircraft to fly closer and closer to thunderstorms which would once have been given the widest of berths. In most cases, passengers experienced nothing more than moderate to severe turbulence, and some spectacular if frightening electrical discharge effects. But with such powerful forces confined to such small areas of sky, the potential is always there for disaster to strike along with the lightning.

On 24 June 1975, Eastern Airlines flight 66, a Boeing 727, was approaching New York's Kennedy Airport at the end of a flight from New Orleans, with a heavy thunderstorm in the vicinity. Observers on the ground reported very heavy rain and strong winds shifting in speed and direction, making flying conditions extremely difficult. One DC-8 cargo flight arrival touched down on runway 22 Left after having received a message from the controller that the wind was only blowing at 15 knots. The captain complained that the winds they met on the final approach meant they should have been landing on one of the other runways instead.

The next arrival was an Eastern Airlines Lockheed TriStar which met such adverse winds that it nearly hit the ground before overshooting and climbing away from the airfield. Conditions were still changing, and two more incoming flights landed safely before flight 66 started to make its final approach. At first the aircraft descended above the glide-path, but when only a few hundred feet above the ground its descent suddenly steepened and its extended undercarriage collided with a series of approach light towers.

These impacts tore away the outboard section of the port wing. Deprived of the lift this provided, the aircraft rolled to port, broke up and burst into flames short of the runway threshold. The only survivors were seven passengers and two cabin crew members in the tail end of the passenger cabin. With no survivors from the flight-deck, the investigators had to depend on the information contained in the flight data recorder and the cockpit voice recorder systems.

The pilots' conversation showed the captain had spotted the runway approach lights when the 727 was approximately 400 feet above the ground. The first officer agreed, and it became clear that both were concentrating more on their view of the ground through the heavy rain than on the instruments. They did not seem to notice the aircraft descending below the glide-path, which would have been shown by the horizontal needle on the ILS display moving upwards on the dial. Only when the first officer spotted what was happening and called for full take-off power, was there any attempt to correct the problem. By then it was too late. Within a brief moment and long before the engines could accelerate to full power, the still descending aircraft brushed the approach lights and the crash was inevitable.

What had caused the sudden and catastrophic increase in the aircraft's rate of descent towards the runway? The pilots ahead of the 727 in the queue to land on runway 22 L made it clear the wind was shifting in strength and direction from moment to moment. Later research into the mechanisms governing thunderstorm cells were to reveal that the approaching flight 66 had encountered a 'microburst', or an area where fierce downdraughts of cold air coming down from high altitude, to balance the warm upcurrents in the centre of a storm cloud, strike the ground at high speed.

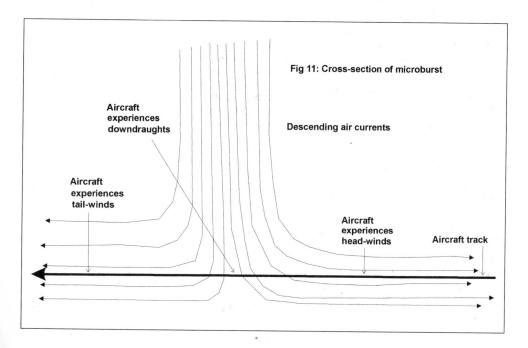

Fig 11: Cross-section of microburst

Aircraft experiences downdraughts

Descending air currents

Aircraft experiences tail-winds

Aircraft experiences head-winds

Aircraft track

As each microburst reaches the ground, the airstream is deflected outwards from the centre of the microburst in all directions. This means that an aircraft approaching the microburst meets a strong headwind which generates plenty of lift. But as soon as it reaches the core of the microburst, it meets a violent downdraught at the centre of the column of cold air. As it flies on towards the other side, it encounters an equally strong tailwind caused by the outflow of air from the microburst in the opposite direction.

This violently fast change in wind speed and direction is called 'windshear' and since the aircraft is still moving at roughly the same speed relative to the ground as it was before, its speed relative to the air drops very sharply indeed. This brings a sharp drop in the lift generated by the wings. Depending on whether the aircraft is taking off or landing, this causes a decrease in the rate of climb, or an increase in the rate of descent, as happened with flight 66. So sharp was the change that the FAA inspectors decided that even if one of the pilots had been concentrating on the ILS indicator, by the time the needle movement showed they were losing height, it was already too late. Even opening the throttles immediately to full take-off power would not have accelerated the aircraft and stopped the descent in time to prevent it hitting the ground.

This is difficult to avoid, for several reasons. Thunderstorms are common in many areas of heavy air traffic, so operators are under pressure to maintain schedules. Warnings of severe windshear are difficult to organise, since much of the airfield-based wind measurement equipment only gives an accurate reading of the wind at ground level, at one spot on the perimeter of the field. If a microburst is passing overhead, the readings at places only a few hundred yards away would show dramatic differences in speed and direction.

When investigators studied the records, they found that in the United States alone, thunderstorm systems were involved in a whole series of accidents during the 1960s, 1970s and 1980s. In the 22 years from 1964 to 1986, an average of just over one crash a year was caused by aeroplanes encountering microbursts and windshear. Furthermore, because the direction of the wind reversed as an aeroplane passed through a microburst, winds of moderate strength could cause disaster, when a wind of equivalent speed blowing in a constant direction would scarcely cause concern.

One of these windshear related accidents involved another Boeing 727 also on a flight from New Orleans, this time bound for Las Vegas on 9 July 1982. On this occasion the microburst struck the aircraft at the start of its flight rather than at the end, as a thunderstorm approached the airport as it prepared for take-off. The 727 belonged to Pan American and had just arrived from Miami on the first sector of flight 759 which would eventually finish its journey at San Diego in California.

When the crew were filing their flight plan for the New Orleans to Las Vegas sector of the flight, the weather forecast was generally good, with no low pressure areas or weather fronts within 100 miles. Humidity was high though, and sporadic thunderstorms were springing up all over the southern USA with little warning. Even when the aircraft was starting its engines a heavy downpour began, and air traffic control amended the wind information from 'calm' to a direction of 040 degrees at eight knots. By the time it joined the queue of departing aircraft waiting to use runway 28, the tower was reporting the wind had shifted to 060 degrees and increased to 15 knots, with gusts reaching a peak of 25 knots.

A few minutes later the wind information changed again to 070 degrees at 17 knots, with a peak of 23 knots, but the tower now issued a low level windshear alert as the storm approached the airport. An inbound Boeing 767 came in over the runway threshold and touched down successfully, reporting a 10-knot windshear on the approach. Once the 767 had turned off the runway, the 727 was cleared for departure and flight 759 started its take-off run.

Witnesses on the ground saw the airliner lift off somewhere near the half-way point on runway 28 and climb to approximately 100 feet. After that, they were horrified to see it begin to sink, still with its nose held upwards in a climbing attitude, until it vanished behind a row of trees. Within seconds of its disappearance there was the noise of an explosion and a column of smoke and flame told its own macabre story.

The pattern of destruction was plain to see. The slowly descending aircraft had struck a group of three trees bordering a road almost half a mile beyond the end of the runway. Banking gently to port, it struck a second group of trees a hundred yards beyond, tearing away parts of the port wing and the flaps. With the loss of lift on the port wing, this caused the aircraft to roll further to port so that its wings passed the vertical before the port wingtip hit the ground and caused the aircraft to crash on its back and explode, almost a mile from the end of the runway.

The wreck destroyed or damaged a dozen houses and killed eight people on the ground outright, in addition to the 145 people who died on board the aircraft. Unfortunately, the wholesale destruction threatened to obscure vital clues as to the causes of the accident. For example, it was difficult to retrieve any information from the flight-deck instruments. On the other hand, the wreckage showed that flaps were correctly set for take-off at 15 degrees, which eliminated the possibility that the aircraft's sudden descent could have been caused by the pilot retracting the flaps too soon and reducing the lift while the aircraft was still climbing away from the runway. The undercarriage was in the retracted position, which eliminated another source of aerodynamic drag, which might have slowed the plane down and reduced the lift generated by the wings.

The next possibility was an unexplained reduction in engine power. Although the engine power readings on the instrument panel had been damaged in the fire, the investigators found it was possible to read that all three engines had been developing sufficient power for a normal take-off in perfect safety when the aircraft had crashed. In addition, the damage to the engines when they hit the ground confirmed they had been operating at high power, and when they were dismantled and checked, there was no evidence of any system failure which could have affected their output.

One by one, the pieces were falling into place. The aircraft had been seen to climb away from the runway and remain in a nose-up attitude, the flaps had been set correctly and the undercarriage safely retracted, and all three engines were delivering sufficient power. Yet the aircraft had clearly lost lift and sunk into the trees. The only remaining cause must be a sudden and catastrophic shift in wind speed and direction.

Fortunately for the success of the investigation, both the flight data recorder and cockpit voice recorder survived the impact. The CVR recording showed that the crew had been aware of the windshear problem, and that Captain McCullers had advised the first officer to let the speed build up past the minimum needed for take-off, as an extra safety precaution. Forty-two seconds after the start of the take-off run, the 727 left the ground at an indicated airspeed of 158 knots, seven knots higher than the calculated take-off speed.

From that point onwards, things went wrong with terrifying speed. Just two seconds after leaving the ground, the captain could be heard saying the aircraft was sinking. In another twelve seconds the ground proximity warning system alarm sounded, with the noise of the aircraft striking the trees being clearly heard just three seconds after that. By comparing the information on the FDR with the CVR recording, it showed that at the moment the GPWS alarm sounded, the aircraft's air speed had dropped to 149 knots, and its height had dropped back from a maximum of 95 feet above ground level to just 55 feet.

In the absence of any weather information from the crew of the crashed aircraft, the investigators had to check with the other crews who had taken off from New Orleans that summer afternoon. The pilot of one DC-9 which had taken off from the airfield's other runway ten minutes before the PanAm flight, said their weather radar showed a thunderstorm cell directly over the centre of the airfield. Another DC-9, which took off three minutes afterwards, reported their weather radar showed storm cells all around the airport, with the most intense one on the ENE side of the field. This second DC-9 met severe windshear on its take-off run and had to lift off below the recommended speed to avoid being blown sideways off the runway and on to the grass.

On the other hand, a third DC-9, which took off just four minutes ahead of the Pan American flight, reported storm cells a few miles from the airport, and encountered no problems with rain, windshear or turbulence during its take-off and climb. The difficulty with conditions changing as quickly as this was that it was very difficult for any controller to take responsibility for issuing an official warning. Even the National Weather Service station at Slidell, 30 miles north east of the airport, found their radar recordings at the time of the 727's fatal take-off attempt showed a storm cell of intensity level 2 over the airfield, which was not regarded as a severe weather system.

When the readings of the air-speed and height recorded on the FDR were analysed and used to show the changing effect of the wind on the aircraft's trajectory, the information produced two conflicting sets of signals. On the one hand, it revealed that between the aircraft starting its take-off run and finally losing height to crash into the trees beyond the end of the runway, the wind changed from a headwind of 18 knots to a tailwind of 36 knots. At its worst, the change involved a shift in airspeed equivalent to a sudden deceleration of 47 knots as the aircraft passed through the peak of its climb from the runway. At this very moment it was also subjected to a maximum vertical downdraught of 18 knots, which conspired with the sudden drop in airspeed to force it back down towards the ground, in spite of anything the crew could do. Even so, the first officer had carried out the approved emergency drill of keeping the nose high, but a sudden increase in the intensity of the rain halfway down the take-off run meant they were now flying on instruments.

This may well have confused the situation, since there would be an appreciable delay for pressure-sensitive instruments like the altimeter and the rate of climb and descent indicator to respond to the change in circumstances and actually show what was happening. Nevertheless, it was a close-run thing. The flight data recorder showed the descent had been stopped at the moment the aircraft collided with the first group of trees. Had they not been there, the 727 might have succeeded in climbing away with no trouble beyond a profound fright for all involved.

If this particular microburst created conditions in which a successful take-off was simply not possible, why had the airfield's own systems not given adequate warning? The airport was equipped with an array of anemometers to measure wind speed at five different points around the airfield boundary, to the south, west, east, north-west and north-east, and one in the centre of the field. If the wind speed and direction readings between any two of these sensors differed by more than a pre-set level, then a windshear alarm was sounded and the controllers were made aware of the situation.

Unfortunately, the anemometers could not detect a vertical component in the wind speed and direction which would indicate updraughts and downdraughts. Secondly, if a gust reached more than one sensor at the same instant, the alarm might not sound. Thirdly, a microburst could be concentrated over a sufficiently small area to pass between sensors, and fourthly, there was speculation that the sheltering effect of the surrounding trees might slow down the apparent wind.

There was another possibility which might have meant their own weather radar failed to warn the crew of the danger they faced. Although these on-board radar systems spotted the presence of thunderstorm cells, they have a number of weak points. They tend to be sensitive to heavy rain. The cockpit voice recorder showed the crew had checked the weather radar display before take-off when the downpour was reaching its height. They had seen no sign of the approaching storm cells to the east of the airport, including the one which proved to be their downfall.

Another problem with weather radar is a phenomenon called a 'contour hole', where an area of extremely heavy rain fails to return any echo at all. The result is that an area of specially severe weather appears, at first sight, as a gap of clear weather which may persuade a crew that it offers an escape route from the rest of a thunderstorm system. This was a mistake which proved fatal for the flight-deck crew and the majority of the passengers of a Southern Airways DC-9 flying from Muscle Shoals in Alabama via Huntsville to Atlanta in Georgia on 4 April 1977.

This was a day of truly terrible weather, with one of the worst storm systems recorded in the United States since records began. There were tornadoes in the area with winds of more than 70 knots, hailstones as large as tennis balls and thunder clouds up to almost 60,000 feet. Nevertheless, the first sector of the flight to Huntsville was smooth enough, though the next sector to Atlanta promised to present more severe problems. As the DC-9 took off for the 25-minute flight, it was already raining and there were several severe weather warnings for the area covered by their route. Other aircraft reported turbulence and severe winds, but nothing which could be seen as threatening aircraft safety.

Nine minutes after take-off, the DC-9 had reached its top of climb altitude at 17,000 feet, and three minutes later it was cleared to descend to 14,000 feet. By this time, the crew had spotted a thunderstorm in their path in the vicinity of Rome, Georgia, some 50 miles from Atlanta. The CVR revealed they were not going to attempt to fly through the heart of the storm, but would make for an apparent gap of clear weather shown on the radar display. Within minutes it was clear that they had been badly misled by the radar picture into entering the most intense area of the thunderstorm. The aircraft was hit by a furious hail-storm which cracked the flight-deck windows, and the port engine failed. Within another 30 seconds, the starboard engine failed too, and the DC-9 started to descend without any engine power at all.

The pilots called up air traffic control and asked for the nearest airfield. ATC gave them a vector to Dobbins Air Force Base which was more or less ahead of them, and closer than Atlanta. The pilots then concentrated on staying in clear conditions long enough to try to restart the engines, which meant turning away to the south-west and interrupting communications with the tower for two vital minutes. By the time it was clear that they were not going to restart, and they had turned back towards Dobbins airfield, it became increasingly obvious that they had now lost too much height to make the 17-mile distance as a power-off glide.

Air traffic control suggested an approach to another nearby airfield called Cartersville, but by now time was running out. The captain wanted to select the largest field they could find for an emergency landing, but the first officer, a forceful ex-navy pilot, insisted they should put the aircraft down on a nearby highway. They made a careful approach on to the two-lane road, but the fact that it was lined with trees and telephone poles made disaster almost inevitable.

Just before touching down on the road, the DC-9's port wing hit two trees, and soon afterwards both wingtips struck a number of other trees in succession before the main wheels contacted the road surface. As they did so, the port wing hit a more serious obstacle in the shape of a roadside embankment which caused the airliner to wheel off the road to the left, and crash through a succession of trees and poles before demolishing a roadside service station and grocery store. The petrol in the pumps, and in a group of cars parked outside, was set ablaze by sparks from overhead power cables brought down in the crash, and the aircraft itself caught fire from its own fuel spillages. Miraculously, 21 of the passengers and both stewardesses survived the crash and the resulting fire, but both pilots died in the impact.

It was clear that the first causal factor in the accident had been the decision of the crew to try to steer their aircraft through what seemed to be a clear patch in the storm system. But the direct cause had been the failure of both engines, and the investigators concentrated on the reasons for the normally extremely reliable power units to fail in such quick succession. A Pratt & Whitney JT8D engine identical to those fitted in the aircraft was run at similar speeds to those used on the flight, and large amounts of water sprayed into it to simulate the effect of flying through an extremely intense downpour.

The investigators found the combination of reducing power settings on the engines, as the pilots slowed the aircraft down according to the procedure laid down for negotiating a storm, and ingesting huge quantities of water, could cause the engine's high pressure rotors to slow down. Eventually they would not be able to drive the aircraft's power generators, explaining the interruptions in power and communications during that phase of the flight.

When they stripped and examined the engines of the DC-9, they also found that the crew's natural reaction to open the throttles when the engines had started slowing down caused a series of power surges which had been noticed by survivors. These surges had caused the low-pressure turbine blades in the engine to collide with the fixed vanes intended to guide the airflow over the turbine blades. Pieces of broken blades and vanes were then thrown back into the high-pressure compressors, to cause much more severe damage. This would spoil the efficiency of the compressors, so that increased throttle settings would cause the turbines to overheat, and signs of this were found in both engines. The sum total of this damage was to make the engines virtually impossible to restart, and from then on the end was inevitable.

Two questions arose from the investigation. There were no signs of hailstone damage in the engines, so that heavy rain rather than hail proved to be the decisive factor. Secondly, at the time that both engines had failed, prompt action by the crew should have enabled the aircraft to glide as far as Dobbins AFB, then less than 30 miles away with the aircraft approximately 13,000 feet above the height of the airfield. Its main runway was almost two miles long, and the field was equipped with precision approach radar and a full range of emergency services. But the delays resulting from a succession of attempts to restart the engines wasted precious height and closed off the options, until a narrow, tree-lined highway was all that remained.

Alerting more crews to the possibility of being misled by contour holes in their weather radar displays could prevent more mishaps along the lines of the DC-9 crash. But severe windshear effects close to the ground caused by thunderstorm microbursts remain a more intractable problem. The extremely transient nature of these conditions means that one flight may encounter no real trouble at all, but another one, only minutes earlier or later, could face the most intractable of threats.

Another accident which demonstrated the power of microburst conditions to bring down even a powerful modern airliner with almost no warning, occurred on 2 August 1985, once again in the thunderstorm-prone region of the southern United States. Delta Airlines flight 191 was a service from Fort Lauderdale in Florida to Los Angeles in California, with an en route stop at Dallas-Fort Worth Airport in Texas. The aircraft in question was a Lockheed TriStar carrying 152 passengers and a crew of 11. The early stages of the flight from Fort Lauderdale had been smooth, though the crew had received permission to divert to avoid one line of thunderstorms along the Gulf Coast.

This brought the aircraft on to a more northerly route which involved holding over the Texarkana navigational beacon in Arkansas until they were given clearance for an approach into the extremely busy Dallas-Fort Worth Airport. By this time, their weather radar showed another intense thunderstorm astride their route, so once again they were given permission to divert to avoid it. As they neared the airport, they were warned of rain showers to the north of the airfield, and given a heading to steer to make an instrument approach and landing on runway 17 Left.

There were two aircraft ahead of the TriStar in the queue for landing. The first one, belonging to American Airlines, touched down safely after reporting heavy rainfall on final approach. Next was a Learjet, followed by flight 191. The controllers ordered two speed reductions, down to an approach speed of 150 knots, and warned of showers in the vicinity. Finally, the Tower controller told them that surface winds were 090 degrees at 5 knots, gusting to 15. The pilots lowered the flaps and undercarriage for landing and, at first, all seemed well, until things began going very wrong indeed.

The controllers saw the big, wide-bodied airliner emerge from a blanket of rain on the northern side of the airfield far too low for a normal approach, and ordered an overshoot. Before the crew could take any action, the main wheels touched the ground on a ploughed field, more than a mile short of the runway. The huge aircraft bounced back into the sky and then sank down again towards a busy highway which skirted the northern side of the airport. It struck a passing car and a lamp-post with the port wing, which swung it round to the left, straight towards a pair of water tanks on the airfield perimeter.

The already badly damaged port wing struck the first tank, swinging the aircraft further round to the left, to impact head-on into the second tank. The aircraft exploded, and the shock of the detonation blasted the whole tail section backwards, clear of the conflagration which destroyed the front half of the aircraft completely. After such an impact, followed in quick succession by fire and explosion, it seems almost incredible that 29 people survived the crash, all of them in the rear section of the fuselage.

For the investigators there were two main questions, as with the earlier windshear accidents. Why had the weather conditions brought this aircraft down so catastrophically short of the runway, when two others had touched

Wreckage of the Delta Airlines Lockheed TriStar at Dallas Fort Worth which was brought down by flying through a microburst on its final approach. (Associated Press)

down perfectly normally only minutes before? Secondly, why were the flight crew not warned in time to abandon their approach and wait until the danger was over before trying again?

The weather records showed that 2 August had been a day of fierce temperatures, exceeding 100 degrees Fahrenheit in places. As the ground heated up, huge columns of warm air rose upwards, displacing the cold air above them to create thunderstorm cells of great intensity, with little or no predictable pattern. One of the airfield fire team said afterwards that the west side of the airfield was bathed in brilliant warm sunshine at a time when the eastern side had thunder, lightning, drenching rain, golfball-sized hailstones and winds gusting to 100 mph or more. With variations like that over a couple of miles, it was small wonder that weather warnings were difficult to sort out from the general meteorological chaos.

Yet one place should have been able to issue a timely alarm. The weather radar watch at Stephenville, just over 70 miles from the airport, spotted a thunderstorm cell in the vicinity of the airport just 17 minutes before the crash. This was rated as moderate intensity, level 2. Within four minutes the observers had regraded it level 3, and spotted another growing storm system, which they tagged cell D, just to the south of it. By 6.4 pm, just two minutes before the crash, the observers called Fort Worth forecast centre and warned them about the growth of cell D. By 6.21 pm, just over 15 minutes after the crash, this cell had grown so fast that its top reached 50,000 feet and it had been rated level 5. This was the storm cell sitting on the approach to runway 17 Left, lying in wait for flight 191.

Unfortunately the airport controller did not consider the information passed on from Stephenville warranted a weather warning, and no special alert was passed to flight 191. The first sign the crew had of the storm cell ahead of them was a remark from the first officer that he could see lightning in the cloud ahead. But they only realised the intensity of the microburst when their indicated air speed suddenly increased from 150 knots to 173 knots. The cockpit voice recorder showed the captain was aware of the danger of it suddenly dropping equally spectacularly. Within seconds it had done just that, falling away to 129 knots. The first officer pulled back on the control column to hold the nose up, the standard procedure for dealing with the situation.

In a really intense microburst, this reduces the tendency to sink at the price of bringing the aircraft closer to the stall. The crew applied full power, but before the engines could fully respond, the TriStar entered a series of vortices which created a succession of updraughts and downdraughts. At one stage the first officer had to ease off the back pressure on the stick when the stall warning horn sounded and the aircraft lifted in an updraught. In less than a second, revealed by the readings on the flight data recorder, the air speed dropped by 20 knots and the airliner began to sink, with fatal results.

In all, the TriStar had encountered sudden cross-wind gusts approaching 70 mph, which had rolled the aircraft 20 degrees left and right at the most difficult part of the approach, and a total windshear of almost 75 knots between the peak headwind and the peak tailwind during its attempt to reach the runway. Small wonder that the crew's determined attempts had failed. Yet these were no novices. Both were especially experienced fliers, well versed in the difficult flying conditions in these southern weather systems. The Captain, Ted Connors, was one of the senior pilots on the airline with an unblemished record, while the first officer, Rudy Price, was rated 'above average' and had been involved in the production of the airline's official training manual. If they had failed to spot the danger in time, given the warning information they had, or had not, been given, what hope was there for other fliers?

The official investigation criticised the lack of weather warnings given to the aircraft as it approached the airfield. Yet the fact remains that, given their adherence to the recovery procedures from the start of the emergency, it might have been possible for the crew to abort the landing and climb away clear of the ground as soon as the first evidence of windshear was encountered. The standard technique involved pulling back on the stick to raise the nose even when the speed is falling off, and setting the engines to full emergency power to blast the aircraft clear of the ground. Given that split-second decisions were needed, the prime requirement is still for more accurate information and for earlier and more reliable warnings, to give pilots the chance of carrying out the recovery technique in full.

Has the microburst peril finally been tamed? New types of warning equipment have been developed, including improved networks of ground sensors. Better performance Doppler weather radar can sense the changing wind speeds which pose the actual threat. This combination of equipment was thought to have saved another airliner from being brought down by an intense microburst over Denver, Colorado in 1989. In the longer term, probably the best solution is offered by aircraft carrying on-board radar sensitive enough to reveal windshear up to 1½ minutes ahead. This has been available for some years, but is still very expensive, so will take time to fit to all aircraft which may need to fly through potential danger areas on a regular basis.

5

Freeze, freeze, thou bitter sky

For much of the history of powered flight, there was a third deadly menace lying in wait to trap the unwary. Along with winds and storms, ice was a potential killer with a long list of victims to its name. As an aircraft struggled to climb through increasingly cold and moist air, icing layers could build up to choke the carburettor air intakes and starve the engines of the power to breathe. Even when carburettor heaters reduced this danger, there still remained the potential of ice to build up on the flying surfaces, increasing drag, adding to the weight and distorting the aerofoil sections of the wings which created the vital lift to keep the aircraft flying.

Time and again wartime flyers, especially bomber crews raiding Germany on freezing moonlit nights, reported having to fight to retain control of their heavily loaded aircraft when icing took hold. Sometimes they managed to climb above the freezing levels, sometimes they were forced down to warmer layers of air, where the ice thawed and broke up. But for every crew that survived, many must have been lost, and assumed to have fallen victim to flak or Luftwaffe night-fighters.

With the return of passenger flying in the post-war world, there was an increasing demand for year-round services, with the minimum of cancellations and postponements. The early piston-engined airliners still found icing a problem in adverse weather conditions. Wartime developments like de-icer boots helped keep the problem more or less under control until the arrival of the jets, by relying on rubber panels in the leading edges of wing and tail surfaces. These could be inflated and deflated in icing conditions to dislodge the ice layer as it formed.

Yet the problem never quite disappeared. Pure-jet aircraft could climb and descend more quickly through the icing layers of the atmosphere, and their engines produced large quantities of surplus heat which could be ducted to warm the wings and control surfaces in extreme conditions. Propeller-turbine aircraft like the Vickers Viscount and Bristol Britannia on the other hand, though they were faster, more efficient and more reliable than the piston-engined airliners they replaced, still flew at heights where icing could be a problem.

How severe a problem this could still be was proved on 18 January 1960, when flight 20 of the American operator Capital Airlines left Chicago for

Norfolk, Virginia. The aircraft was a Viscount 746D and it made one en-route stop at Washington DC, before taking off into the winter darkness to resume its journey with 46 passengers and a crew of four. It was cleared to fly at 8,000 feet for the relatively short sector, and the local weather was a mixture of mist and scattered showers.

At approximately 10.20 pm local time, the Viscount came down in a forest near Charles City, some 30 miles south east of Richmond in Virginia and approximately 50 miles from its destination. The wreckage caught fire after the impact, and all on board were killed. But what had caused this apparently well-maintained aircraft to come to grief in such relatively calm conditions?

Crash investigation almost 40 years ago was less well equipped with recording mechanisms on board the aircraft. Set against that was the fact that it was cruising at a much lower altitude than most present-day flights, so that witnesses on the ground were able to describe its movements in more detail. For example, their recollections showed the aircraft was much lower than its designated height just before the crash, and it flew very slowly, making two complete left-hand circles before losing speed and plunging to the ground.

Examination of the wreckage showed the aircraft hit the ground in a flat attitude. The wings and fuselage were impaled by trees, showing the Viscount had little or no forward velocity at the time of the crash. Checking the control surfaces showed no obvious signs of malfunction to explain the two complete circles and the final stall into the ground. This rather suggested engine problems, and the known weather conditions at the time made it possible that icing could be involved.

Inspection of the power units showed that the two port engines must have failed during the flight, and had not been restarted. One possible explanation was that the crew had failed to realise the danger of icing, and had not switched on the anti-icing system. With at least two engines out, the aircraft had clearly descended to a lower altitude either for lack of power, or in the hope of clearing the problem and restarting the engines.

Engine failure on a Viscount activated the automatic feathering system, which turned the propeller blades edge-on to the airflow to prevent them windmilling and to reduce drag to the minimum. The crew must have decided to put the aircraft into a shallow dive in the hope of unfeathering the propellers and turning the engines over to persuade them to restart. However, the descent to warmer temperatures probably caused the other engines to fail, either by melting ice entering the intakes or because the anti-icing system had now been switched on, and left on during the descent into warmer air.

Whatever the reason, the relighting attempts were unsuccessful. One problem might have been a drop in battery power after all four engines stopped, though opening the throttles prematurely before the restart procedure had been completed would cause the autofeather mechanism to take charge once again, turning the propeller blades to stop them spinning in the slipstream. It takes little imagination to understand the crew's haste to restore the power, with the aircraft dropping towards the ground from such a low altitude.

Witnesses' statements made it clear they only succeeded when time and height had almost run out, and they managed to restart the starboard outer engine. Unfortunately, running this up to full power to arrest the descent produced a huge asymmetric thrust, and turned the plane through two complete circles, while they struggled to restart another engine. When they succeeded, it was the starboard inner engine, which produced extra power, but at the expense of an increase in the asymmetric thrust. The aircraft was now only seconds from impact, and all the crew could do was pull up the nose to avoid the ground. By now the aircraft had lost so much speed that it stalled and fell nearly vertically in a flat attitude, with almost no forward movement.

What were the lessons to be drawn from this disaster, to ensure it should never happen again? When the investigators studied the company's checklist procedures for their flight crews, they found that the emergency section on restarting engines recommended they first descend to warmer temperatures before carrying out the relight procedure. This was to be replaced by an instruction to restart engines at any height, but to be careful to employ the exact procedure in full. Crews were also to be reminded of the need to switch on the anti-icing system whenever there was any possibility of meeting icing conditions.

The problem with the Charles City accident was that so much of the explanation for what happened involved informed speculation. This in turn highlights the major difficulty with investigating accidents where icing might be a factor. No evidence in the whole field of crash investigation is as perishable as that of icing. An aircraft which might come to grief because of iced-up wings might be completely clear of ice within an hour. Equally, an aircraft which crashed without icing being involved could collect ice on its wings and control surfaces simply by the action of winter weather, before the investigating teams could assemble.

This is what had been the cause for sharp differences of opinion and a measure of injustice resulting from an accident almost two years before the Capital Airlines Viscount suffered its multiple engine failures. In February 1958, the Manchester United football team and a party of pressmen and team managers were returning from a European Cup match against Red Star of Belgrade, the Yugoslav champions. The aircraft, registered G-ALZU, was a twin-engined Airspeed Ambassador of British European Airways, known by its BEA name of Elizabethan, and flight 609 was a charter from Manchester to Belgrade and back, with an intermediate stop at Munich in each direction to take on more fuel.

The match had been a three-all draw, which left Manchester winners as a result of the earlier tie played at home, and there was an element of celebration among the 38-strong party as the Elizabethan took off from Belgrade. The two pilots were, unusually, both Captains. James Thain was sitting in the right-hand seat, although he was in command of the aircraft, while Ken Rayment as the senior pilot, standing in as a favour to Thain on this non-scheduled trip, took the left-hand seat. Though this was strictly an infringement of BEA's operating procedures, it was not against Civil Aviation Authority rules.

The weather was cold and damp, and Rayment had to land on instruments at Belgrade at the end of the outbound trip to pick up the team. While en route to Munich, and descending through cloud at 18,000 feet, the pilots had switched on the airframe de-icing system. This directed currents of warm air, heated to 60 degrees Centigrade by fuel burners in the wings, under pressure to vents in the leading edges of the wings, tailplane and the triple fins of the

Elizabethan. Once again they had to make an instrument approach, but they broke through into clear weather at 500 feet above the airport.

The landing at 2.15 pm local time was normal enough, though the nose-wheel was throwing up huge waves of slush. Although the temperature was just above freezing at ground level, the steady and persistent drizzle was turning to sleet in the darkening winter afternoon as the Elizabethan taxied over to the apron for refuelling.

Because there was only one licensed engineer on duty, they could not use the underwing pressurised fuelling system, so local ground staff had to use the emergency fillers. This meant clambering on top of the wings, which were still warm from the anti-icing applied on the descent and approach, and snowflakes hitting the wing surface were melting and running off the trailing edge. They had no difficulty keeping their footing on the smoothly curving metal, even when some of their colleagues on the ground made them dodge snowballs.

When the aircraft was ready to leave, the pilots could have had de-icing fluid sprayed on the wings, or had the snow brushed clear, but neither seemed necessary. At 2.20 pm GMT (3.20 pm local), they called the tower to ask for clearance, and though there was almost an inch of slush on the runway, this was given. As the aircraft started its take-off roll, with Rayment at the controls, Thain called out the increasing speeds. Suddenly there was a change in the engine note, and Thain dropped his eyes to the pressure gauges where the needles were flickering ominously. Rayment called, 'Abandon take-off' and slammed the throttles closed, trapping Thain's fingers.

The apparent problem was one of 'boost surging', which was thought to be caused by opening the throttles too quickly, producing an over-rich mixture in some of the engine cylinders. It was more prevalent in high airfields where the air was thinner, and Munich was at an elevation of 1,700 feet. They decided to backtrack down the runway, and try again, opening the throttles more slowly. When this was approved by the tower, they went back to the end of the runway, opened the throttles to 28 in of boost against the brakes and then started the take-off roll.

With the throttles set to full power, the starboard engine remained at a steady 57.5 in boost pressure, but the port engine went past 60 and off the clock. Once again the take-off was abandoned. The tower offered them the chance to backtrack and try again but the pilots decided to go back to the apron. After discussion with the engineer, they decided not to have the engines retuned, which would mean stopping overnight, but to try once more, opening the throttles even more slowly. Even though this would mean lifting off much further down the runway, this did not seem to be a problem.

During the final take-off run, the throttles were advanced very slowly, though Thain noticed slight surging on the port engine at around 85 knots. Soon afterwards, Rayment pulled back on the control column to raise the nosewheel clear of the slush and reduce the drag. Thain eased back the port throttle until the surging ceased, and then slowly opened it again. Both boost indicators were now showing 57.5 in with no surging and the speed was now 105 knots, with acceleration slower than normal, but this could have been due to the extra care and time taken in opening the throttles.

Slowly, it reached 110 knots, and crept up to V1 at 117 knots, after which the aircraft was committed to take-off. V2 would be at 119 knots, but by now the aircraft was so far down the runway it was entering the deepest area of slush, and one which had not been disturbed by earlier aircraft movements. To Thain's horror, the ASI needle hesitated at 117 knots, and then dropped back to 112 knots, and then back further to 105 knots, as the aircraft left the paved stretch of runway.

It crashed through a fence, crossed a small road outside the airfield boundary and headed for a house and tree directly in its path. Thain pressed the throttles hard against the stops, while Rayment tried to lift the aircraft off the ground, and called for the undercarriage to be retracted to cut the drag as it became airborne. It seemed to lift off, and then swung to the right to head between the house and a tree. The port wing struck the house and was torn off outboard of the engine, the tail unit was ripped off and the house set on fire.

The aircraft then struck the tree, which tore open the port side of the flight deck, trapping Rayment, and 100 yards further on the right-hand side of the fuselage hit a wooden garage containing a truck, which tore off the complete tail section. Twenty people had died, including seven players, the coach, the trainer, the secretary, and one of the club's directors, seven of the press party, the steward and a Yugoslav passenger.

The survivors were rescued and taken to hospital, and a team from the Luftfahrt Bundesamt accident investigation department arrived at the site at ten o'clock that night. With snow still falling and the temperature dropping, they found a thick blanket of snow on the wreckage. On the wing it had formed a powdery coating which was easily brushed off, but underneath this was a rough layer of ice, frozen firmly on to the skin of the wing.

Wreckage of the BEA Airspeed Ambassador at Munich in February 1958 following the third failed attempt to take off from the slush-covered runway. (Popperphoto)

The Germans seemed to have made their mind up, that icing and the consequent loss of lift were the causes of the accident. When they interviewed BEA station engineer Bill Black for his personal opinion as to why the accident had occurred, Black replied 'One possibility I feel could be the amount of drag caused by excessive slush on the runway'. By the weekend a BEA engineering team arrived to check the engines and find they were in perfect working order. The following day, the German authorities simply sold the wreckage for scrap, precluding any further detailed examination.

There were now two opposing camps. The Germans insisted, on the basis of what they had found when the wreckage had been lying in the open for six hours after the crash, under steadily falling snow, that icing on the wings had caused the disaster, so that the pilots were to blame. The British investigating team felt that this explanation could not be consistent with the fact that the runway was covered with slush and melting snow at the time of the take-off. In their view, because the wings were still warm from the anti-icing applied from the descent into Munich a relatively short time before, the extra drag of slush on the runway must be what had caused the accident.

In the end, because the evidence was so ephemeral, both sides dug in behind their entrenched positions. A German professor of aerodynamics said that if the ice found on the wings that night had been present at the time of the take-off, it would have stopped the aircraft becoming airborne, though it would not explain the deceleration on the take-off run.

A BEA engineer calculated that up to three inches of ice would be needed to interfere with the aerodynamic properties of the Ambassador wing. Furthermore, even that much ice would not have impeded the aircraft's acceleration on the ground. In addition, a British meteorologist pointed out that only ⅛th of an inch of snow actually fell while the aircraft was on the ground, between landing at Munich and the time of the crash. Since a full 1.75–2 inches would be needed to form the layer of ice found at 10 pm, there was no chance that this was present at the time of the accident.

Nevertheless, the German enquiry found that ice on the wings (effectively a pilot's responsibility) rather than slush on the runway (where the airport authorities would bear a measure of responsibility) was the only decisive factor. BEA disagreed, but complained that Thain, as captain of the aircraft, was sitting in the right-hand seat, even though his senior and more experienced fellow-captain Rayment, sat in the left-hand seat. This was within CAA regulations and could be interpreted as a legal requirement, but it also contravened BEA Flying Staff Instructions. Thain's licence was revoked, and he never flew again.

Five years after the disaster, trials conducted by the Royal Aircraft Establishment at Farnborough showed the disastrous effects of slush on the take-off performance of several types of aircraft. In the case of the Ambassador, a depth of only ⅛th of an inch meant the aircraft needed one and a half times as long to leave the ground as on a dry runway. Given the engine problem which required a slow build-up of power, this made the accident virtually inevitable.

Still neither side would budge. New evidence showed that many crucial witnesses had not been called to the German enquiry and their statements had been ignored, and a British enquiry, without the co-operation of the German authorities, but with the help of many German witnesses, was held in the summer of 1969. It found that the cause of the accident was slush on the runway, and reserved its opinion on the possible presence of wing icing, saying that it was 'unlikely'. Captain Thain was exonerated, though he never flew again and died six years later. To this day the German authorities do not accept the findings of the British commission of enquiry.

Perhaps the best testimony to what happened on that cold February day in 1958 is the fact that an infinitely more powerful present-day 747 is restricted from attempting to take off if there is 13 mm (½ in) of slush on the runway. Though the thickness of the slush layer at Munich was in dispute, the airport management admitted they had checked the surface and found 20 mm of slush before Thain and Rayment's first take-off! Pilots who landed later, claimed it was actually much thicker, especially where the layer of trapped water covered the final third of the runway. This was where the Elizabethan desperately tried to build up speed for its third take-off attempt.

Examples like these may imply that icing is no longer a problem for pure-jet aircraft, operating at altitudes far above the levels where ice tends to form in engine intakes and on flying surfaces. Yet even the most powerful jet has to start from somewhere, and it can be as vulnerable on take-off as Thain and Rayment's Elizabethan at Munich. One terrible example of the power of the weather to disrupt an otherwise perfectly routine operation occurred in Washington DC on the afternoon of 13 January 1982.

Snow had been falling heavily all day, and Washington's National Airport had actually been closed for an hour to give the snow removal teams a chance to clear runway 36 which was used for instrument departures in conditions of poor visibility. This time, there was no doubt about the need for de-icing on planes waiting to depart once the airfield re-opened at just before 3 o'clock local time, and Air Florida's flight 90, a Boeing 737 bound for Fort Lauderdale and Tampa in Florida, was no exception. The de-icing team had sprayed the port side of the aircraft with a mixture of glycol and water when there was an announcement that the planned re-opening of the airport at 2.30 pm would be postponed. By this time there was a big backlog of flights waiting to depart from the cramped and crowded airfield, and the 737 was twelfth in line. The Boeing 737 could only move from its place on the apron after the airport had re-opened and half of the waiting aircraft ahead of it in the queue had left. So Captain Wheaton, concerned that ice could build up again during the continuing delays, told the de-icing crew to stop what they were doing.

At 2.50 pm, with the airport about to re-open, the captain called back the de-icers who then started to spray the port side of the aircraft all over again and then treated the starboard side too. Snow was still falling heavily, with a coating of approximately three inches on the ground, and a light dusting on the newly cleared wing surfaces of the 737. The captain called ground control for permission to push back from the apron and start moving to join the queue for departure. At 3.23 pm clearance was given, but the towing vehicle skidded on the frozen ground and failed to push the 737 back.

The flight crew tried to help by selecting reverse thrust on the engines to help the tug. When that too failed, they stopped the engines and called for a towing vehicle fitted with tyre chains. Fifteen minutes after its original clearance the 737 was finally ready to join the lengthening queue of 16 aircraft, all waiting to take off from runway 36. After another 15 minutes, the 737 was second in line, and was cleared to hold at the end of the runway.

At long last, within a few seconds of 4 o'clock, the aircraft was given permission to take off, and it accelerated down the runway into a blinding snowstorm. As soon as it lifted off the runway, it pitched up in an unusually nose-high attitude and climbed hesitantly to between 200 and 300 feet above the ground, before sinking towards the icy Potomac river. It struck the 14th Street road bridge, then jammed with crawling late-afternoon traffic, before tearing away a section of bridge parapet and collapsing into the icy waters.

In spite of all the devoted efforts of rescuers, only four of the 70 passengers and only one member of the five-strong crew survived the crash, and the immersion in the freezing river for more than 20 minutes. Four more people had been killed in the vehicles on the bridge which were struck by the aircraft. The two pilots were among the dead, so the investigators were forced to rely on the FDR and CVR retrieved from the river-bed by divers, for clues as to what had caused the unsuccessful take-off.

The FDR told its own sorry tale. After lifting off the runway at 147 knots, the 737 had climbed at the price of a drop in airspeed. Within 15 seconds the aircraft had reached 240 feet, but the speed had fallen back to 144 knots. In another seven seconds, it had climbed to a peak of 352 feet, but the speed had now fallen back to 130 knots while the aircraft began a shallow turn to the left as it started on its fatal descent.

What had caused this unusual behaviour? Crews of other aircraft at Washington National that day noticed large amounts of ice on the 737 as it queued for the runway. One passenger on another aircraft took a picture of the 737 which clearly showed layers of ice on the wings and fuselage. One of the survivors, a former US Navy pilot, noticed that when he boarded the plane, there were no footsteps in the snow to show the flight crew had walked around the aircraft to inspect conditions for themselves.

Other witnesses were convinced the 737 only succeeded in leaving the ground after passing the intersection with runway 33, which was almost three-quarters of the way along runway 36. They also felt its take-off run and climb seemed unusually slow, and witnesses on the 14th Street bridge had seen sheets of ice falling from the 737 as it crashed down on to the parapet.

The cockpit voice recorder showed that the crew had been aware of the build-up of ice on the aircraft since the de-icing spray had been applied. They could be heard going through the after start checklist, but when the first officer called out 'anti-ice', the captain's response was indistinct. Only after a long and exhaustive analysis of the recording under laboratory conditions was it determined that the response was 'off', a fact confirmed by the system settings in the recovered pieces of wreckage. For some reason the crew, who were not experienced in cold weather flying, had decided they did not need to operate the anti-icing system, even though it was almost half an hour since the aircraft had been sprayed.

The accumulation of ice which had built up in that period would have added to the weight of the already heavily loaded aircraft, increased the drag and reduced the lift. But it was far from certain that this on its own was enough to explain its lack of speed and the long slow plunge into the Potomac. Later on the CVR recording, there were signs that the pilots realised something was amiss with the engines. While waiting in the take-off queue, the first officer noticed discrepancies between the readings on the two sets of engine instruments, which they put down to the effects of the jet exhaust from the aircraft ahead of them in the queue.

The tail of the Air Florida Boeing 737 being lifted from the River Potomac after the icing-induced crash on take-off from Washington DC. (Associated Press)

During the take-off itself, the captain referred to the engines being 'real cold' as the speed increased. The first officer seemed dubious as the speed readings increased on the air speed indicator, and just two seconds after take-off, the sound of the stick-shaker (part of the stall warning system) could be heard operating. However, the most vital evidence was not the conversation between the pilots, but the engine noise in the background. Using a sound spectrum analyser, the investigators were able to determine the engines were emitting a noise with a frequency of 3,189 cycles per second, instead of the normal 3,545 cycles per second at take-off power.

This meant the engines had only been delivering partial power, which in addition to the ice on the wings, would have accounted for the aircraft's catastrophic attempts to climb away from the runway. When the sound spectrum results were supplied to Boeing, they ran an analysis of the aircraft's predicted performance at the actual weight of the Air Florida jet and with the engines running at the reduced power setting indicated by the change in noise frequency. The result was very close to the 737's actual take-off run, though not to its crippled stagger into the air and fall back to impact with the bridge. Nevertheless, the question remained as to why the crew had not attempted to increase the power to the correct setting.

During the take-off run, the instruments which told the crew how much throttle to apply were the engine pressure rating, or EPR instruments. These compared the pressure of the air being taken into the engine at the intake with that being ejected in the exhaust. The higher the ratio, the higher the power being delivered. But the probe at the engine intake was susceptible to blockage by ice, which would have been cleared by the anti-icing system being switched on. As anti-ice was off, there was a strong possibility the probes were blocked, causing a falsely high EPR reading to be displayed on the instruments.

A blocked probe would mean the instruments would show the correct take-off power, at a pressure ratio of 2.04, when the true pressure ratio was only 1.70. In other words, the aircraft was being made to take off at about three-quarters power. Nevertheless, the Boeing analysis showed that this would certainly affect take-off performance, but would not have brought the aircraft crashing out of the sky in itself.

Clearly, the ice on the wings would have been another powerful brake on the aircraft's ability to recover from its terrible situation. Tests have shown that a layer of ice on the wings of an aircraft can distort the aerofoil section to the point where lift is reduced by half. But the most effective recovery action the crew could have taken, given the aircraft's steep nose-up attitude, would have been to open the engine throttles to full power. The reason they did not, despite the extreme position in which they found themselves, is that they were convinced that the engines were already delivering full power, and increasing the power settings would overstress them. So they held back from the one step which might have saved their lives.

In theory, one other avenue of escape remained. Calculations showed that, had they acted on the concerns they expressed during the take-off run, they could have aborted the take-off even after the aircraft had reached 120 knots, and stopped before reaching the end of the runway. However, the tower had broken safety regulations to try to clear the traffic backlog by accepting an

inbound Eastern Airlines Boeing 727 to land on the same runway, while the
Air Florida 737 was still taking off.

Was anything learned from the disaster which would make future cold-
weather take-offs safer? One factor was the relative inexperience of the pilots
in ice and snow. The captain had made only eight landings or take-offs in
snowy weather, and the first officer had only flown 737s in icing conditions
twice. Their lack of experience with the changed priorities caused by freezing
weather might have meant they were unaware of the importance of de-icing
for the aircraft and the need to select the anti-icing system before take-off.

Even when weather conditions are not so extreme at ground level, the
menace of icing can still cripple a powerful and well maintained jet long after
a successful take-off, in more insidious ways. On 1 December 1974, a
Northwest Orient Boeing 727 was making a 40-minute positioning flight with
a flight crew of three, from John F. Kennedy Airport in New York to Buffalo,
to pick up a football team and its supporters on a charter flight.

The aircraft took off from JFK at 7.14 pm, and was cleared, first to 14,000
feet and then to 31,000 feet. Three and a half minutes following the second
clearance, the New York Air Traffic Control Centre was appalled to receive an
emergency transmission from the aircraft, reporting it was out of control, and
descending through 20,000 feet. The controller asked for more information,
and the crew replied that they were now descending through 12,000 feet and
the aircraft was in a deep stall.

There were no more messages from the aircraft, and the wreckage of
the 727 was found the next morning in Harriman State Park on the edge
of the city. All three flight crew had been killed in the impact. The investigators began by examining the pattern of the wreckage which had been found
on a shallow mountain slope. The fact that most of the wreckage lay within
a very compact area showed the 727 had hit the ground with very little
forward speed.

The pattern of damage also showed the aircraft had hit the ground with its
nose down and banked to starboard, but there were two more significant clues
in the debris. The only major pieces missing from the main wreckage were the
tips of both elevators, and the whole of the port side tailplane. These were
found at different distances from the main wreckage, showing they must have
broken away before it hit the ground.

The other, even more significant clue was the presence of ice in two of
the aircraft's pitot heads. These are pressure tubes which provide the information for several instruments, including the air speed indicators. Two more
pitot heads were too badly damaged to reveal the presence of ice, and a fifth
was clear. Other checks were carried out to the aircraft's engines, where
damage showed that they had been running at high power settings at the time
of the impact.

Because fire had not broken out after impact, the flight deck revealed still
more useful information. The instruments which showed the attitude of the
aircraft had been damaged in such a way as to preserve their readings. They
showed the aircraft had been nose down by 20 degrees at the moment of
impact, which confirmed the wreckage analysis. The most significant finding
of all though, was the setting of the pitot heater switches on the roof panel

above the first officer's seat. These were not only in the 'off' position, but the switch handles had themselves been bent in the impact to show that they were switched off before the crash.

The next step was to check the FDR and CVR. Running these in parallel, it was clear to the investigators that the flight seemed to be proceeding perfectly normally until the aircraft reached 16,000 feet. Then, for no apparent reason since the engine power settings remained the same, the indicated air speed began to increase, as did the rate of climb. The air speed increased from 305 knots to 340, and the rate of climb shot up from 2,500 feet per minute to an astounding 5,000 feet per minute.

In reality these figures were totally impossible, but the crew's voices could be heard discussing the reason for this strange behaviour, and explaining it by the fact that the 727 was light, with no passengers or baggage on board. If the air speed really was increasing to such uncomfortable levels, the answer was to pull back on the controls and climb. This they did, but the apparent acceleration continued to 405 knots, when the overspeed warning horn could be heard sounding. By now the crew were at a total loss to explain what was happening, while the recording, and the instruments, showed the 727 was rocketing into the sky at a totally unbelievable 6,500 feet per minute.

Their response was to pull back on the control column still harder. The overspeed warning sounded again, but ten seconds later the crew made an error which was to cause their deaths. The stall warning system activated the stick-shaker mechanism, to alert them to the grim truth that far from climbing faster and faster, the aircraft was wobbling on the point of a stall. So locked was their mind-set that they believed the literally incredible readings on the instruments, and ascribed another reason altogether for the shaking of the controls. They assumed the reason for the vibration was the only possible cause consistent with the situation they *thought* they were in – the aircraft buffeting as it approached the speed of sound.

A moment's calm thought would have revealed the impossibility of their heavy airliner having the performance of a jet fighter, but these were men under terrible pressure. Their response was to pull back still harder on the controls, and to close the throttles in a desperate attempt to kill this unwanted speed. The sound of the undercarriage warning alarm, designed to remind pilots closing the throttles on a landing approach that the landing gear hadn't been lowered, could be heard on the cockpit recording. Two seconds later the inevitable stall sent the plane tumbling out of the sky, reaching a true descent rate of a fearful 15,000 feet per minute.

From that moment, their fate was sealed. The Boeing 727 has a high-mounted tail, which is vulnerable to a deep stall. This occurs when the aircraft is in such an extreme nose-high attitude relative to the airstream that the tail is blanketed by the turbulence streaming back from the stalled wings. Effectively, the crew have no way of using the elevators to recover control and pull the aircraft out of the stalled condition.

In the event, they tried lowering the wing flaps, which would cause a change in the aircraft's pitch attitude. This might have been enough to divert the airflow so that the elevators recovered some of their normal effect, but by now the speed was so high that the airstream tore away part of the tail when they applied more effort to the controls to try to pull out of the dive. From that point onwards, the aircraft became a missile heading for the ground, immune to any action on the pilots' part.

In the view of the accident investigators, there could only be one cause for the impossibly high readings of air speed and rate of climb, which tricked the pilots into stalling their aircraft so completely. The pitot-head senses the dynamic air pressure caused by the aircraft moving through the air by means of a pressure sensor fed by a narrow tube. The static air pressure is measured by vents elsewhere on the fuselage, and the system uses the difference between the two pressure readings to calculate the aircraft's speed through the air, and its rate of climb and descent. The static pressure alone controls the altimeter reading, to display the height reached by the aircraft.

If the pitot heads had been blocked by ice, as seemed likely from the inspection of the wreckage, then as the aircraft climbed, the static pressure would have fallen with increasing height, as the static vents were *not* blocked. The blocked pitot heads would have maintained the dynamic pressure at the same as it would have been at ground level, so the difference between the two would have increased steadily. The system would have displayed this as increasing speed and an increasing rate of climb, even though the aircraft was performing completely normally.

The crew reacted to this by pulling back on the stick to reduce speed. This would indeed cause the speed to drop, but because the height was still increasing, the pressure difference would also continue to increase. The instrument readings would rise even faster, so they then pulled back on the stick still harder. Eventually, the aeroplane fell into a deep high-speed stall, because of the actions they had taken to recover from a spurious problem. Had they checked with the instruments which were not affected by the pitot system, like the artificial horizon, they might have realised something was at fault, and lowered the aircraft's nose before it stalled.

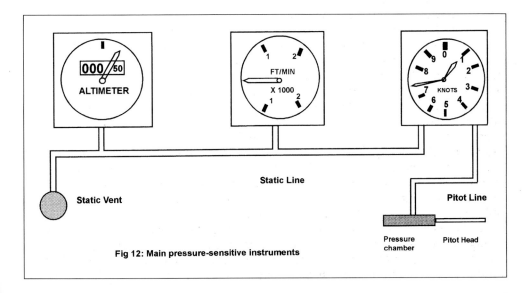

Fig 12: Main pressure-sensitive instruments

Iced-up pitot heads would have had one more fatal effect on their actions. The power-assisted controls on the 727 have a feed-back system to effectively tell the crew how much force to apply to the controls when climbing or diving. But a blocked pitot head system would effectively disable this system, so there was no 'feel' in the controls to tell them when they were pulling too hard. Particularly in the final dive, when extension of the flaps might have offered an escape route from the stall, the stick forces needed at that speed were very small indeed. There was no way for the crew to sense this, so the indications were they pulled back much too hard, causing the tailplane to fail.

How could all five pitot heads possibly suffer from the same problem at once? There was only one possible explanation. The crew must have left the pitot heater switches in the 'off' position. When the investigators checked the early part of the cockpit recording, where the crew were carrying out the pre-take-off checks, they found that at one moment the question-and-response litany slipped out of sequence. The flight engineer missed out the 'engine heat' query and went straight on to 'pitot heat'.

The first officer replied 'off and on', which they concluded was in answer to the normal sequence of questions. He then asked specifically if engine heat was required. There was no response to this, except for the sound of five distinct clicks, which the investigators concluded was the switch for the engine heat being set to 'on' and the pitot heaters being selected 'off'. When they checked the wreckage, they found that in addition to the previously spotted 'off' setting of the pitot heat switches, that the engine heating warning lamps had been 'on' at the moment of impact.

In other words, the first officer, who was relatively inexperienced on Boeing 727s, had been confused by the missing items in the checklist and had in fact set the switches to the reverse of what was really intended. This was not the only time that an aircraft has encountered this problem. In at least two other cases, the willingness of crews to disbelieve their pressure-operated instruments and concentrate on the readings of other signals to reveal the true state of affairs has proved their salvation.

Fortunately for future fliers, the issues raised by these two disasters are reasonably easy to deal with, by ensuring that pilots who may not have direct personal experience of icing conditions are briefed on exactly what precautions to take. Additionally, the exposure time of jet aircraft to this danger is limited mainly to the take-off and ensuing climb. Propeller driven aircraft still pose more of a problem, since not only do they operate in these altitudes all the time, but it is possible that in one particular area, modern designs may actually make the problem worse.

Two crashes involving a French-Italian turbo-prop aircraft, the ATR72, in icing conditions, caused warning bells to ring in the minds of safety experts. Both occurred in similar circumstances: the first one in 1987, when one of these aircraft stalled and crashed in the Italian Lakes en route from Milan to Cologne, and the second in 1994 when a Chicago-bound flight stalled and flew into the ground while holding for a descent to the airport at the end of its journey.

In both cases, the crews were well aware of the need to use the anti-icing systems, and the evidence showed that these were working properly. It was only when the National Transportation Safety Board carried out its own tests on the aircraft that they found it was susceptible to a build-up of ice behind the de-icer boot, creating a ridge of ice on the upper surface of the wing. This appeared to be a function of the design of aerofoil used on this particular aircraft, which had very low drag and high lift, to produce a capable and fuel-efficient design.

In certain icing conditions, droplets of freezing rain hit the leading edge of the wing and were blown across its surface by the slipstream, to cool down and freeze behind the area protected by the de-icer boot system. Unfortunately, the presence of this ridge, which built up relatively slowly during the course of the flight, broke up the airflow over the top of the wing. Ultimately this reduced the lift to the point where even at normal cruising speed, the wing was stalled, so recovery was impossible.

A problem identified is a problem half-way solved. If pilots knew about this danger, they could take steps to avoid the freezing-rain conditions which caused the ridge to build up to this dangerous level. Unfortunately, it was difficult for them to see it on the wing surface. There were also sharp differences of opinion between the authorities in the countries making the aircraft, and those which, like the NTSB, represented the companies operating it in areas where these freezing-rain conditions were common.

The real solution was to fit a modified de-icer boot to the wing of the aircraft, able to extend its influence further backwards along the upper surface and melt the ice before the ridge could build up. That effectively eliminated the problem, but it also reminded the aviation industry that icing was still a danger calling for positive and effective defences to keep it at bay.

6

Flames
in the sky

As flying becomes more popular, the sky grows more crowded. Even the development of wide-bodied airliners carrying far more passengers than the earlier generation of jets and turbo-props seems to have little effect on the overall upward trend in airline traffic. In general the airways system works well, with strict guarantees of safe separation built into the system. For example, on busy airways like the Transatlantic routes, aircraft fly in different height bands depending on whether they are westbound or eastbound, and these height bands are a thousand feet apart. Within a particular flight level, the separation between any aircraft and the one ahead of it or astern of it is equivalent to ten minutes' flying time.

Other regulations govern the ascents or descents made by aircraft to go to and from the upper flight levels, where they must not usually take more than five minutes to cross each operating flight level. When aircraft approach an airfield where there is a queue of flights for landing, the controllers order them to orbit a particular beacon at specific heights. The aircraft forming the 'stack' of orbiting flights are also layered at thousand-foot intervals, with the first aircraft in the queue at the bottom of the stack, and the most recently arrived aircraft at the top. When each aircraft at the bottom receives clearance to leave the stack and approach the airfield, all the other aircraft are then cleared to descend by a thousand feet.

Choke-points still remain in the system however. At the final approaches to busy airports, or where one busy air route crosses another, or where other types of flying conflict with the carefully regulated, carefully controlled airline traffic, the threat of mid-air collisions arises. In the early post-war period, especially in countries where visibility was generally good, much reliance was placed on the ability of pilots to look out for conflicting traffic, sometimes with disastrous results.

Relatively little was known about the difficulty of spotting another aircraft on a conflicting course at a lower altitude, for example. If the courses of the two aircraft were converging, the position of the other aircraft would appear constant, and it was easy to miss it against the dark background of the ground below. On the other hand, the limitless blue of the sky at altitude gave nothing on which the eyes could focus outside the cockpit. Research later showed that when looking out of the aircraft, the eyeball tended to relax so that the lens took up a short-distance focus. The result was that another aircraft could be in the vicinity, but invisible until its image was large enough to trigger the reflexes and cause the eye to refocus.

One of the worst mid-air collisions of the fifties happened over the Grand Canyon in the western United States on 30 June 1956. Two different flights had left Los Angeles for different US destinations. The first was TWA flight number 2, a Lockheed Super Constellation bound for Washington DC with 64 passengers and a crew of six, with a first stop at Kansas City, Missouri. The second was United Airlines flight No. 718, which was a Douglas DC-7 carrying 53 passengers and a crew of five bound for Newark in New Jersey, but with an intermediate stop at Chicago.

Both these aircraft were given IFR (instrument flight rules) clearance on the same airway, but at different flight levels to guarantee the separation the system demanded. The United DC-7 was cleared to 21,000 feet, with the TWA Super Constellation cleared to 19,000 feet. During the course of the flight, the TWA aircraft found it was flying into cloud, and asked for clearance to climb to 21,000 feet, but since this slot was already taken up by the DC-7, permission was refused. Instead, the TWA flight was given permission to fly at a thousand feet above the cloud layer. The crew complied with this clearance, but found they were flying at 21,000 feet in any case.

Even then all might have been well, apart from a loophole left open in the air traffic control system at the time. Either aircraft could leave the airways system and switch to VFR (visual flight rules, or 'see and be seen') if they wanted to take a short cut in clear weather, for a more direct course to their destination. Both aircraft took up this option, and it later became clear their tracks would eventually cross one another over the Grand Canyon. Nevertheless, this was strictly by the rules, and it was the responsibility of the two crews to keep clear of one another.

The only message received from either of the aircraft after half an hour's silence was a garbled message from the DC-7 saying 'we are going in'. Next day, the wreckage of both aircraft was found on the western side of the canyon a short distance from one another. When the investigators examined the debris, they found patterns of scratches and flakes of paint which showed the two aircraft had been at the same height, and on courses which had converged at an angle of approximately 25 degrees to one another, with the slightly faster DC-7 overhauling the other aircraft.

The DC-7's port wingtip had hit the centre tail fin of the Super Constellation and then the outboard section of that same port wing had struck the top of the Super Constellation's fuselage. There was a series of cuts in the fuselage skin inflicted by the port outboard propeller of the DC-7. The direction of the scratches also showed the DC-7 was banking about 20 degrees to starboard, away from the other aircraft, which might have been due to a last-minute attempt to avoid the impact.

The pattern of the wreckage also showed the tail section of the Super Constellation had been broken off by the initial impact, causing a total loss of control as well as an explosive decompression, similar to that of the Comet or the Japanese 747. Deprived of the lift provided by the tail, the Constellation pitched over into a vertical dive, and finally crashed on its back into a mountain called Temple Butte. The DC-7 meanwhile lost its port outer wing in the impact, which caused the aircraft to fall into a spiral dive and crash into the top of Chuar Butte, approximately a mile away from the other aircraft. All 117 passengers and 11 crew on both aircraft were killed in the crash, and with the lack of additional information from any form of flight data recorder or cockpit voice recorder, the investigators could not be more definite about why the crews of the two aircraft had not seen each other.

In any case, it was clear the system could not guarantee keeping aircraft out of one another's way, and following this disaster the rules on fixed airways and assigned height levels were tightened up. However, two more aircraft from the same two operators were involved in another collision disaster just 4½ years later, on the opposite side of the country. Apart from the fact that the total casualties were the same in this instance, the system under which the flights were being made was totally different. Both crews were operating under IFR clearance, they were reaching the ends of their journeys, and were actually making for different airfields.

On the morning of 16 December 1960, the weather over New York was overcast, with cloud down to approximately 5,000 feet, and patches of fog, with snow or sleet showers. TWA's flight 266 was another Super Constellation, this time on a service from Dayton and Columbus in Ohio, to New York's La Guardia domestic airport, with 39 passengers and a crew of five. It was approaching the city on a heading of 115 degrees or just south of east, until it reached the Solberg VOR navigational beacon, where it turned on to a heading of 096 degrees under the control of La Guardia Approach.

At the same time, United flight 826 was a service from Chicago being operated by a DC-8 jet airliner, carrying 77 passengers with a crew of seven and bound for New York's international airport, then called Idlewild but later renamed after John F. Kennedy. The DC-8 was approaching on a more southerly course and considerably higher at 25,000 feet than the piston engined Super Constellation. When crossing over Allentown in Pennsylvania, some 80 miles from its destination, and beginning its descent from cruising altitude, the DC-8 was ordered by New York air traffic control to take a short-cut to the Preston Intersection, where the jet could expect to join a stack orbiting the intersection point and wait for landing clearance.

This routine instruction caused two problems. Most holding points are located over a single navigational beacon, which makes homing on to that beacon a fairly straightforward exercise. Unfortunately, the Preston Intersection had no navigational beacon of its own. It was simply a point in the sky defined by the crossing of two navigational beams, the 120 degree radial from the Solberg navigational beacon to the west, crossed by the Super Constellation on its way to Idlewild at just after 10.26 am, and the 346 degree radial from the Colts Neck VOR to the south.

Normally, this was acceptable since aircraft usually have two different VOR receivers, so that each could be set to one of the two beacons in question. On that particular morning, the DC-8 had only one receiver working properly. The air traffic controller had no way of knowing this, nor the fact that the crew would have to switch backwards and forwards between the

114.7 MHz frequency of Solberg and the 115.4 MHz of Colts Neck, in addition to retuning to the appropriate radial bearing in each case. This was a time-consuming operation needing a great deal of concentration. As if this were not enough to deal with, as the DC-8 approached the interchange, the controller told the crew to switch to the Idlewild Approach Control frequency.

Meanwhile, the Super Constellation was being given headings to steer by a different controller at La Guardia to line it up for the runway on which it was due to land. At 10.32 am local time, the DC-8 was almost over the Preston Interchange, while the Super Constellation was ordered to turn right on to a heading of 130 degrees. The La Guardia controller, spotting another radar echo approaching quickly from the south west, told the TWA crew there was unidentified jet traffic one mile away on their starboard side. By that time, the DC-8 had called Idlewild Approach and reported it was nearing the Preston Interchange at 5,000 feet, although the post-crash investigation showed it was already more than ten miles beyond the interchange.

On the controller's screen the two echoes merged into one. The two aircraft collided at 5,000 feet over an army airfield on Staten Island called Miller Field, with the Super Constellation falling to earth within the airfield boundaries. The DC-8 carried on flying for another eight and a half miles to crash in flames at the junction of Seventh Avenue and Sterling Place in Brooklyn. Though three passengers were found alive in the TWA wreckage, and a small boy survived the United DC-8 impact, all four died within hours of the crash. Once again, as in the previous impact, all 128 passengers and crew on the two aircraft had been killed, but this time six people on the ground also died at the point where the jet airliner finally came to earth.

When the US Civil Aeronautics Board investigators studied the wreckage of the two aircraft, they found a truly chilling set of clues to what had happened a mile above Miller Field that December morning. Amid the wreckage of the Super Constellation was the starboard outer engine of the DC-8 and the whole of the starboard wing outboard of the engine. Inside the engine, they found pieces of cabin insulation from the Super Constellation and fragments of human remains, showing the engine had smashed its way into the other aircraft's passenger cabin when the two planes collided.

By analysing the patterns of tears and scratches on the fuselage and wing panels of the two aircraft, they found that the Super Constellation had been banking to port when the DC-8 had caught it up and hit it at an angle of approximately 110 degrees, with the starboard wing of the jet striking the fuse-lage and shattering the other aircraft into three main pieces. Evidence from the flight data recorder of the DC-8 showed it had been travelling at approximately 350 mph, which was an unusually high air speed for carrying out complex manoeuvres in controlled airspace in the vicinity of airfields.

With the crew concentrating on the complexities of navigation, and switching between two different air traffic control authorities, no-one may simply have had time to keep a lookout through the cockpit windows for other traffic. In any case, in controlled airspace, and in the absence of any radio warning, they may not have felt this was a very high priority.

The main cause of the accident was clearly the DC-8's overshoot of the designated holding point by more than ten miles. Why had an experienced and professional crew made such a lethal mistake? The investigators noticed that the overshoot was almost exactly equal to the distance saved by the short-cut they were instructed to adopt by air traffic control in making for the Preston Intersection, and it was at least possible they had not revised their estimates of the time and distance needed to reach it. This mistake would certainly have been compounded by the difficulties they had in trying to pinpoint the intersection with only one VOR receiver.

One possibility suggested by the investigators was that the crew had simply tuned their sole VOR receiver to one of the beacons, and used the automatic direction finding system (ADF) to tune to the nearby Scotland low-frequency beacon to provide cross-bearings. Although this would have worked in theory, it would have carried with it the danger of confusion between the ADF readings and the correct VOR readings which a second receiver would have provided. The ADF readings would actually have resembled the expected VOR display at a point close to the collision site.

Once more, the positive legacy of the collision was another tightening up of the air traffic control system. All jet airliner flights came under positive radar control, together with all flights down to 8,000 feet on busy airways. In addition, strict speed limits were to be imposed on flights within 30 miles of their destination, and the procedure of handing over responsibility between one air traffic control authority and another was more strictly specified. All aircraft except the very smallest light aircraft operating in United States airspace were required to have transponders fitted, so that their radar echo on the controllers' screens could be positively identified. Finally, more navigational beacons were to be fitted with distance measuring equipment (DME) so that pilots could be made more aware of their position at any moment.

These changes proved extremely effective, and the menace of a collision involving two passenger airliners has been kept at bay ever since, so far as American airspace is concerned. Since then, the only collisions in the USA involving passenger aircraft have been between an airliner and a totally different type of aircraft, such as military planes or light, general aviation aircraft, that have intruded into controlled airspace. On the other hand, the danger of a two-airliner collision remains possible, and there are times when even a near collision can turn into a disaster for one of the aircraft involved.

This was the case, once again in the very crowded airspace over the approaches to New York, on the evening of 8 February 1965. Eastern Air Lines flight 663 was a propeller driven Douglas DC-7B which had landed at Kennedy Airport from Boston, and was now departing for Atlanta in Georgia, at the same time as a Pan American Boeing 707 was approaching New York from the south, on a flight from Puerto Rico. Once again both aircraft were under positive radar control, flying under instrument flight rules, with the controllers responsible for maintaining adequate separation between flights.

The weather that dark evening was clear, with scattered cloud cover over a base of 10,000 feet, and a visibility of seven miles. The crew of the DC-7B had signed off from local control, but two minutes afterwards the PanAm 707 reported a near miss with another aircraft. The controllers checked the screens, and noticed that the echo which was tagged with the transponder code for the Eastern flight had disappeared. The 707 came in to a routine landing, and later searches found that the DC-7B had crashed in shallow water 15 miles from the airport, killing the 79 passengers and the crew of five.

The aircraft had exploded on crashing into the sea, but in spite of having to dive to locate the wreckage, searchers managed to find more than 60 per cent of it. Detailed checks failed to find any evidence of failure in the aircraft structure and systems, and the investigators turned instead to the flightpaths of the two airliners which had so narrowly missed one another. The northbound 707 was following a heading which would take it well to the east of the airfield, but the DC-7B was climbing on an easterly heading which might take it dangerously close to the flight path of the jet. The departure controller told the DC-7B to turn southwards and to climb until it was at least a thousand feet above the height of the 707, which had begun its descent.

That order was prudent enough in theory. Unfortunately, by the time the controller spotted the possible conflict, the DC-7B's turn would carry it straight over the track of the 707 on an opposite course. From the actions of the Eastern aircraft, it would seem they spotted the 707 heading for them at a lower altitude, but because of the lack of a distinct horizon in the darkness, they thought it was approaching them at the same height. They therefore started to descend to avoid the apparent danger. Certainly the 707 crew, who had spotted the DC-7B descending towards them, tried to avoid it by steepening their own descent.

From the viewpoint of the Eastern captain, his evasive action seemed to have no effect. If he pulled up and flew over the top of the 707, the other aircraft might do the same thing. The collision avoidance rules allowed either aircraft to make a sharp turn to starboard. The DC-7B was in a vertical bank when it passed the still descending 707, although it had actually crossed its course and was passing it on its starboard side. It seemed to the inspectors that in carrying out this extreme but unnecessary manoeuvre, the Eastern crew became disoriented, and were unable to recover from the vertical bank before the aircraft turned over and plunged into the sea. Ironically, had the crew not made the steep turn, they would have crossed the 707's course well ahead of the jet, and suffered no more than a severe fright.

Even with the present level of sophistication of air traffic control regulations, collisions do still occur, even in clear weather. On 20 September 1969, an Air Vietnam Douglas DC-4 was approaching Da Nang air base in South Vietnam on a service from Saigon, at the same time as a US Air Force F-4E Phantom fighter on its way back from a combat operation. It was four o'clock in the afternoon, visibility was good, and the two aircraft were cleared to land on parallel runways, the DC-4 on runway 17 Left, and the Phantom on runway 17 Right. Unfortunately, the DC-4 pilot heard the tower's message to the Phantom confirming clearance to land on 17 Right as being addressed to him. His reply was recorded as 'Roger, 17 Right' and he turned into the path of the descending fighter.

The two aircraft collided at a height of 300 feet, with the Phantom tearing away the DC-4's starboard tailplane. The transport aircraft tried to overshoot and make a second approach, but the lack of control due to the missing tailplane caused it to crash into a field and explode on impact, killing 69 passengers and a crew of six, together with two people on the ground, leaving only two injured passengers alive. The navigator of the Phantom ejected and was injured on landing, but the pilot managed to land the damaged fighter successfully.

More significant, however, is the type of collision which involves an airliner operating under strict air traffic control rules, and a light aircraft. Unfortunately, two of these disasters have happened over California where the density of local traffic and the generally clear visibility makes potential conflicts more common. For example, 25 September 1978 was a perfect flying day, with a cloudless sky and clear visibility for ten miles in any direction.

Pacific South-West Airlines flight number 182, a Boeing 727 on its way from Sacramento to San Diego via Los Angeles was approaching its final destination with 128 passengers, and a crew of seven. At 8.53 am local time, the 727 was handed over to San Diego Approach Control, and was given clearance to descend through 11,000 feet. Four minutes later, the captain reported the 727 was at 9,500 feet and the airfield was in sight. So far, everything seemed completely routine.

At 8.15 that same morning, while the 727 had been on the ground at its intermediate stop at Los Angeles International Airport, a single-engined high-wing Cessna 172 Skyhawk light aircraft had taken off from Montgomery Field. This was a small general aviation field just six miles north-east of the 727's destination at San Diego International. The object of the flight was instrument flying practice, with an instructor, for a pupil who already held a commercial flying licence. The lesson would include carrying out instrument landing system (ILS) approaches, but these could only be done at a major airfield, so the Cessna was cleared to carry out a series of practice approaches, without actually landing, at San Diego International.

At 8.59 am, as the 727 continued its descent, the air traffic controller warned it of the presence of the Cessna ahead. The 727 crew confirmed they had spotted the other aircraft. The Cessna then called approach control to report it had reached 1,500 feet and was now steering north-east. The controller told the Cessna to maintain a heading of 070 degrees before being steered back to the airport to practise another approach, but to remain at or below 3,500 feet. The controller then warned the 727 that the Cessna was three miles ahead of it, climbing through 1,700 feet, and the captain of the 727 confirmed the Cessna was still in sight.

After that several changes happened quickly. The 727 turned to port to take up its easterly downwind heading for San Diego at a height of 3,200 feet. At the same time, control was handed over to San Diego tower, where the 727 captain reported he was on the downwind leg of his approach, flying parallel to the runway heading but in the opposite direction. The tower controller then warned them again of the presence of the Cessna, now one mile ahead of them.

Unfortunately, the Cessna had also altered course. Instead of following the approach controller's orders and staying on a heading of 070 degrees, which would by now have taken it clear of the 727's heading, it had turned on to an easterly course too and was continuing its climb. The airliner was now descending towards it, and rapidly catching it up. Furthermore, because it remained under Approach Control, the two aircraft were communicating with controllers on different frequencies.

The next warning was a conflict alert signal which began flashing on the controllers' screens, to warn them the two echoes were getting dangerously close. This happened around a dozen times a day in the crowded airspace near the approaches to an airport as busy as San Diego. As each aircraft had been repeatedly warned of the presence of the other, and the 727 had specifically confirmed having the Cessna in sight, the approach controller took no action beyond repeating the warning to the Cessna. There was no reply to his warning message.

Witnesses on the ground watching the two aircraft saw the 727 descend on top of the Cessna, so the light aircraft hit the under surface of the starboard wing of the airliner. The wreckage of the Cessna fell to the ground, together with fragments of the 727 wing. The stricken airliner began descending in a shallow starboard bank, with plumes of white smoke followed by flames emerging from the damaged wing. The angle of both the dive and the bank steepened, until the airliner crashed in the San Diego suburb of North Park, killing all 135 people on the aircraft and seven on the ground. It was just two minutes past nine, and the two pilots of the Cessna were already dead, lying in the wreckage of their light aircraft just over half a mile away.

When the NTSB investigators inspected the wreckage, much of it had been destroyed by the fire which originally broke out as a consequence of the collision. However, amid the wreckage they found the Cessna's port wing fuel

Wreckage of the tail section and centre engine of the Pacific South Western Boeing 727 which crashed in the suburbs of San Diego after colliding with a Cessna 172. (National Transportation Safety Board)

One of the engines of the PSW Boeing 727 lying amid the wrecked houses in the San Diego suburbs. (National Transportation Safety Board)

tank. When they checked the remains of the Cessna they found that in addition to the wing tank, part of the port wing was missing, and the fin and rudder had been bent over to the left by a heavy impact and the upper side of the fuselage was crushed. Several pieces of the 727's wing leading edge flaps were mixed up in the wreckage of the Cessna, which accounted for a loss of lift on that side which produced the airliner's increasing bank to starboard as it dived to earth.

Why did the crews not see each other in those crucial moments before impact? The NTSB carried out a series of tests showing how the two aircraft would have appeared in one another's field of view. It should have been possible to see the light aircraft from the flight deck of the 727 with sufficient time to take avoiding action, but with both aircraft on the same heading, and the much smaller light aircraft appearing tail-on, against the background of the suburbs below and into the rising sun, it would have been much more difficult to spot. From the viewpoint of the Cessna's pilots, the high-wing design of the aircraft and the fact that the 727 was approaching from astern, meant they would only see the airliner as it flew over them, just before the impact.

The final conclusions of the accident enquiry flagged up a number of causal factors. Some were the responsibility of the 727 pilots, like their failure to warn air traffic control when they lost sight of the Cessna. Others were laid at the door of the air traffic controllers, like the failure to warn either aircraft that a conflict alert had been triggered in the ATC Centre, or the failure to order the 727 to keep to a minimum height of 4,000 feet when crossing over the traffic area covering Montgomery Field. The undeniable fact remains that in spite of all these individual failings, had the Cessna maintained the heading given by air traffic control, it would have crossed the path of the 727 with an ample safety margin, and the two aircraft would never have come anywhere near each other.

With most aircraft accidents, the positive result can be a new regulation, a new device or a new operating method which will make a recurrence of that particular type of accident either impossible, or considerably less likely. In the case of these conflicts and collisions though, curing the problem completely has proved rather more difficult. One loophole was closed off in this particular case by designating the area around San Diego a terminal control area or TCA. Here, *all* traffic has to be under positive ATC control and proper standards of separation have to be maintained. In theory, a repetition of the conditions that occurred on 25 September 1978 would not now produce such a tragic result.

There still remain the accidents that happen because, in spite of a watertight system, someone makes a fatal mistake. On the late morning of the last day of August in 1986, again over California, an Aeromexico Douglas DC-9 was making for Los Angeles International Airport under positive ATC control within the Los Angeles TCA at the end of a flight from Mexico City and Tijuana. Once again, the weather was clear, with 15 miles visibility, as a Piper Archer light aircraft took off from Torrance Municipal Airport carrying a family of three on a trip to Big Bear in the San Bernardino Mountains. Because the Piper was flying under visual flight rules, it was strictly forbidden to cross the boundaries of the Los Angeles TCA, so there should have been no possibility of a collision.

Unfortunately, the Piper strayed off course as it followed an easterly heading, and it wandered across the TCA boundary. The DC-9 was descending at the time, making for Los Angeles on a north-westerly heading, and at an altitude of 6,500 feet the two aircraft met each other in a violent impact. The tailplane of the DC-9 sliced with terrible precision into the cockpit of the Piper killing the three occupants instantly, before being torn away in the crash. The loss of the stabilising influence of the tailplane sent the airliner plunging beyond the vertical into the ground more than a mile below, exploding into a fireball on impact. The total death toll was made up of 58 passengers and six crew aboard the DC-9, two parents and their daughter in the Piper and 15 people on the ground.

This was a different type of investigation from the norm. The immediate cause of the accident was as clear as the California weather that August morning. The Piper had wandered off course and crossed the flightpath of the DC-9 to cause this terrible collision. Why had it done so? A post-mortem examination of the Piper pilot revealed a potentially serious heart condition, but the radar recording of his aircraft's progress showed it was flying under control right up to the impact. Colleagues described him as a careful and methodical pilot, and investigators found a chart in the Piper cockpit which clearly showed the TCA boundaries.

The investigators could only suggest he had made a mistake over his navigational checkpoints. But given that such a mistake was possible, why hadn't the system prevented it from causing a disaster? The approach controller claimed the echo of the Piper did not appear on his radar screen, though when the recording was played back, the light aircraft's transponder echo could be seen quite clearly. On the other hand, the controller had been distracted during those vital few minutes when the possible conflict was becoming apparent.

The reason was that not one, but two, light aircraft flying on visual flight rules strayed across the TCA border at almost the same time. The second was a Grumman Tiger which actually called ATC to ask for help. The controller dealt with this emergency, and when he returned to the DC-9 found its echo had disappeared from the screen. Several other factors may also have been important. The investigators found the Piper's transponder did not give a positive readout of the aircraft's height, so from the controller's point of view it might have been flying well below the traffic routes. Finally, he had been asked to relay a message to the DC-9 notifying its crew of a change in runways to be used on arrival at Los Angeles International, all of which conspired to distract his attention from the danger signs on his display. Against these workings of chance, even the most watertight of systems battles in vain.

7

Losing
the plot

At one time, the concept of 'pilot error' was criticised by pilots' professional groups as being a catch-all term used to explain accidents where other, more accurate explanations could not be produced. Then, such a thought carried a grain or two of truth. In the relatively early days of flying, pilots had almost none of the support provided by the complex and powerful control, navigation and communications systems the industry relies upon today.

If a pilot of the past tried to descend below cloud to find his destination airport, without any idea of his position beyond the glorified guesswork of dead-reckoning navigation, he was all too likely to collide with the nearest high ground. If he was unlucky enough for that to happen, the reason might well be described as 'pilot error'. With the technology of the times, a pilot of the highest possible ability and experience would almost certainly make the same mistake. The real error lay in not being superhuman.

Today, thanks to much higher safety standards and sophisticated techniques of accident investigation, when some responsibility for an accident is laid on the pilot the criticism is more justified than it was in the past. For when failures of engineering, of communications, of aircraft systems, of maintenance routines, of weather prediction or any other part of the machinery of flying have all been checked and absolved of blame, there still remains a minority of accidents where genuine pilot errors bring disasters in their train.

They may well be unwitting and unintentional. There is a saying in flying that the pilot is always the first to arrive at the scene of any crash, and that alone should be a powerful incentive to try as hard as possible not to make a mistake. At one time, the most common mistake a pilot could make was to lose track of his aircraft's position, at night or in bad weather. In making an approach to an airfield in mountainous country, an error of only a mile or two could make all the difference between a safe descent down a valley to the runway, and a headlong flight into a vertical mountain face.

On the evening of 3 July 1970, a Dan-Air Comet 4, registration G-APDN, was approaching Spain on a holiday charter flight from Manchester to Barcelona. It was routed over the Berga reporting point on its way from France into Spain, but the Barcelona approach controller had not noticed it had deviated some 15 miles to the east. The Comet was then steering for the Sabadell non-directional navigational beacon, but there was no automatic read-out to tell the crew how far away it was. At 30 seconds short of 6 o'clock local time, the crew contacted Barcelona Approach Control and confirmed they were descending from 13,000 feet.

The approach controller told the aircraft to turn to port from 197 degrees to a heading of 140 degrees. The crew said they expected to reach the Sabadell beacon in seven minutes, but then revised that to five minutes. Approach Control then ordered them to fly direct to the Sabadell beacon. Further messages from the approach controller cleared the aircraft to descend to 6,000 feet and asked for confirmation when it had passed the Sabadell beacon. At 6.2½ pm, roughly half the time the crew had estimated would be needed to reach the beacon, they reported they were passing it. The approach controller, confused as to which echo on the screen represented the Comet, asked the pilot to turn on to a south-easterly heading, and descend to 2,000 feet. The airliner crew read back the clearance, and asked for the number of the duty runway. Two minutes later the approach controller asked for their altitude. The crew confirmed they were then passing through 4,000 feet.

Seven seconds later the Comet crashed into the cloud-covered peak of Los Angudes, roughly 30 miles north of where the crew, and the approach controller, believed it to be. All 105 passengers and seven crew on board the aircraft died in the impact. Though nothing was found in the wreckage to explain the crash, the investigators were at a loss to explain why the pilots had thought they had passed the Sabadell beacon when they were still 28 miles short of it.

With the equipment in use at the time, there was no way the approach controller could have identified the Comet's echo on his screen with any certainty. Unfortunately, there *was* an aircraft on his display crossing past the Sabadell beacon at the right moment, travelling with the right kind of speed for a Comet. He ordered it to turn to port on to a heading of 140 degrees, to steer it for the airport and to identify the echo. He also cleared it down to an altitude of 2,800 feet, which was the approved safety height to the south-west of the beacon. Before he could discover the true whereabouts of the Comet, the aircraft had hit the mountain.

Since then, the introduction of secondary surveillance radar and transponders would show the controller exactly where the echo of the Comet was from moment to moment. Even if the crew made the same fatal mistake about their position, the controller could have corrected them, and the accident could not happen.

In spite of the closing of loophole after loophole, there are still chinks in the safety armour where inattention or false assumptions by the pilots can admit disaster. Just two months before the Dan-Air Comet crashed in the Spanish mountains, a Douglas DC-9 of Overseas National Airways, on charter to ALM Dutch Antillean Airlines with a total of 57 passengers and a crew of six, was flying 1,400 miles from Kennedy Airport in New York to Juliana Airport on the Dutch West Indian island of St Maarten. The aircraft had taken off at 11.14 from New York, and it cruised over the Atlantic at 29,000 feet. After the halfway point, the weather took a turn for the worse, and the DC-9 was steered round a succession of thunderstorm cells, reducing speed to cope with windshear and turbulence, and eventually descending to 27,000 feet.

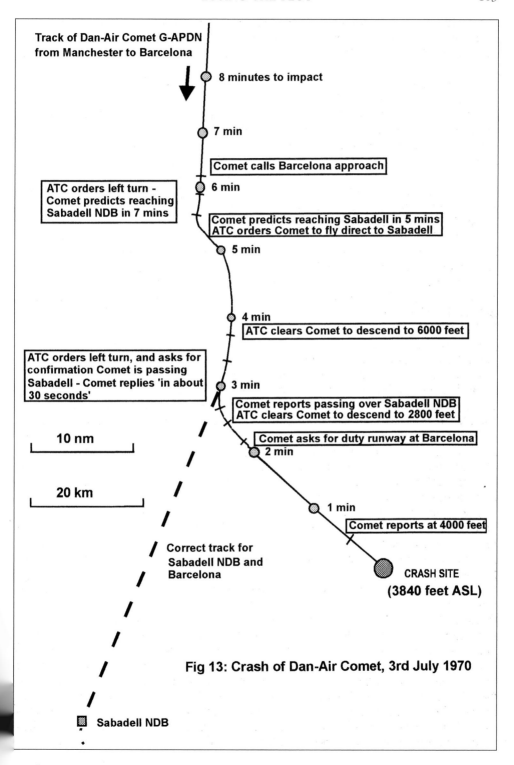

Track of Dan-Air Comet G-APDN from Manchester to Barcelona

8 minutes to impact

7 min

Comet calls Barcelona approach

ATC orders left turn - Comet predicts reaching Sabadell NDB in 7 mins

6 min

Comet predicts reaching Sabadell in 5 mins
ATC orders Comet to fly direct to Sabadell

5 min

4 min
ATC clears Comet to descend to 6000 feet

ATC orders left turn, and asks for confirmation Comet is passing Sabadell - Comet replies 'in about 30 seconds'

3 min

Comet reports passing over Sabadell NDB
ATC clears Comet to descend to 2800 feet

10 nm

Comet asks for duty runway at Barcelona
2 min

20 km

1 min

Comet reports at 4000 feet

Correct track for Sabadell NDB and Barcelona

CRASH SITE
(3840 feet ASL)

Fig 13: Crash of Dan-Air Comet, 3rd July 1970

Sabadell NDB

More and more thunderstorms were encountered, and the crew asked for permission to descend to 25,000 feet. By the time they were 180 miles from their destination, the fuel state was 8,600 pounds remaining, which would probably leave a margin of around 6,000 pounds when the aircraft touched down at St Maarten. Unfortunately, within 15 minutes, the airfield reported the weather was closing in, and the crew asked for a diversion to San Juan in Puerto Rico.

At 2.46, the DC-9 swung on to a course for San Juan at a height of 21,000 feet. Within five minutes, another report from St Maarten told the crew that weather conditions had improved, and the airliner was given a revised clearance at 2.51 to land at its original destination. By now the fuel load had dwindled to 5,800 pounds, with 110 miles to the airport, where there should be a margin of 4,400 pounds remaining.

At last the DC-9 arrived over the island, and made its first approach to the airfield. The aircraft descended through cloud layers into clear weather, following a course to the local non-directional navigational beacon, but was wrongly aligned to land on the relatively short runway. The captain selected full power for an overshoot, and flew a circuit at low level to stay in sight of the airfield. Their second attempt was baulked by a rain shower blotting out visibility, and another high-power, low-level circuit followed. The crew then emerged from a rain shower to find themselves in line with the runway, but too high for a successful landing.

At this, Captain de Witt decided enough was enough, and asked for clearance to divert to the island of St Thomas, in the US Virgin Islands, a slightly nearer destination than San Juan. The distance was 110 miles and the cleared altitude was 4,000 feet. Unfortunately, the crew were appalled to notice the fuel tanks contents gauges were now beginning to fluctuate ominously. The captain called San Juan Control to ask for a higher altitude to conserve fuel and avoid a slower aircraft ahead of them, and they were cleared to climb to 12,000 feet.

With the danger of the engines running out of fuel at any moment, the crew discussed the possibility of diverting to the island of St Croix, which was ten miles closer than St Thomas. This was approved and the aircraft started a low-power climb only to find itself wrapped in cloud. The captain was now very worried about the need to ditch if the engines should fail, and decided it was better to stay within sight of the sea. Messages were passed to air traffic control and the passengers and crew prepared for an emergency landing in the sea. With consummate skill, Captain de Witt managed to bring the DC-9 down to a successful crash-landing on the water just after the engines ran dry and stopped.

Though the impact was fierce, the aircraft stayed mainly intact. Before it sank beneath the swell, more than half the passengers managed to make their escape. While none of the life rafts were released, most survivors were wearing life jackets, and others managed to hold on to the inflatable escape slide which acted as an impromptu life raft. Within an hour and a half of the ditching, rescue helicopters arrived and managed to lift off five of the crew and 35 passengers. The remaining 22 passengers and a stewardess either died in the impact or went down with the aircraft.

This time, the investigators had no wreckage to examine, though the evidence of the fuel state of the DC-9 told its own story. What had seemed a perfectly prudent safety margin at the start of the flight had been eroded by the changes of course to avoid the thunderstorms, the reductions in speed and the descent to a lower flight level. By 2.40 pm, when the DC-9 should have been safely on the ground at St Maarten, it was still more than 120 miles short of its destination.

The abortive diversion to San Juan followed by the flight back to St Maarten ate deeper into this safety margin, but the really expensive luxury had been the three missed approaches, with the low level circuits and the high power overshoots, which consumed fuel much faster than cruising flight. Had the pilots realised their danger earlier, they might have decided to switch to San Juan after the first missed approach, and the fuel might have lasted long enough to do that. Once they elected to try again, as so often happens in flying, a bad decision started to close off their options.

A number of 'pilot error' accidents tend to repeat this same theme. A flight-deck crew is faced with a short-term priority, like the need to make every effort to reach their intended destination in spite of all obstacles. Disaster strikes when they fail to keep longer-term imperatives like the remaining fuel, firmly in mind. Another example, in very different circumstances from the St Maarten ditching, occurred over the Florida Everglades in the evening of 29 December 1972, when a Lockheed TriStar of Eastern Airlines was approaching Miami Airport on a flight from New York. The weather was calm and fine, with ten miles visibility in the moonless conditions, and it seemed to be a routine arrival.

The aircraft had just turned on to its final approach for the runway, when the first officer lowered the landing gear. Only two of the three indicator lights on the instrument panel showed a green 'clear' indication. The light for the nosewheel remained obstinately unlit. Either the lamp circuit had failed, or the nosewheel leg had failed to lock in position. The pilots raised and lowered the landing gear several times, but the lamp still failed to light.

When they told the air traffic controller the situation, the TriStar was cleared for an overshoot and a climb to 2,000 feet. The flight engineer came forward to check the light assembly to see if he could to make the lamp light up, but without success. By this time, approach control had ordered the aircraft to turn left on to a northerly heading at the same height. The captain then ordered the first officer to put the aircraft on to autopilot while the crew sorted out the problem. Air traffic control then ordered another left turn, to a heading of 300 degrees, while the crew continued to fiddle with the lamp. The engineer took a flashlight and started to climb down into the nose of the aircraft, from where he could see if the gear appeared to be locked in position.

In the meantime the first officer managed to remove the lamp from the panel, but could not unscrew the tiny bulb. Air traffic control ordered another left turn, on to a downwind leg of 270 degrees, and the crew gave up trying to replace the lamp, as the engineer tried to make out the position of the nose-wheel leg. A company technical man, occupying the flight deck jump seat because the aircraft was full, climbed down into the nose to help the flight engineer.

By now the TriStar was out over the darkness of the Everglades, and the approach controller called for a progress report. The captain asked for clearance to turn and make a second approach. Clearance was given for a left turn on to a heading of 180 degrees, but as the first officer banked the aircraft, he sensed something was wrong. The 'altitude' lamp on the autopilot display showed the aircraft was being kept at the cleared height of 2,000 feet, but the altimeter told a different story. At the same time the radio altimeter monitoring the aircraft's height above the ground, started sounding an alarm, and the aircraft hit the ground and broke up into a trail of wreckage.

The air traffic controller noticed the altitude readout changing from 2,000 feet to 900 feet as the aircraft began its turn back towards the runway. This could have been an error of the equipment, but before it could be checked, he had to deal with two other flights. When he looked again, the TriStar's echo had vanished. There were no replies to his calls, but an explanation was provided by other aircraft in the vicinity, which reported seeing 'a big flash' in the TriStar's last known position.

When the searchers arrived in helicopters and airboats, it seemed incredible that anyone had lived through the total destruction of the large wide-bodied aircraft. The truth was that many of the passengers and crew had survived the impact, among them most of the flight-deck crew, but some had drowned in the swamps before rescue arrived. The first officer had been killed, the captain and flight engineer had been fatally injured, but the company technical representative had been less badly hurt. In all, 77 passengers out of the 176 on board had lived through the crash, though all were injured, 60 of them seriously.

The investigators faced a daunting task. It was clear the TriStar's port wingtip had struck the ground first, as it banked to port to make for the airfield, and 50 feet further on there were the marks of the tricycle landing gear which had still been lowered at the moment of the crash. Ironically, the scars on the ground confirmed that all had been well with the nosewheel all along, although the landing gear had collapsed almost immediately under the shock of the impact.

The aircraft spread itself across the landscape in a series of fragments, starting with the port engine and wing, then the starboard wing and finally the main fragments of fuselage, where most of the survivors had been found. So completely had it broken up that it was virtually impossible to check the working of the main control systems, but some clues did emerge. The flap lever showed they were set at 18 degrees, and the position of the starboard wing flap actuator showed the same setting. Part of the starboard wing had escaped damage, and confirmed that the leading edge slats were fully extended, so the aircraft was correctly set up for an overshoot and second landing approach. The autopilot controls showed '2,000 feet' in the altitude hold window.

The landing gear warning lamps for the nosewheel were also found to have burned out, while the nosewheel leg was found in the wreckage, damaged but firmly locked in the 'down' position. Although the captain died before being freed from the wreckage of the flight deck, and the flight engineer had died in hospital, the investigators had been able to retrieve the FDR and the CVR from the scattered wreckage. Detailed checks of both confirmed that everything had proceeded perfectly normally, apart from the fault in the warning lamps for the landing gear, yet something had caused the aircraft to descend from the height selected on the autopilot, without the 'altitude hold' lamp being extinguished.

One possible factor emerged when a post-mortem examination of the captain revealed he had suffered an undetected brain tumour which could have affected his peripheral vision, but interviews with close associates led to that being discounted as a possible cause of the accident. The next most likely factor was something which could have unlocked the autopilot from its altitude hold setting, without switching off the lamp on the first officer's panel. When the investigators checked the flight data recorder information again, they spotted a spike on the vertical acceleration trace, followed by a shallow descent of approximately a hundred feet.

This was aligned with the cockpit voice recorder, and it was found that the loss of height happened as the captain was telling the flight engineer to go down into the nose and check the nosewheel. To do this he would have had to turn right round to address the flight engineer, sitting behind the two pilots. There was a strong possibility that in doing so, he might have inadvertently pressed on the control wheel strongly enough to disengage the altitude hold of the autopilot.

From this point onwards, the FDR showed the aircraft was descending very gradually towards the ground. Had either of the pilots been watching the instruments, they would have seen the altimeter reading unwinding with the loss of height, but they were too preoccupied with the problem of the undercarriage warning lamp. To confuse them even more, any disengagement of the autopilot by the captain would have left the 'altitude hold' display in front of the first officer, who was flying the aircraft, reading as it had done before.

Once again the result was that two skilled and experienced pilots failed to notice the approach of a potentially disastrous situation because they were locked into total concentration on a problem which was trivial by comparison. All that was needed was for someone to climb down into the nose for a visual check, while the pilots continued to fly the aircraft. That unnecessary diversion of attention was an error which ultimately cost them their lives.

Ironically, another undercarriage fault proved the undoing of the crew on a United Airlines Douglas DC-8 bound from New York to Portland in Oregon, via an intermediate stop in Denver, Colorado. It was six years almost to the day after the Miami crash. The aircraft topped up its fuel tanks in Denver, and took off for the final sector of the flight at 2.47 pm local time with 181 passengers, a cabin crew of five and a flight-deck crew of two pilots and a flight engineer. The flight would take 2½ hours, and the aircraft carried a margin of almost 50 per cent of extra fuel.

At 5.6 pm the DC-8 was descending through 10,000 feet when Captain McBroom called Portland Approach Control to ask for clearance. He was asked to maintain his present heading for a visual approach to runway 28. At 5.9 pm, air traffic control cleared the DC-9 to descend to 6,000 feet, and the first officer asked for 15 degrees of flap and then for the landing gear to be lowered. The captain moved the undercarriage selector but the normal sequence of noises and trim changes was replaced by a pronounced vibration and a sudden swing to starboard.

The crew checked the instrument panel. Only the nosewheel light showed a comforting green, but the lamps relating to the port and starboard main landing gear remained unlit. At that moment Portland Approach asked the aircraft to switch its communications to the frequency for Portland Tower. The captain reported the problem, and asked for clearance to stay at their present height of 5,000 feet and their present speed of 170 knots, while they tried to sort out their landing gear malfunction.

The controller cleared them to make a turn to port, away from the runway, and then to turn back parallel with the runway where they could orbit the airfield edge until the trouble was dealt with. It amounted to a re-run of the Miami TriStar situation, where the crew tried to see whether the indications on the instrument panel were a true reflection of what had happened to the actual undercarriage. In this case, it was the main wheels which were involved rather than the nosewheel, and the noises and the sudden yaw to starboard were worrying signs that something really was wrong. For more than 20 minutes the controllers steered the DC-8 on a series of manoeuvres around the hills to the south-east of the city, approximately 20 miles from the airport and clear of all other arriving and departing flights.

In this case it was impossible to check the landing gear from the nose of the aircraft. The DC-8 was fitted with mechanically actuated indicators in the upper surfaces of the wings, so the flight engineer went back into the passenger cabin and shone a torch into the darkness to check. They seemed to be in place, showing the gear had lowered normally, but in the pitch blackness outside the windows and in view of the strange noises and yawing effect, it was impossible to be certain.

At 5.38 pm, the captain radioed United Airlines' Line Maintenance Control Centre in San Francisco for advice. He estimated they still had just over 7,000 pounds of fuel remaining, and said that if they failed to solve the problem he would spend another 15 to 20 minutes preparing the crew and the passengers for an emergency landing and evacuation. The flight engineer then discussed the symptoms with the maintenance engineers, and the captain said they would try to land at approximately 6.5 pm.

At 5.47 pm, the flight engineer reported 5,000 pounds of fuel left. Two minutes later, the fuel pump lights on the instrument panel started to flicker, which was usual when the fuel reserves dwindled to this figure. The captain then confirmed he planned to try a landing in 'another 15 minutes', but the flight engineer muttered his concern that this would 'really run us low on fuel'.

By 5.51 pm, the flight engineer had finished talking to San Francisco. They had decided not to raise and lower the landing gear again as an extra precaution, in case something had broken and the gear might fail to lower properly. The captain then told the flight engineer that he expected to land with about 4,000 pounds of fuel in the tanks, and confirmed on the radio they would be touching down at about 6.5 pm. At 6.1 pm, the flight engineer warned the captain they had no more than 3,000 pounds of fuel remaining, and told Portland Approach Control they would be landing in 'about five minutes'.

At that moment the DC-8 was five miles from the airport but flying away from it on a south-westerly heading, and for just over three vital minutes the flight crew discussed some of the implications the undercarriage problem might have on their landing. The aircraft was then 17 miles from the airport, when the starboard outer engine showed symptoms of fuel starvation. Despite trying to select crossfeeds from the other tanks, they were unable to stop the engine failing, at a moment when they were now 19 miles away from the airfield and actually turning away from it to begin another orbit.

Portland Approach was clearing them for an immediate approach to the runway, but the starboard inner engine instruments were now showing zero fuel remaining. At 6.13 pm, with the runway still 12 miles away, the two port engines started to run down, and the captain told the first officer to call air traffic control and declare a Mayday emergency. Two minutes later, and now ten minutes past their declared landing time, the DC-8 came down in a wooded area on the north-eastern side of the city, just six miles from the runway.

The airliner hit a house which tore away the port wing, and the landing gear was smashed against a roadside embankment, leaving the fuselage to come to rest in the ruins of another house. Fortunately, both houses were empty, and the lack of fuel aboard the aircraft prevented the risk of fire breaking out. In all, 156 people were able to climb from the wreckage, while another 20 passengers from the badly damaged forward section of the cabin survived with more serious injuries. The crew casualties numbered two, the flight engineer and the senior stewardess, which in the circumstances, was almost miraculous.

The investigators had two priority objectives. They needed to determine why the landing had been delayed until the ample fuel reserves had all been used up, and they also had to check the undercarriage problem which caused the original emergency. It was clear that the aircraft's fuel consumption on the flight from Denver had been normal, and that when the emergency occurred over Portland, there had been 13,800 pounds of fuel remaining. From then on, by checking the conversations revealed on the CVR, it was clear that, as at Miami, the undercarriage problems had distracted the pilots from monitoring how much fuel remained in the aircraft's tanks.

Unfortunately, flying a holding pattern at low level with the landing gear and flaps extended uses up fuel at a high rate. When they finished their call to the airline maintenance service at San Francisco, they still had ample fuel remaining to complete a landing, but the safety margin was already dwindling. The fuel monitoring system would have shown the reserves would finally run out at around 6.15 pm, which turned out to be an extremely accurate prediction.

Yet at 5.50 pm, the Captain declared he would land in 15 minutes time with 4,000 pounds remaining. Had he actually landed on time, the reserves would have amounted to less than 1,000 pounds. The landing attempt was not actually started until triggered by the first engine failure when he had already passed his estimated time, with the aircraft nearly 20 miles from the airport. The engines and the fuel system had performed exactly as they should, and the reason for the total engine failure was simply that the landing had been delayed for too long, due to the crew concentrating on one problem to the almost total exclusion of everything else.

None of this would have happened without the initial undercarriage problem. When the investigators inspected the wreckage, they found that all the major assemblies of the aircraft had been present when it hit the ground, and all the damage had been caused by the consequences of that impact. The four engines had all suffered damage in the crash, one of them having been torn away from the wing, but when the investigators checked them, they found they were all otherwise capable of running normally. Internal damage, however, showed that none of them was running at the time of the impact.

Turning now to the undercarriage, the investigators found both the main landing gear legs had been torn from their mountings by impact with the embankment during the crash. Closer examination showed they had been fully extended, and would have supported a normal landing, but there were signs of corrosion in the threads of a bolt holding the piston rod in the hydraulic actuator cylinder, which was part of the mechanism for retracting the starboard undercarriage. The bolt had pulled away from the rod when the undercarriage started to lower, and the descending landing gear leg had pulled the piston rod out of the actuator cylinder.

This allowed the starboard landing gear to fall into the extended position, where it locked in the normal way, but with a thump which first alerted the crew to the fact that all was not as it should be. As the undercarriage fell into position, the landing gear door opened with it, more quickly than that of the port landing gear, which was lowering in the ordinary way against the drag of the actuator mechanism. This temporarily increased the drag on the starboard side of the aircraft, producing the yaw to the right, though once all three landing gear legs were fully extended, the aircraft flew normally once more.

The investigators also found the shock of the starboard main wheels dropping into the lowered position damaged the sensors which controlled the lights on the instrument panel. The end result was that the landing gear was perfectly safe for a landing as scheduled, but in the light of the noises and the sudden yaw to starboard, and the darkness which prevented them confirming all was indeed well, the crew was presented with symptoms of an emergency which did not actually exist. In coping with this emergency, they were drawn into a real crisis, with much more tragic results.

Even with today's much more sophisticated navigation systems, the potential still exists for emergencies to arise from an error in the precise position of an aircraft, in places where this can literally mean the difference between life and death. The world still remembers the tragedy of the Korean Air Lines 747 which was bound from Anchorage in Alaska on the final sector of its flight 007 service from New York to Seoul in South Korea on 1 September 1983. During the course of its flight across the North Pacific, the airliner edged into Soviet airspace, flying across areas of great military sensitivity. Having apparently failed to establish contact with the airliner, the Russians scrambled Sukhoi Su-15 jet fighters to intercept.

At first they failed to find the airliner, but when it later re-entered Soviet airspace over Sakhalin Island, the pilot of one of the fighters made visual contact. American monitoring of his radio messages to ground control revealed he never referred to it as anything other than a 'target'. He apparently closed up to the aircraft, interrogated the IFF (identification friend or foe) transponder code, and fired his cannon in an attempt to attract attention and signal the aircraft to follow him to land at a Soviet airbase.

There was no response, and recordings of the 747's transmissions to air traffic control revealed the crew did not even see the Russian fighter. Finally, the

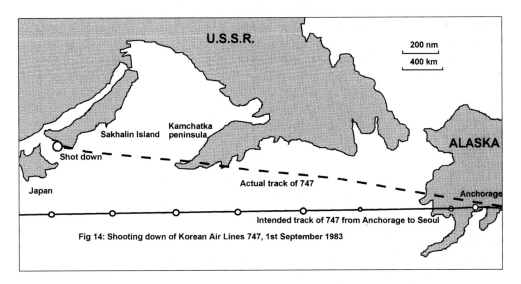

Fig 14: Shooting down of Korean Air Lines 747, 1st September 1983

airliner began to climb from 33,000 feet to 35,000 feet and, in doing so, its forward speed decreased so that the fighter overshot it. The fighter pilot then relocated the 747, locked his missile radar to the target and fired two air-to-air missiles, before reporting that the 'target' had been destroyed. There was one more transmission from the stricken 747, a distress call referring to rapid decompression, before it crashed into the sea, killing all 269 people on board. The wreckage completely disappeared, and the only remains were some floating bodies and small items of debris left on the surface of the sea.

In the absence of any material evidence, there was little to guide the investigators to an explanation of the disaster. The result was an elaborate network of conspiracy theories, casting the airliner as a deliberate or unwitting decoy for a genuine US spy plane on a snooping mission along the Russian coast at the time. Others claimed the aircraft itself carried surveillance equipment, and was obeying CIA orders to stray from its course to trigger responses from the Soviet defences.

Certainly there were precedents for this kind of undercover civil flying from the other side. At one time, before the British withdrawal from Singapore, overshoots taking incoming aircraft over sensitive defence installations in one part of the harbour almost invariably involved airliners from Warsaw Pact countries. In this case, however, the Korean denials of any involvement seemed genuine enough.

There were two more convincing theories involving different ways in which the navigational computers could have been mis-programmed. Possibly the flight crew might have left the autopilot set in the heading mode. This would initially have been set to a course of 246 degrees to take the aircraft towards the first navigational beacon on its route, the Cairn Mountain non-directional beacon. After this the normal procedure would have been to switch over to the inertial navigational system, which would then steer the aircraft towards the Bethel VORTAC beacon on the way to the coast, and then down the succession of reporting points to its destination.

If the crew had left the autopilot heading mode selected, the airliner would have stayed on that heading instead of being turned further south, which could have accounted for its passing 15 miles to the north of the Bethel beacon, and thereafter showing a steadily increasing deviation from its intended course. This required a high degree of inattention on the part of the flight crew, since the 'INS' lamp on the instrument panel would fail to light up, showing the navigational system was not steering the aircraft. It would, however, explain why the Soviet fighter pilot reported the target was on an approximate heading of 240 degrees several hours later.

The second possible explanation concerned the inertial navigation system itself. On the 747 there are three INS systems, each of which monitors the aircraft's position by responding to its acceleration in three dimensions. Each system also checks itself against the other two, and displays a warning if any of the three shows an obvious discrepancy. The INS systems have to be updated with the aircraft's precise position on the ground before take-off, and when they have been programmed with the position co-ordinates of the different reporting points on the designated airway, they can control the autopilot system to steer the aircraft along its route, making allowances for the effects of wind en route.

The explanation for the aircraft straying from its planned course involved an error in keying in the original position of the aircraft on the INS. If a longitude of 139 degrees West had been typed into the system instead of 149 degrees West, it would account for the progressive misalignments shown on the air traffic control radar recordings in the earlier stages of the flight, and the position where the 747 was finally spotted by the Soviet fighter and shot down. If the mistake had been due to typing the wrong key though, it would only have been entered into one of the INS systems. The other two would have the correct positional information entered into them, would have detected the discrepancy, and warning lights would flash on the instrument panel. This would have been more difficult to ignore than the unlit condition of the INS warning lamp.

Two more pointers should have alerted the crew that all was not well. Their steadily diverging course would mean they failed to pick up signals from the next navigational beacons down their route, at St Paul's Island and at Shemya in the Aleutians, which ought to have prompted them to check the system. Furthermore, if their weather radar system had been switched to ground-mapping mode, the unmistakable outlines of, first, the Kamchatka Peninsula and Sakhalin Island showing up where there should have been nothing but sea, would have provided positive proof that something was wrong.

Could the crew have made a mistake in reading the positional information for Anchorage airfield, so that the 139 degrees West longitude was entered into all three systems? If that had been the case, then all three INS systems would effectively confirm to them all was working normally. The lack of signals from navigational beacons en route might have been put down to weather or technical problems, and they might have felt no need to check the radar display, where they would expect to see nothing but ocean.

There matters rested for ten years, until the Russians admitted they had recovered the aircraft's flight data recorder from the bottom of the sea. They handed it over to the French accident enquiry bureau as impartial observers who could keep an objective point of view between themselves and the Americans over the disaster. When the information on the FDR was analysed, it became clear that the aircraft's course had followed a constant magnetic heading, modified by the winds blowing at the time. This could only mean that the autopilot *had* been left in heading mode, and for some reason the INS was not selected, or had failed to control the autopilot. In either case, the problem became a catastrophe because of the crew's failure to monitor their position, and check the other monitoring systems with which the aircraft was equipped.

Another terrible illustration of the consequences of navigational inaccuracies had been demonstrated by a disaster involving another wide-bodied jet almost four years before, at the other end of the world. During the late 1970s, Air New Zealand operated an occasional sight-seeing service with Douglas DC-10 aircraft from New Zealand to Antarctica and back, during the brief Southern Ocean summer. On 28 November 1979, the fourth and last of these trips for the year departed from Auckland with 237 passengers and a crew of 20 at 8 o'clock in the morning for a trip of 6,000 miles, spending between 11 and 12 hours in the air.

The highlight of this day-long flight was the close-up view of the Southern Continent itself, its wealth of wildlife and its frozen wastes, and the sense of wonder engendered by the last great unspoiled wilderness left on the planet. Usually, when the weather was clear, the aircraft could fly at low level over the Ross Ice Shelf, up McMurdo Sound and over the New Zealand Scott Base and the US Navy McMurdo station, before leaving for the long haul back to Christchurch and Auckland. This involved radar control from McMurdo station, under strictly specified conditions.

Normally, aircraft were given a minimum altitude of 16,000 feet in clear visibility for more than 12 miles, and were allowed to descend to 6,000 feet passing over McMurdo station. However, if the McMurdo controllers approved, they were able to descend even lower, in most cases to 2,000 feet or even less, for spectacular close-up views of the ice shelf and the Antarctic coast. Time was strictly limited, since this low-level flying burned off much more fuel than altitude flying, and the DC-10s were close to the limit of their range with full tanks.

Navigating so close to the South Pole created problems with conventional latitude and longitude, particularly since the only navigation beacon was the military beacon at McMurdo station. Instead, the flights were operated on a special navigational grid, reinforced by the aircraft's inertial navigation system. Like that of the ill-fated Korean airliner, this was programmed with the co-ordinates of a number of waypoints on their routes to and from the Pole.

In the case of the Antarctic flights, the crew entered these flight-plan co-ordinates manually from a computer printout supplied by the airline. There were actually two alternative routes, offering a choice of overflying McMurdo Sound if weather conditions were favourable, or of following a different course after overflying the Balleny Islands on the coast, crossing the Ninnis Glacier and then heading westwards to the South Magnetic Pole, returning by way of Macquarie Island. The choice had to be made before reaching the Balleny Islands, depending on weather reports from McMurdo station.

This time, the McMurdo controller reported cloud cover above 3,000 feet, but as Captain Collins could see the Antarctic coastline sharp and clear, it was decided to carry on for McMurdo in the hope of conditions improving. As the aircraft drew nearer, McMurdo reported an overcast at 2,000 feet, with occasional snow showers, but clear visibility under the cloud layer to a distance of approximately 40 miles. The controller offered them radar guidance once they were within 40 miles of the base down to 1,500 feet over the Sound. All these early transmissions were on high frequency radio, but when the DC-10 was 114 miles away, the crew were asked to switch to one of two VHF frequencies to call McMurdo control tower.

For the next 18 minutes the crew of the DC-10 struggled to establish VHF contact with McMurdo Tower, until at last, at 1.35 pm local time, the tower broke through loud and clear. The DC-10 was cleared to descend to 10,000 feet in clear visibility and the crew were able to ask for radar guidance through the cloud layers before communications broke up once again. After three minutes the McMurdo controller heard the aircraft call on HF asking for a clearance to approach McMurdo under visual flight rules, and the controller asked the crew to continue to report their height as they descended towards the base.

Four minutes later, the crew reported the DC-10 was at 6,000 feet, and was descending to 2,000 feet, still in clear conditions. After five minutes, the controller called the aircraft, concerned there had been no report of it levelling off at 2,000 feet. There was no reply, on either HF or VHF channels. The controller called all American aircraft in the area, in an attempt to relay messages to the DC-10, but nothing more was heard from the airliner. It never appeared over the base, and there were no more messages, as the delay extended into hours.

Communications breakdowns were common enough in the area, and it was clear nothing appeared to be amiss on board the airliner when the VHF contact was broken. There had been several more conversations with air traffic control on HF radio, so it was possible some form of radio failure or some meteorological fluke had interrupted communications. It was only when time passed without any news of its return, past the point where its fuel must have run out, that the fear of disaster became a certainty.

The next day, a US Navy C130 Hercules was flying over the northern side of Ross Island, when the crew spotted scattered and burned out wreckage on the icy slopes of Mount Erebus on the side from which the DC-10 would have approached. When the first accident investigators flew over the site by helicopter, the pattern of the wreckage showed the aircraft had hit the ice in a level attitude rather than an uncontrollable dive. Moreover, the length of the trail of wreckage, spread over the best part of a mile, and the degree to which the pieces had been smashed, suggested the aircraft had impacted at cruising speed, rather than in an attempt to carry out an emergency crash landing.

When they checked at ground level, it became clear that nothing had broken away from the aircraft before the impact, and all three engines had been delivering power at the moment of the crash. The enormous mass of fuel needed for the return flight to Auckland had burst into flames, but some of the material recovered from the wreckage included a collection of cameras belonging to the passengers. The film was removed and processed at the base, and the images studied for clues as to the aircraft's route on its way to Ross Island. These pictures showed the DC-10 seemed to have made its approach over North Victoria Land in clear weather according to the flightplan, before making a series of descending turns through a gap in a cloud layer which seemed to extend down to approximately 2,000 feet over the coastline.

The searchers also retrieved the computer memory modules for the inertial navigation system. When these were checked, it was clear the crew had entered the flightplan from the computer printouts without any errors at all. The flight data recorder showed that the aircraft had made two descending turns, one to port of the flightplan track and one to starboard, before continuing its descent towards McMurdo. It had finally levelled out at 1,500 feet and continued flying on a steady course at this height, until it had suddenly nosed up with an increase in engine power just before impact.

Even more significantly, the investigation showed an error in the list of computer co-ordinates entered into the INS. This error had been made more than a year before, and its effect was to move the co-ordinates for the TACAN beacon at McMurdo 2 degrees and 10 minutes, or approximately 30 miles to the west of its true position. As the other trips conducted with this incorrect flight plan had been lucky enough to cross this section of the route in clear visual meteorological conditions, the error had not been discovered until the night before the fatal flight.

The error had been corrected, but the crew of the DC-10 had not been told. The effect of this was to shift the flightplan course from the safe approach up the waters of McMurdo Sound, to cross the slopes of Mount Erebus instead. This extinct volcano is a full 12,000 feet high, and the reason why 16,000 feet had been set as the minimum altitude in conditions of poor visibility. Even then, if the weather had remained clear, the peak would have been unmistakable evidence that they were not where they thought they were. But the cloud conditions existing over McMurdo that day, with a layer of overcast to provide light without shadows, and a featureless white ground surface invariably give rise to a condition called 'whiteout', where all definition and horizon are blotted out in a featureless white glare.

Not only does this cause severe disorientation, it can also disguise even the most obvious features of the landscape. Under these conditions, it would be difficult to make out anything except the dark lines of the cliffs of Lewis Bay on the north coast of Ross Island, which would look very like the similar cliffs lining the entrance to McMurdo Sound. The fatal difference was that the whiteout in the centre of their field of view did not conceal the flat surface of the Sound, but a steadily rising ice slope, trending upwards to the still unseen peak of Mount Erebus.

Evidence from the CVR, though difficult to unravel in places because the polar flights carried almost a double flight crew of two first officers and two flight engineers, showed they were progressively more uneasy as the visibility ahead deteriorated. At one point a voice was heard to ask, 'Where's Erebus in relation to us at the moment?' Another replied, 'Left, about 20 or 25 miles, about 11 o'clock'. But the effect of the unreported correction of the earlier computer error was that the icy slopes of Erebus were almost dead ahead, and the aircraft had just over three minutes flying time left.

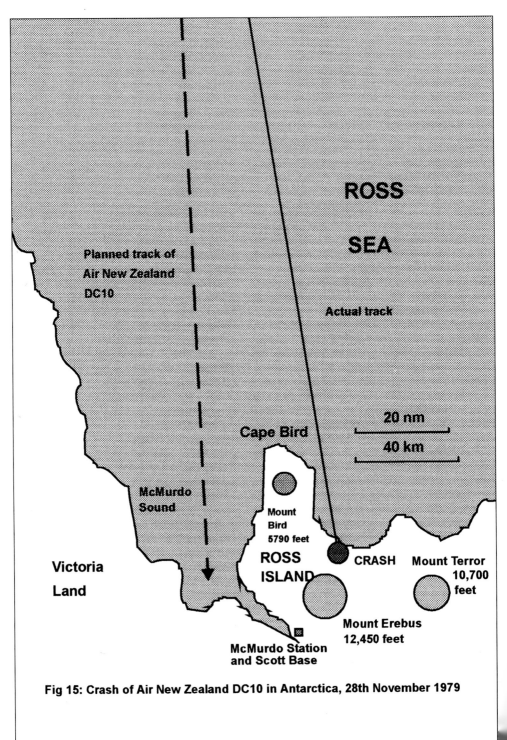

Fig 15: Crash of Air New Zealand DC10 in Antarctica, 28th November 1979

The captain was actively considering climbing to a higher altitude in the hope of better visibility, or carrying out a 180 degree turn to reverse their course. Unknown to them, their worries were amply justified and their time had run out. The reading on the radar altimeter, showing the height above ground, suddenly started to drop and almost immediately the ground proximity warning system sounded. Calmly, the captain called for 'go-round power', but it was already too late. A second later, the DC-10 slammed into the mountain and it was all over.

The initial official enquiry put the blame squarely on the captain, for descending at low level into conditions of poor surface definition. A subsequent Royal Commission reversed the enquiry's decision and placed the blame on Air New Zealand and its management. With the advantage of hindsight it seems highly probable that the real cause was a combination of both factors. The airline made a mistake with the computer printout and then corrected it without notifying the crew, but the captain risked a descent to low level in an unforgiving part of the world, in less than perfect weather conditions. Either factor on its own would probably not have caused an accident. The combination of both was lethal, and no more flights were made over Antarctica.

8

Everything
under control

In most aircraft accidents, the air traffic controllers remain the helpless spec-tators of an unfolding disaster, powerless to influence events which develop a momentum of their own. In many cases, they are important witnesses, through the communications between them and the aircraft involved. In others, they are able to mitigate an emergency situation by isolating it, and preventing it from escalating into a major catastrophe. But controllers remain as human as pilots and flight engineers, passengers and cabin crew, and there are times when they too make mistakes, which can have fatal consequences for those under their responsibility. Fortunately these are rare, but at times the system has to be brought under the objective scrutiny of the accident investigators.

One reason why air traffic control errors are so potentially serious is that they usually involve a failure to maintain the separation between aircraft, where a breakdown in the system automatically involves a possibility of a high casualty toll. For example, on 19 July 1967, a Piedmont Airlines Boeing 727 on a flight from Atlanta to Washington DC took off from an intermediate stop at Asheville Municipal Airport for the next leg of the flight to Roanoke in Virginia, while a twin-engined Cessna 310 was inbound to the same airfield on a flight from Charlotte. The time was two minutes before midday, and both aircraft were flying under instrument flight rules and positive radar control.

The Cessna was cleared to fly over the Asheville VOR radio-navigation beacon and then to head for the Asheville non-directional radio beacon to the north-west of the airport, maintaining an altitude of 7,000 feet. With the 727 climbing away from the runway on a south-easterly heading, there should have been no conflict between the two flights. What actually happened was that the Cessna deviated from its cleared heading, swinging away to the south west until it approached the position where the 727 was turning to port, on to its assigned heading to pass over the Asheville VOR for the flight to Roanoke.

At that point, with the Cessna now ten miles from its assigned track, the two aircraft collided at a height of 6,000 feet over the edge of the town of Hendersonville, some 15 miles south-east of Asheville proper. It was just over one minute past midday, and the three people aboard the Cessna, together with the five crew and 74 passengers aboard the airliner, were all killed in the crash.

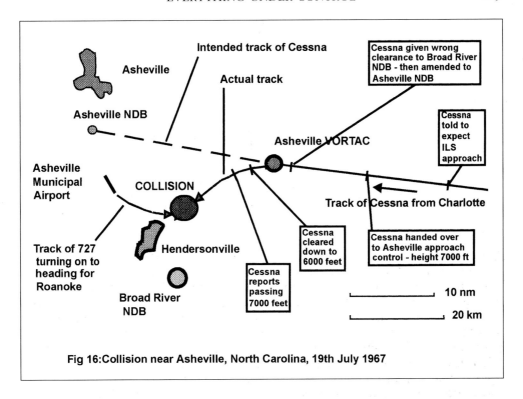

Intended track of Cessna

Actual track

Asheville

Cessna given wrong
clearance to Broad River
NDB - then amended to
Asheville NDB

Asheville NDB

Asheville VORTAC

Cessna
told to
expect
ILS
approach

Asheville
Municipal
Airport

COLLISION

Track of Cessna from Charlotte

Cessna
cleared
down to
6000 feet

Cessna handed over
to Asheville approach
control - height 7000 ft

Track of 727
turning on to
heading for
Roanoke

Hendersonville

Cessna
reports
passing
7000 feet

10 nm

Broad River
NDB

20 km

Fig 16:Collision near Asheville, North Carolina, 19th July 1967

When the accident investigators examined the wreckage, the pattern of scratches and impact damage found on the skin panels of both aircraft showed the Cessna had flown straight into the airliner, striking the forward fuselage section of the 727 with its nose and the tip of its port wing. They also showed the airliner was banking gently to port, in accordance with its turn on to its newly assigned heading. Eyewitnesses on the ground said the collision took place in an area of sky clear of cloud cover, and reported that the Cessna seemed to pull up sharply just before the impact, indicating that its pilot might have seen the 727 when it was too late to avoid it. There was no indication that the 727 crew had attempted any avoiding action, and the airliner turned over on its back and dived steeply into the ground, where it exploded on impact.

A search of the burned and scattered wreckage of both aircraft revealed no mechanical reason for the disaster. It was clear the principal cause was the Cessna's failure to stay on the heading it was given by air traffic control, and turning through a change of heading which amounted to around 40 degrees. This was far beyond what might have been explained by sloppy flying or inadequate navigation. In any case, one of the two pilots aboard was an experienced commercial flyer and the other was a qualified private pilot. This hinted at a deeper underlying cause.

At the time of its clearance to the Asheville navigational beacons at 11.51 am, the Cessna was controlled by the Atlanta ATC Centre. When the investigators checked the messages between the controller and the aircraft, they found the Cessna pilot had been told to expect an ILS (instrument landing system) approach to Asheville. This was only an advance warning rather than an actual clearance, but its implications were serious. The ILS approach involved aircraft first flying over the Broad River non-directional beacon before turning towards the airfield to pick up the ILS localiser beam. And the Broad River NDB was to the *south-east* of the airport.

A minute and a half later, the Cessna was handed over from Atlanta Centre to Asheville Approach Control. The pilot reported his height, and called soon afterwards to report crossing a bearing of 340 degrees from the Spartanburg beacon. So far the aircraft was on its assigned track, and all was well. The controller then made a mistake which, though trivial enough in itself, compounded the confusion which may have been caused by his opposite number at Atlanta giving the Cessna early warning of an ILS approach to the airfield. He actually cleared the Cessna to the Broad River beacon. He immediately corrected his mistake, substituting 'the Asheville radio beacon' and ordered the Cessna to report passing the Asheville VOR beacon.

Five minutes after that, the Cessna pilot called the approach controller once more, to report passing over the Asheville VOR beacon. Their final words were garbled, but they appeared to say that they were heading for 'Asheville now'. The controller replied by clearing the Cessna to descend and maintain a height of 6,000 feet, at the precise moment the Piedmont Airlines 727 was starting its take-off run. Just over a minute later, the Cessna was cleared for an ADF (automatic direction finder) approach to runway 16, and instructed to report when passing over the Asheville radio beacon inbound.

This should have alerted the Cessna pilots to the fact that the earlier warning of an ILS approach to the airport was actually wrong, since they were now being cleared to approach the runway from the opposite end to that equipped with the ILS system. But they had now been given two different descriptions of their approach to the airport by two different controllers, and they had had a reference to the Broad River beacon, which was correct for the first (ILS) approach mentioned, replaced by a reference to the Asheville beacon, which was correct for the second (non-ILS) approach.

When the investigators had examined the wreckage of the Cessna, they had found the ADF receiver was set to 379 kHz which was the frequency of the Broad River beacon, and not 357 kHz, which was the frequency for the Asheville beacon. Even more significantly, they found an out-of-date edition of the Asheville Airport approach chart in the cockpit, which showed the Broad River beacon, but showed only one Asheville beacon. This was the Asheville VOR beacon the Cessna had already passed. There was no sign of the Asheville non-directional radio beacon.

The investigators then checked the precise wording of the Approach controller's message to the Cessna five minutes before the crash. The controller had actually said 'Three-one-two-one Sugar (the callsign for the Cessna) cleared over the VOR to Broad River. Correction, make that the Asheville radio beacon...over the VOR to the Asheville radio beacon, maintain seven thousand, report passing the VOR.'

It was possible that the Atlanta controller's earlier reference to an ILS approach, which would be clearly shown on the chart carried in the Cessna as involving a heading over the Broad River beacon, might have caused the pilots to assume this would be their final route. When the approach controller also mentioned the Broad River beacon, and then amended it to the Asheville beacon, the pilots would have found the reference confusing, since there was only one Asheville beacon on their chart, the VOR over which they were about to fly. They may have concluded the Asheville and Broad River radio beacons were one and the same, as no other Asheville beacon was shown on their chart, or that the controller had become confused between the Asheville VOR and the Broad River beacon.

Whatever the reason, they clearly assumed their clearance allowed them to steer for the Broad River beacon, which they did with such tragic results. The official enquiry concluded that the lack of an up-to-date approach chart in the Cessna was partly responsible for the accident, since the presence of an Asheville VOR and an Asheville radio beacon on the chart should have enabled the pilots to realise exactly what the approach controller's clearance referred to. Another factor was the lack of any information from air traffic control to correct their mistake before it led to disaster.

Against this, it was only fair to say the local controllers did not have secondary surveillance radar. This would have identified the Cessna's echo with its height and transponder code, so they could have seen it change its course from that on which it was cleared. Also, the Cessna pilots failed to ask for clarification, when the clearance they were given seemed to contradict the information shown on their approach chart.

In total, it was a highly unsatisfactory outcome, where confusion was piled on confusion and assumption piled on assumption, from the Atlanta controller warning them of an ILS approach when the approach controller had a totally different routeing in mind. One positive result was the later introduction of a Federal Aviation Administration requirement that all aircraft had to carry approach charts displaying all the available navigational beacons in the area covered by the chart.

In theory, this kind of accident should be less likely on a busy airways intersection, with professionally trained commercial pilots in aircraft equipped with every kind of navigational aid, and controllers having the latest secondary surveillance radar at their disposal. But on 10 September 1976 the crowded skies over Yugoslavia imposed a burden on the Zagreb Area Control Centre which caused its organisation to buckle under the strain. Finally it brought about a disaster through a chain of six errors, each one trivial in itself, but terrible in their cumulative consequences.

British European Airways flight BE476 from London Heathrow to Istanbul had taken off at 8.32 am GMT with 54 passengers on board and a crew of nine. The aircraft was a Trident 3B, and the flight was expected to take approximately 3½ hours. An hour and a quarter later, the cabin crew served breakfast to the passengers, and the aircraft reported passing Munich at 9.43 am GMT. It was flying on airway Upper Blue 1 at an altitude of 33,000 feet towards the Villach radio beacon in southern Austria. It crossed into Austrian airspace five minutes later, and the atmosphere on the flightdeck was relaxed, with Captain Dennis Tann and First Officer Martin Flint, the third pilot, helping First Officer Brian Helm finish his crossword puzzle.

At that moment, Flight JP550 of the Yugoslav charter airline Inex-Adria Aviopromet, took off from Split bound for Cologne. The aircraft was a DC-9, and was almost full with 107 West Germans and one Yugoslav passenger. The flight was likely to take approximately 2½ hours, and the aircraft carried a crew of three stewardesses and two pilots, Captain Joze Krumpak and First Officer Dusan Ivanus.

Both aircraft were making for the Zagreb radio beacon, which marked the junction of three airways, Upper Blue 5, Upper Blue 9 and Upper Red 22. Upper Blue 40 bypasses Zagreb to the south, but Upper Amber 40 starts there and connects direct to Sarajevo. As if this were not more than enough, Zagreb is also the site of what was then Europe's second busiest air traffic control centre where, at the time, a team of 30 controllers was struggling to cope with traffic levels which really needed 60 controllers to deal with them properly.

The centre was beset by problems. A major training programme had been introduced, but there was still a shortage of experienced controllers. Three years earlier, a Swedish secondary surveillance radar system had been installed, but it was still not properly calibrated and the Yugoslav authorities complained it hadn't met the contract specification. Until these problems were sorted out, the centre relied on procedural control with each aircraft being entered on a flight progress strip, updated by pilots reporting their progress, with these reports then being monitored on radar.

It was a far from watertight system, at the one place where pressure was greatest. The airspace over the Zagreb Centre was divided into three height bands. The lower section covered altitudes below 25,000 feet, the middle section covered altitudes between 25,000 feet and 31,000 feet, and the upper section covered altitudes greater than 31,000 feet. Because of staff shortages, the normal complement of three controllers per section had been relaxed to two in the middle and upper sections, with each controller working a 12-hour day split into two-hour watches, each one followed by an hour's break. As a result, the strains were beginning to show. A total of 32 near-misses had been reported in the five years since 1971.

The BEA Trident was due to pass over Zagreb in the upper section of airspace, while the DC-9 was cleared to pass through the middle section. At 9.55 am GMT the DC-9 called Zagreb lower sector control and was cleared to climb to 24,000 feet. One minute later Zagreb gave the aircraft clearance to climb to 26,000 feet, and asked the crew to call when passing 22,000 feet, at which point the lower sector controller would remind the pilot to retune to the frequency for the middle sector controller. The DC-9 crew wanted to climb to 31,000 feet, but they could not be given clearance to do this as all the upper levels were occupied with overflying traffic. At 10.2 am GMT the DC-9 reported passing through 22,000 feet, and was told to switch frequencies. The crew had to wait 30 seconds because of heavy radio traffic before making contact with the middle sector controller.

The controller ordered the DC-9 to change its transponder code. Because traffic was so heavy over Zagreb, the radar displays were crowded with echoes. Aircraft in each of the three height sectors were given codes in three different sequences. Those flying in the middle sector for example had codes from 2500 to 2577, while those flying in the upper sector had codes ranging from 2300 to 2377.

The radar system was programmed to display only those codes relating to the appropriate sector in each case. The middle sector radar display would identify all the aircraft in its height bands carrying codes within its range, and all other aircraft would appear as unidentified echoes. By following the controller's instructions and changing its transponder code to 2506, the DC-9 would now appear on the middle sector radar display, but its echo would carry no identifying code on the upper sector display. However, if an aircraft strayed between sectors without proper clearance, its label would appear automatically. There was also a facility which allowed a controller to interrogate an unidentified echo, but only by going to use a keyboard which took him away from radar monitoring.

The first problem arose when the DC-9 climbed into the middle sector of airspace, as its flight progress strip had not been prepared in advance. Each strip was eight inches wide by one inch deep held in a metal frame, and recorded the aircraft's type, call sign, the flight level asked for, the airways routeing and the transponder code. All the strips relating to aircraft under a given controller's direction were slotted into racks beside the controllers. Checking them, updating them and arranging them were the responsibilities of the assistant controller, and in this case the matter was dealt with safely enough.

In the upper sector, the pressure was mounting. The controller's relief had not arrived, so the controller went to look for him, leaving his assistant to cope in his absence. At 10.2 am GMT, the BEA Trident passed over the Klagenfurt radio beacon on the border between Austria and Yugoslavia. The Vienna ATC Centre told the crew to call Zagreb, which they did two minutes later. They reported flying at 33,000 feet and estimated they would be passing over Zagreb in ten minutes time. The controller ordered them to set their transponder code to 2312.

The Zagreb upper sector assistant controller, still working on his own, found the pressure mounting. He had to speak to a Vienna-bound Turkish airliner at 35,000 feet, which the Trident crew glimpsed as it flashed past over their heads. He then had to ask for clearance for an Olympic Airways flight making for Sarajevo, which meant making a telephone call to the Sarajevo upper sector controller, to feed the flight into the Sarajevo pattern. While he was doing this, he also responded to calls from three other aircraft, all in the space of just over one minute.

Meanwhile, in the middle sector, the DC-9 was now levelling off at its cleared altitude of 26,000 feet, northbound on airway Upper Blue 9. Once again the crew asked for clearance to climb to higher altitude. The middle sector controller asked if they would be happy with 35,000 feet and they agreed enthusiastically. They were told to stand by for more instructions.

On his way out of the control room to look for his replacement, the upper sector controller found him at the door. The two men broke the regulations by stepping outside to discuss the traffic situation and to hand over duties, out of sight of all the other controllers. This was error number one. At the same time the assistant upper sector controller was still working on his own, and the middle sector controller was trying to attract his attention to agree clearance for the DC-9 to climb to 35,000 feet through the intervening flight levels.

Gradimir Tasic, the assistant upper sector controller saw the middle sector controller wave his hand, but as he was far too busy to speak to him, he waved him away. The assistant middle sector controller, Gradimir Pelin, moved across Tasic's radar screen and pointed at the echo representing the DC-9, which was still unidentified because at this stage the transponder code was still set for the middle sector, and asked him for clearance.

This was another fatal mistake. Tasic thought that Pelin was merely drawing his attention to an unidentified aircraft, but Pelin thought Tasic was aware of what he wanted and had given him the clearance he needed. He moved back and told the middle sector controller, Bolan Erjavec, that all was now clear. This was error number two.

Erjavec then radioed the DC-9 and gave the crew clearance to climb to 33,000 feet. Meanwhile Tasic, still on his own and unaware of what his colleagues had assumed he had agreed to, was dealing with a London to Istanbul BEA Airtours flight which meant he now had to ring Belgrade control. The DC-9 was now heading for 33,000 feet while the BEA Trident was crossing its path at that altitude, expecting to pass over Zagreb at 10.14 am. At 10.11 am the Trident altered course slightly from 121 degrees to 115 degrees. At that moment the DC-9 was climbing through 31,000 feet, and it reported to the middle sector controller.

Erjavec now instructed the captain to set a stand-by code on his transponder, so as to release his previous code for another middle sector aircraft. This was all in order if Tasic had been aware of it, as he would then immediately have allotted it an upper sector code. Until he did so, its code would not now appear on the radar scope as a warning that it was climbing into the upper sector. This was error number three.

The crew of the DC-9 changed radio frequency to call the upper sector controller, but the now seriously overstretched Tasic was dealing with a Finnair flight, and could not be contacted. Before he finished doing this, he was passed the flight progress strip for the DC-9. However, instead of a new strip, he was handed the old middle sector strip, but with the height altered. This was error number four.

By now the still single-handed Tasic was doing the work of three controllers, controlling a total of eleven different aircraft. He switched to processing a Lufthansa flight bound for Belgrade, when his relief finally arrived, and Tasic's attention was drawn to briefing the new man on the situation. For the first time he was able to look at the flight progress strip for the DC-9, but the amended altitude information was simply written as 350. There was no arrow with the figures to give a warning that the aircraft was climbing through traffic on other flight levels to reach this height. This was error number five.

In the next 60 seconds he had to deal with an Olympic flight and another BEA Airtours flight. Meanwhile the DC-9 had reached 32,500 feet and was climbing steadily towards the BEA Trident. Only when the DC-9 called him to report did the terrible truth dawn on Tasic for the first time. He asked it for its height, and the crew reported they were passing through 32,700 feet. In the clear upper air the Trident was leaving a long trail of condensation, while the DC-9 was climbing with the sun behind it. The Trident crew would have found it difficult to spot the other aircraft coming up from below, especially as the relative bearing was not changing because they were on a collision course. The two aircraft were approaching each other at almost 1,100 mph.

Realising the horror of the situation at last, the desperate Tasic tried to separate the two aircraft. A turn would take too long, but the Trident's height was shown (incorrectly) as 33,500 feet. If he could hold the DC-9 at its present height of 32,700 feet, there might still be a chance of the two aircraft missing each other. He called the DC-9 and gabbled instructions in Serbo-Croat to hold at its present height and report when passing Zagreb. The puzzled crew asked what height, and Tasic warned them to hold at the height they were climbing through, because there was another aircraft in front of them, passing from left to right.

Sadly, in spite of the incorrect label on the radar screen, the BEA Trident was flying at exactly 33,000 feet. Tasic's action had eliminated the last faint hope that the DC-9's continuing climb would have taken it safely past the British aircraft. This was error number six, in a chain of mistakes which doomed the passengers and crews of both airliners to death more than six miles over the Yugoslav countryside. At 14 minutes and 41 seconds past 10 o'clock GMT, the DC-9's port wingtip sliced through the Trident's flight deck, the wing broke off and the port engine separated. As the aircraft began its fiery plunge to earth, the tail broke away.

The Trident, with its crew all dead from the impact, lost its fin and rudder in the collision and plunged to the ground almost seven miles below. In all, 176 people were killed. The entire shift of Zagreb middle and upper sector controllers was arrested and replacements brought in. The defendants contradicted one another, and finally only Tasic was found guilty of criminal negligence and sentenced to seven years in prison. An appeal was launched by the International Federation of Air Traffic Control Associations, the case was reopened in April 1978, and the sentence was halved. Five months later an IFATCA sponsored petition to President Tito led to Tasic's release.

Yet the terrible toll of the Zagreb collision was dwarfed by that of another catastrophe just six months later. Once again pressure on an inadequate air traffic control system, compounded by errors made by pilots, created the world's worst flying disaster without the aircraft involved properly managing to leave the ground. Once again, it was a catastrophe brought about by a chain of small mistakes which added up to the most terrible final price ever demanded. The first of these was the detonation of a terrorist bomb at Las Palmas Airport on Gran Canaria, the principal island in the Canaries group, on 27 March 1977. The bomb injured eight people, and as there was a threat of another bomb hidden in the airport, it was closed for searches to be carried out. Traffic was diverted to the smaller Los Rodeos airport on the nearby island of Tenerife.

Two of the aircraft diverted to Los Rodeos were Boeing 747s. One belonged to KLM and was operating a charter service from Amsterdam to Gran Canaria and back, and the other was a Pan American charter from Los Angeles via New York carrying passengers joining a cruise ship for 12 days in the Mediterranean. The PanAm aircraft's journey had been so long that the crew, on hearing that Las Palmas was expected to reopen soon, had asked air traffic control for permission to fly a holding pattern close to the airport until they could be given clearance to land. This would save their passengers being subjected to all the additional delays of landing at another airport, joining the queue of aircraft which would then want to make the short repositioning flight once Las Palmas reopened, and then adding another take-off and landing to their already stretched schedule.

Air Traffic Control refused, and the second 747 joined a group of airliners crammed on to the restricted apron and adjacent taxiway at the single-runway Los Rodeos airfield. When the reopening of Las Palmas was announced, the smaller aircraft were able to leave by taxiing in the wrong direction up the runway until clear of the queue, and then swinging on to the parallel taxiway to take them to the far end of the runway for their eventual take-off. But for the PanAm 747 waiting to start the short trip to Las Palmas, there was no room to inch past the equally large bulk of the KLM aircraft. This was being refuelled from tanker vehicles for the eventual return to Amsterdam, since Captain van Zanten thought additional delays would be inevitable if he tried to refuel at Las Palmas. As things stood, he could only complete the trip within his flight time limitations if he left soon, and he was becoming increasingly anxious.

Unfortunately, his decision to refuel not only cost him another half an hour, but meant the increasingly frustrated PanAm crew had to wait for the operation to be completed before their aircraft could be moved at all. In the meantime the weather was poor, with mist and light rain showers drifting across the runway and bringing down the visibility from six miles to less than a mile at times. Finally, by the time the KLM 747 had finished refuelling, and asked for permission to start engines and prepare for departure, curtains of mist had brought the visual range down to a mere three hundred yards.

The clearance given to them in English was confusing. When the KLM crew asked if they should turn left at taxiway 1 to follow the parallel taxiway to the end of the runway, the controller told them to taxi straight ahead to the end of the runway, and then to 'make a backtrack'. The mist was now thickening further, but the KLM 747 edged along the runway to turn round at the far end and await take-off clearance.

At 5.2 pm local time, the crew of the PanAm 747 called the tower and asked for confirmation that they were to taxi down the runway which was still occupied by the KLM aircraft. The tower controller confirmed they should do exactly this, but that they should turn off the runway 'third to your left'. The crew could not be certain whether he actually said 'first' or 'third', and visibility was now so poor, they could not actually be sure which was the third turn-off from the runway. They passed the first turning, which was a 90 degree turn to the left. Then the controller confirmed the third turning was the one they should use, and that they should report back when they were clear of the runway.

In the meantime, the KLM 747 reported passing the fourth turning, and was told by the tower to carry on to the far end of the runway before making a 180 degree turn and wait for take-off clearance. The PanAm aircraft was crawling through the mist, with the crew watching patiently for the third turning off the runway. As they passed the second turn-off, the KLM aircraft turned round and faced back along the runway, ready for take-off. Just after 5.5 pm, the PanAm crew were horrified to hear messages which suggested the KLM aircraft was starting its take-off run. The Pan Am captain radioed the tower to remind them they were still on the runway. Calmly the controller reassured them, repeating that they were to report once they were clear of the runway, and they continued to search for the turn-off on to the parallel taxiway.

Unfortunately for the PanAm crew, they had become confused over the third and fourth turnings because of the layout of the airfield, and the mist which shrouded the different taxiways. They were actually heading for the fourth turn-off when they saw powerful lights approaching them through the fog from further down the runway. Within seconds it was clear they were approaching with increasing speed, and Captain Grubbs opened the throttles to turn off the runway as fast as he could. It was too late. Catastrophe was bearing down on them, driven by four jet engines running at full take-off power, and there were just 8½ seconds left. The nose of their 747 was barely over the runway boundary when the other aircraft loomed over them, leaving the ground reluctantly as it sought desperately for height.

The impact was terrible. The KLM aircraft's nosewheel skimmed over the top of the PanAm 747, but its main wheels tore away the top of its fuselage, before the Dutch aircraft crashed back on to the runway and both aircraft exploded into flames. The controllers in the tower had no idea what had happened, as the mist blanketed the fearful sight from them. Only when airport workers and crews from the parked aircraft reported seeing flames on the airfield were the emergency services directed to the spot.

They found that all the 234 passengers and 14 crew of the KLM had been killed in the crash or the resulting fire, a blaze which was not finally extinguished until the following morning. Another 326 people had died in the wreckage of the other 747, 317 passengers and nine members of the cabin crew. Amazingly, there proved to be 70 survivors from the PanAm aircraft, though nine of these later died from their injuries. Most of those who survived the crash had been in the forward section of the fuselage, which escaped being struck by the other aircraft because of Captain Grubbs' desperate swing off the runway. All those in the centre and rear sections of the fuselage, as well as those in the upper deck section behind the flightdeck, were killed by the impact or engulfed in the resulting fire.

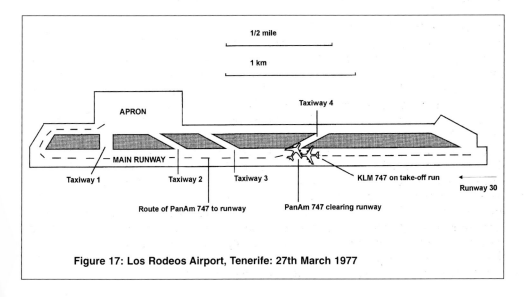

Figure 17: Los Rodeos Airport, Tenerife: 27th March 1977

Because the disaster had occurred with both aircraft on the ground, the investigators' objectives were limited. For once they had no need to determine from the wreckage what pattern of failures had brought two aircraft together with explosive effect high above the earth. In this case, it was all too obvious why both aircraft were in the positions they occupied before the crash. What defied explanation was why the KLM 747 had accelerated towards a take-off attempt, when they could not see the whole of the runway, at a time when other aircraft had been manoeuvring around the cramped confines of the airfield.

Certainly there was no reason to suppose that any mechanical failure aboard either 747 had contributed to the collision. Nor was the mist which shrouded the cramped airfield that fatal afternoon anything more than a secondary factor in determining the course of events. Mist or no mist, there was no way on earth that one aircraft should have been taxiing along a runway while another aircraft was starting its take-off run in the opposite direction. The answer, if there was one, was to be found in the communications between both crews and the tower controller, and the conversations on each flight deck, as revealed by the cockpit voice recorders.

In the end a huge investigation team assembled, with representatives from Spain (as the airfield was on Spanish territory), from Holland and the USA (as the countries where the two aircraft were registered) and from KLM and Pan American, numbering 70 experts in all. The focus of their attention was the recordings of the messages between the flight deck crews and the tower, and once again a chilling tale of progressively mounting errors, mistakes and assumptions was found to have led to the final tragedy.

As the PanAm crew were crawling painfully through the fog and low cloud, looking for their designated turning point to leave the runway and continue down the parallel taxiway, they made the first mistake. They identified the first connecting taxiway when they spotted it crossing to the left of the runway at a right angle. The second taxiway turned back the way they had come, so they would have had to make two laborious turns through 135 degrees in quick succession, a dog's leg course to reach the parallel taxiway.

They then made out a third taxiway connection, but this too was angled back the way they had come, whereas their airport chart showed the fourth taxiway connection was an ideal 45 degrees left turn from the runway. After the earlier confusion over whether the controller had said 'first' or 'third' taxiway, they made the assumption that instead of the 'third' taxiway and its inevitable sharp turns, that he had really meant the fourth taxiway connection, and they carried on down the runway towards it.

The effect of this error was that they would remain on the runway that much longer before it was cleared, so the KLM aircraft's take-off would be delayed. But as they and the tower controller knew they would report as soon as they were clear of the runway, there was nothing inherently dangerous in their mistake. In the meantime though, the KLM 747 had reached the end of the runway, turned round to face back along its length. The pre-take-off checks were complete, and the captain started opening the throttles and the aircraft began to move forward.

The first officer reminded him they had not yet received their take-off clearance, and the captain told him to radio the tower and ask for it. The controller then made a second mistake, which still should have been safe enough if the system had worked properly. Instead of reminding them there was another aircraft on the runway, he simply read them their airways clearance to Las Palmas. His message was 'KLM4805, you are cleared to the Papa beacon, climb to and maintain flight level 90, right turn after take-off, proceed with heading 040 until intercepting the 325 radial from Las Palmas VOR'.

This was what Captain van Zanten, increasingly stressed and frustrated at the continuing delays, had been waiting for. While his first officer acknowledged the clearance, he released the brakes and started pushing the throttle levers forward for take-off power. As the first officer finished reading back the clearance to the tower, he added the line 'We are now at take-off'. As this could have been interpreted as 'we are now taking off', or as 'we are now waiting to take off', this was mistake number three. The crew of the Pan American 747 were worried by the implications of what they heard, and they called the tower to remind them they had not yet left the runway.

This was the moment when fate took a hand, to compound a string of fairly trivial mistakes and turn them into the most terrible accident in the history of civil aviation. As the Pan American crew spoke to the tower, the controller was assuming the KLM aircraft was *ready* for take-off and was still waiting for clearance. He told the KLM crew 'OK, stand-by for take-off, I will call you' at exactly the same instant as the incoming message from the PanAm aircraft. The result was a howl over the Dutch crew's headsets caused by two transmissions at the same moment on the same frequency. They never heard the last warning which could have given them a fighting chance of stopping their aircraft in time.

What the KLM flight engineer clearly heard was the message immediately after the PanAm 747's first call, where the tower instructed the PanAm crew to 'report the runway clear'. His anxious voice could be heard on the recording asking 'Did he not clear the runway then?' 'Oh yes' said the captain, making the final mistake which was to cost him his life, along with all his fellow crew members, his passengers and most of those aboard the other airliner. The first officer called out 'V1' as the accelerating 747 reached the speed at which they were now committed to take-off.

At almost the same moment, the captain must have seen the PanAm 747 sideways-on ahead of him. With no chance whatsoever of stopping his speeding aircraft piling into the other aircraft, there was only one avenue of escape. He hauled back on the control column to try to leapfrog over the obstacle in their path. The investigators found a 20-yard scrape along the runway near to the centre-line markings just 80 yards from the Pan Am aircraft, which had been caused by the tailskid of the KLM 747 as Captain van Zanten hauled the nose up to try to clear it.

Even so, he very nearly made it. When the investigators examined the wreckage of the PanAm aircraft, where the tail assembly had been torn away by the port wing of the KLM 747, they estimated that had Captain van Zanten succeeded in gaining as little as 25 feet of extra height, all might have been well. As things were, the starboard outer engine of the KLM airliner tore open the upper deck of the PanAm 747 just to the rear of the flight-deck, and the main wheels of its undercarriage ripped off the roof from the PanAm main passenger cabin.

The investigators found one of the KLM 747's massive main-wheel under-carriage bogies lying on the runway just beyond the wreck of the PanAm aircraft. They also found the KLM 747 had remained airborne, though crippled, for another 150 yards before it crashed back on to the tarmac, breaking up in a trail of wreckage lasting another 300 yards before its take-off speed was finally dissipated. It was an appalling disaster, and one which was made no less tragic by the realisation, in the resulting report, that if any one of the chain of mistakes had not been made, it could so easily have been avoided.

From the terrorists planting the bomb at Las Palmas, to the air traffic controllers refusing the PanAm 747 permission to fly a holding pattern until the airfield was reopened, some of the causes of the accident were remote from where it took place. The haste of the Dutch crew to leave before their flight-time limits were exceeded, and their decision to refuel before the short hop to Las Palmas, contributed to what happened. So did the PanAm crew's assumption that the tight turns needed for an aircraft as large as the 747 to negotiate the third taxiway must have meant that the controller was mistaken. There was the unfortunately ambiguous way in which the controller gave the KLM 747 its airways clearance without reminding them they were still not actu-ally cleared for take-off. Finally, the coincidence that the alarm of the PanAm crew at what they, rightly, feared might happen, caused them to interrupt the one message from the tower that might have warned the KLM crew to abort their take-off attempt quickly enough to avoid the collision.

With all the dangers of collisions at altitude, it remains a final irony that the most terrible death toll caused by any air accident was caused by two aircraft still to all intents and purposes on the ground. And any comfort resulting from the long chain of mistakes and coincidences should quickly evaporate when considering another ground-based collision, at Madrid's Barajas airport almost seven years later.

Several factors linked the two accidents, in that both involved an aircraft taxiing to its take-off point and another which was actually taking off, both involved conditions of poor visibility and both involved confusion about the right route to take through a confusing maze of taxiways. Fortunately, the death toll in this accident was much lighter at 93, rather than 583. This was due to the aircraft concerned being much smaller, though once again all those aboard one of them perished in the crash, together with the majority of those on the second aircraft.

The collision occurred on 7 December 1983 at approximately 9.40 am local time. An AVIACO Douglas DC-9 was operating an internal flight to Santander on the north coast of Spain, carrying 37 passengers and a crew of five. It was cleared to taxi to its holding point at the end of runway 01, but visibility was poor, with misty conditions which were still above the airport operating limits. Unfortunately, in threading their way through the network of taxiways in the fog, they made one wrong turning. This actually led them at an angle across runway 01, where at that instant an Iberia Boeing 727 was making its take-off run on a flight to Rome, with 84 passengers and a crew of nine.

Once again, the plane on its take-off run did its best to take avoiding action Once again it failed. In this case the port wing and the port main landing gea were torn off the speeding 727 in the impact, so the aircraft swung round or the runway before coming to a stop and bursting into flames. A total of 50 passengers and one member of the crew were killed in the impact and the fire. The DC-9 was less fortunate, with all of its occupants losing their lives in the disaster.

In this case there was no specific criticism of the actions of the air traffic control team, since the fog was too thick for them to see the DC-9 taking its fatally wrong turning. But there had been widespread criticism of the airport authorities from pilots who had been concerned at the lack of marker lights and painted stop signs where the taxiways reached a potentially active runway. Had these been in place on the day of the accident, it almost certainly would not have occurred, but they were due to be installed during the course of the following year. As so often happens in aviation disasters, the workings of chance seek out the weakest link in the system and through it are able to render all the other safety systems powerless.

9

Pressing the
wrong button

Not all mistakes that happen on the flight-deck are because of pilots losing their bearings, or concentrating on an immediate but relatively trivial problem to the exclusion of an ultimately much more serious one. From the very first days of flying, it was always possible for a pilot, particularly when stressed by mechanical failures or bad weather or other external factors, to misread an instrument, pull the wrong lever, or press the wrong button. For all the systems designed to prevent him doing that, sooner or later the workings of chance and coincidence will turn the trivial into the terrible, leaving the air crash investigators to determine the cause, and the actions needed to prevent it happening again.

In some cases, it doesn't even take a mistake. An incorrect decision taken in response to all the available evidence has caught out innumerable pilots over the years. One of these disasters involved another epic of crash detection, when a Royal Air Force jet bomber disappeared without trace on a flight over the Irish Sea in August 1959. The aircraft was the prototype Victor Mark 2, a crescent wing design powered by four jet engines, which took off from the Boscombe Down test airfield at 10.35 on the morning of 20 August.

Its mission was to climb to 52,000 feet, and to carry out a series of tests during a one-hour flight down the length of the Irish Sea, including high speed turns. It was then to dive at high speed to 35,000 feet for further tests, and then carry out a third set of tests at 10,000 feet, before returning to Boscombe Down in the early afternoon. Nothing further was heard from the aircraft, and when it became clear it could no longer be airborne on the fuel load which it carried, the emergency services were alerted.

The BBC broadcast the news that the Victor was missing, and the item was heard by the crew of a small coaster called the *Aquiety*, passing the south-western tip of Wales on their way from Liverpool to London. The master had been on the bridge with the mate and the steersman, keeping a careful look out because of patches of sea mist off the groups of rocks lining the Pembrokeshire coast. At approximately 11.40 am, when the Victor should have been completing its first, high-altitude series of tests, they emerged into clearer weather as they neared a group of islands called the Smalls, crowned by lighthouse and about 15 miles due west of Skomer Island.

The three men then saw a splash in the water. They estimated the distance at five miles and the height of the splash roughly 50 feet. They heard two sharp cracks, like distant gunfire, and after hearing the news broadcast they put in an immediate radio call. The accident investigation team decided to follow up the report, since the time and area sounded roughly correct for the Victor's intended flightpath. They checked all the filmed displays from all RAF radar stations, and they finally struck gold with the station at RAF Wartling near Eastbourne in Sussex, a full 240 miles away.

This showed a track beginning at the time and place of the recording taken by Boscombe Down air traffic control at the start of the Victor's flight. Because it was such a clear trace from such a long distance away, it suggested that the aircraft causing it was flying higher than 35,000 feet. It ended 17 miles away from the position reported by the coaster, and three minutes earlier than the time they recorded, as the aircraft dipped below the area swept by the distant radar coverage. This was conclusive enough for a sea search to be ordered in the area. A fleet of 16 trawlers was assembled, with a naval salvage ship equipped with a diving chamber, an underwater television system and heavy lifting gear which could raise pieces of wreckage weighing up to 20 tons. It seemed like an eerie re-run of the Comet salvage expedition, but now in British waters and five years afterwards.

At first, progress was disappointing. Not one single item of wreckage from the missing aircraft was found for more than four months. Then, on 5 January 1960, a trawler called *Picton Sea Lion*, which wasn't even part of the search team, hauled up a piece of corrugated metal in its net. The fragment was shiny and clean, with little corrosion and small traces of marine growth. The experts identified it as a part of the trailing edge of the Victor's starboard wing. But no more pieces were found until the original search area was widened, and it was discovered that the delay between spotting the splash and writing it up in the log had produced a position five miles away from the true impact.

By the time the search was completed, more than 40 ships had been involved. Between them, over a total of a year and three months, they retrieved almost 600,000 pieces of wreckage, amounting to almost three-quarters of the aircraft's structure. The items identified included the watch worn by the co-pilot of the Victor, stopped at the moment of impact, exactly 46 seconds after 11.30. Another smashed instrument was a voltmeter from the aircraft's flightdeck which showed a faint mark caused by the instrument's needle when it was crushed by the impact forces. When examined through a microscope, it revealed the circuits were carrying full power at the time of the crash, so electrical failure could not have been a factor in bringing about the disaster.

A long and painstaking examination of the wreckage showed that the Victor had been almost intact at the moment when it struck the sea. Only the wingtips and bomb doors had become detached during its final dive, and there was no sign of any in-flight fire. All four engines had been running normally, and the position of the throttles showed that the engines were running at nearly full power. However, there were signs which were inconsistent with the Victor flying normally at high altitude. Curiously, the leading edge flaps on both wings were all in the extended position. Secondly, a device called the auto-mach trim actuator was jammed at a position indicating 0.855M, which was equivalent to a speed of 0.855 times the speed of sound. The purpose of this system was to counteract a tendency for the nose of the aircraft to pitch upwards as it approached the sound barrier. It automatically lowered the elevators to push the nose downwards and correct its longitudinal trim.

When the investigating team turned their attention to the two wingtips, they found another significant clue. The port wingtip still carried its pitot tube, although it was bent back through a right angle by the forces of impact, but the starboard wingtip pitot head was completely missing from its mounting sleeve. The two pitot heads operated different systems aboard the Victor. The port pitot head supplied the information for the co-pilot's air speed indicator and machmeter, but the missing starboard one not only operated the captain's air speed indicator, but also the aircraft's stall detector which operated the wing leading-edge flaps and the auto-mach trimmer.

The experts suggested that the starboard pitot tube might have been loosened by the wing buffeting caused by the sequence of deliberately planned high speed turns. If so, the captain's air speed indicator and machmeter would show the aircraft speed dropping quickly. To add to the confusion, the stall warning system would extend the Victor's leading edge flaps, and the auto-mach trimmer system would lower the elevators, so the aircraft's nose would drop and it would plunge into a high-speed dive. The only clues in this frightening emergency would be the co-pilot's air speed indicator and machmeter which would show the speed actually increasing. In that moment of crisis, there was nothing to tell the crew which instruments were actually telling the truth.

The crew would only have a brief opportunity to take the correct recovery action, and to ignore their basic pilot training and the evidence of most of their instruments. If they concentrated on the co-pilot's air speed indicator and pulled up the nose of the aircraft to reduce speed immediately, they might have been able to regain control. All the signs were pointing to a sudden and unexplained high speed stall, and the correct recovery action drummed into every pilot from basic training is that recovering from a stall means lowering the nose and increasing the speed. Here the correct action, when the aircraft's own systems were already doing just that, could only make things worse.

The result was a dive against which even the power-assisted controls were helpless to level it off before it crashed into the sea. The question remained that if all this had been caused by the loss of the pitot head from the starboard wingtip, what had actually let it become separated from its mounting sleeve? The investigators checked the sleeve more closely, and found that the two tapered collars which held the tube in place were still in position, but there were signs that the inside surface of the sleeve had been lined with too thick a coating of protective paint.

As stress and vibration wore away the paint, the collars' grip on the tube would have loosened, to the point where the wing buffeting in the high speed turns could have shaken the tube free. After all the complex, costly and time consuming investigation, the solution was simple. A change in the design to provide a more positive lock for the tube within the mounting sleeve, meant this particular disaster could never occur again.

In some cases weaknesses in the design or layout of controls, or changes between different variants of a particular design, have turned a potential emergency into an actual disaster. Before the ergonomics of flight-deck design were carefully monitored, there were several cases of crews regressing to the control layouts of earlier variants of the aircraft they were currently flying. As a result they shut down the wrong engine or switched to the wrong fuel tanks, and created an emergency. Though now much rarer, these kinds of error accidents still occasionally happen.

In the case of a British Midland Airways Boeing 737 on a flight from London Heathrow Airport to Belfast on a Sunday evening, 8 January 1989, the aircraft itself was brand new. It had only flown a total of 520 hours prior to take-off, it was powered by two high bypass turbofan engines manufactured by the French company SNECMA under licence from General Electric in the USA, and it was fitted with the latest type of 'glass cockpit', with monitor screens replacing many of the traditional ranks of instruments. It had already flown one trip to Belfast and back earlier in the day, when there had been no sign of any trouble at all. Finally, at 7.52 pm it took off from runway 27 Right on its second journey of the day, carrying 118 passengers and eight crew members, up through the Midlands and across the Irish Sea to the Ulster capital.

All went well until 13 minutes into the journey, when the aircraft was climbing through 28,300 feet on its way up to its cruising height of 35,000 feet. A sudden repeated impact noise, accompanied by severe vibration, broke out. Smoke entered the cabin through the ventilation system and there was a strong smell of burning. Passengers and crew at the back of the passenger cabin saw flames and sparks pouring from the jet pipe of the port engine. The vibration and smoke were noticed on the flight deck too, and Captain Kevin Hunt disengaged the auto-pilot and took over manual control.

He checked the engine instruments display on the cockpit's main monitor screen, but noticed no unexpected readings. Because of the smoke and smell penetrating the passenger cabin, he assumed the starboard engine must be the source of the trouble, because of his knowledge of the aircraft's ventilation system. He turned to the first officer, David McClelland, and asked him which engine was causing the trouble. He started to reply that it was the 'left one', but hesitated and said 'it's the right one'. The Captain ordered him to throttle it back, and then to shut it down, but before he could carry out the instruction, he was ordered to keep it going for the time being.

Captain Hunt then decided to divert to British Midland Airways' maintenance base at East Midlands Airport at Castle Donington in Derbyshire, which was then only a few minutes flying time away. He called the company for permission, then radioed the London controller for clearance to make the diversion. The aircraft was cleared to descend to 10,000 feet and told to switch to Manchester ATC for further clearance. In the meantime the first officer shut down the starboard engine, while the captain throttled back the port engine to begin the descent.

On the face of it, this was a routine emergency, with no particular threat. From the captain's point of view the offending engine had been identified as the starboard one. This had been shut down and the power had been reduced for a single-engine approach and landing at Castle Donington. The noise and vibration had ceased, and within minutes the smoke and the burning smell had cleared, and all seemed well. Manchester air traffic control passed a series of course and altitude changes to the crew of the 737, and when it was finally cleared down to 4,000 feet, handed it over to East Midlands Approach Control.

The approach continued normally until the 737 was lining up with the runway 3,000 feet below and 13 miles ahead of the aircraft. The pilots increased power on the port engine to flatten the descent, and then the flaps were lowered in stages to slow the aircraft down and increase the lift generated by the wing. At 2,000 feet they intercepted the localiser beam for the instrument landing system for runway 27, and the captain called for the landing gear to be lowered. They passed the outer marker with just over four miles to go, and they could see the lights of the runway ahead. A couple more minutes would see them safely on the ground, so that the passengers could be disembarked and the problem investigated. One minute later, with the aircraft down to 900 feet and the runway 2½ miles ahead, the port engine failed.

It had done so at the worst possible moment, with the aircraft flying slowly at low altitude and the runway too far away for a glide approach. The captain called to the first officer to restart the starboard engine, while he raised the nose to trade speed for height as long as possible. At the same time he called over the intercom for the passengers and cabin crew to prepare for a crash landing. Within seconds the aircraft's speed fell so low that the stall warning system activated and it sank gently but inexorably, still in a nose-high attitude towards the ground below.

Unfortunately, the approach to runway 28 at the East Midlands Airport lies across one of the busiest stretches of motorway in Britain, the M1, linking London with Yorkshire, which comprises six lanes with heavy levels of week-end traffic. The powerless 737 hit a grassy slope on the eastern side of the motorway which tore away the main landing gear. It crashed through a row of trees and a boundary fence and across the southbound carriageway which at this point runs in a shallow cutting. It brought down a lamp standard in the strip between the carriageways, carried on across the northbound carriageway and crashed into the slope of the western side of the cutting, just a thousand yards short of the runway.

The aircraft decelerated from around 90 mph to a total stop in less than the length of the fuselage. Terrible destructive forces split the fuselage into three main sections, with the nose continuing furthest up the slope, the centre section following behind and the tail section flipping over and coming to rest almost inverted. Fortunately, the airport fire services were standing by beside the runway, waiting for the emergency landing. They arrived within five minutes and put out a fire which had started in the remains of the port engine, and laid a foam carpet to prevent the spilled fuel from igniting.

In the circumstances, the fact that 79 of those aboard the aircraft survived, although all but five had injuries of varying degrees of severity, was remarkable. So was the fact that the aircraft had avoided crashing into any of the vehicles using the motorway. Nevertheless, 39 passengers were killed in the impact, with another five dying later from injuries sustained in the crash. From the statements made by cabin crew and passengers, and the course of unfolding events, it was all too clear that the pilots had shut down the wrong engine, and as the simultaneous throttling back of the port engine had effectively

Wreckage of the British Midland Boeing 737 at Kegworth with the M1 motorway to the right.
(AAIB)

eliminated the noise, vibration and smoke, there was nothing to alert them to this before the final stages of the approach, when safety margins had been lost.

The investigators had to concentrate on two questions. What had caused a nearly new engine to fail, with disastrous results? Secondly, given the failure, what had caused two competent and well-trained pilots to close down the wrong engine, and turn a situation involving delay and diversion and inconvenience into a full-scale crash? They looked for answers to these questions in the first instance by checking the information provided by the flight data recorder.

Sketch of the impact path of the British Midland Boeing 737 at Kegworth. (AAIB)

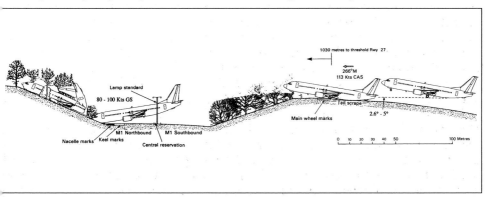

This evidence was clear. At the time when the initial 'rattling' or 'thumping' sound could be heard clearly on the cockpit voice recorder playback, the FDR tracks indicated severe vibration, fluctuations in fan speed and fuel flow, and a rising gas temperature, all relating to the *port* engine. This confirmed what the witnesses in the passenger cabin reported, though the crew could not see the condition of the two underwing engines from the flight-deck. At no time was there any unusual indication on the FDR tracks relating to the starboard engine, up to the time when this was shut down. On the other hand, the FDR data confirmed that at the time of the onset of the noise and vibration problems, the disengagement of the autopilot produced a slight but definite roll to port, a clear indication that the power delivered by the port engine was fluctuating, but one which was not corrected at the time.

So why had the crew closed down the starboard engine in response to the problem? When the investigators checked the CVR recording more closely they found that the captain's question produced a hesitant answer from the first officer. He had actually said 'It's the le... it's the right one'. To the captain this reinforced his own estimation that, because of the layout of the cabin ventilation system, it had to be the starboard engine which was producing the smoke and smells of burning which filled the fuselage.

From that point onwards, neither pilot questioned the decision. They were so convinced the starboard engine was causing the trouble that after they shut it down, they assumed the reduction in vibration and the lessening of the smoke in the cabin was a direct result of their action. In reality, the port engine compressor was running slower than normal, and its exhaust gas temperature was higher than normal. The engine vibration continued at its maximum value together with fluctuating fuel flow, until the port engine was throttled back for the 737 to start its descent for East Midlands Airport.

The captain's error was due to inexperience with this particular variant of the 737. On the aircraft he had flown prior to the 737-400, the cabin air-conditioning supply *was* ducted from the starboard engine, but in this particular type the system was also fed from the port engine. So what had caused the first officer to hesitate, and then to declare positively that the starboard engine was to blame, never afterwards admitting the possibility of a mistake?

The official report concluded that neither pilot was really sure which engine was responsible. It assumed that they both considered that the other one had reasons for believing the starboard engine was at fault, and therefore they went along with the decision. The final arbiter should have been the engine instruments, displayed on the monitor screen in the centre of the cockpit display.

The layout of this display was criticised at the enquiry. It contained the primary engine instruments, covering engine speed, exhaust gas temperature and fuel flow in two vertical columns, one for each engine, set in the left-hand side of the display. The secondary instruments, covering oil pressure, oil temperature, vibration and hydraulic pressure were also in two vertical columns of smaller dials on the right-hand side of the display. These secondary instruments were not only a mere three-quarters of an inch in diameter, but their pointers were composed of three electronic dashes in line, and were much more difficult to read than those of the colour-coded primary instruments.

It is possible that the vital discrepancy in the readings of the vibration meters was either not noticed in the heavy workload which the pilots had to deal with, or the position of the dial which *did* show the abnormal indication was misread. Whatever the reason, neither pilot linked any abnormally high vibration reading to the port engine as shown by the instruments. The investigators questioned whether a change in the layout would have eliminated the confusion. For example, both primary and secondary instruments could be grouped together in two equal halves of the display, with the port engine instruments in the left half next to the appropriate thrust lever, and the starboard engine instruments in the right half.

A number of other factors contributed to the sequence of events. If one of the cabin crew had reported the flames and sparks from the port engine, it might have shaken the pilots out of their conviction that the seat of the trouble lay in the starboard engine. The FDR trace also showed that when the port engine power was increased during the approach to reduce the rate of descent, the vibration level rose quite sharply, and would have been displayed on the engine instruments. At that point there was still sufficient time to restart the starboard engine.

What had caused the original engine problem which initiated the disaster? The two engines were retrieved from the wreckage and flown to the SNECMA factory in France for more detailed study. It was clear that the starboard engine damage was limited to that caused in the impact, and its internal condition was normal for an engine which had not been delivering power at the time. There were no signs of a fire, or any other abnormal condition. The port engine, however, showed signs of severe damage both outside and, more significantly, on the inside as well.

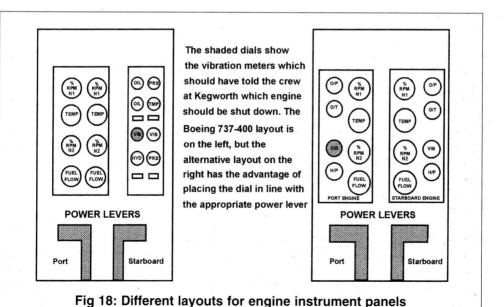

Fig 18: Different layouts for engine instrument panels

Twenty-nine of the 38 fan blades had been damaged, with the ends broken off. There were signs of damage from hard objects drawn into the compressor stages, and the central core of the engine showed deposits of soot which seemed to originate from a damaged combustion nozzle, while there was also soot found inside the high pressure compressor case, and inside the low pressure shaft. There was fire damage outside the engine, but the pattern showed this had not been spread by a high velocity slipstream, so that it had almost certainly broken out after impact.

They then turned their attention to the individual fan blades, and the nature of the break with the ends which had become detached. In all cases except one, these were overload fractures. The one exception was blade number 17, which seemed to show signs of a fatigue fracture. It was cleaned and microscopically examined, and the break was found to originate at a fatigue failure close to the leading edge of the blade. Was this likely to be a one-off occurrence, or was it a potential weakness?

The answer came just five months later, when a Dan-Air Boeing 737 with the same type of engines, suffered an identical set of symptoms at 25,000 feet over the Channel. Again it was the port engine which suffered the noise and vibration. The difference was that the flight-deck crew checked the vibration meters, shut down the port engine and made a safe approach and landing on the starboard engine alone. Two days after that, another British Midland Airways 737 on the same London to Belfast service, also suffered a run of the same symptoms, and once again the crew located the problem, closed down the correct engine and made a safe landing.

In both cases, the engine problems were due to identical fatigue failures of individual fan blades. The cause of the problem was traced, after an extensive test programme, to a particular pattern of vibration which tended to build up when using climbing power, particularly between 25,000 and 30,000 feet. Detailed changes to the damping of the fan blades effectively cured the problem, and another safety loophole had been well and truly plugged.

The 737 crash at East Midlands Airport was a tragic case of a mistake being made in dealing with a genuine emergency. In other cases though, crews' mistakes with perfectly serviceable aircraft have led to disaster. One of a series of accidents which hinged on the difficulty of presenting information to the flight crew in such a way that it could not be mistaken involved a Boeing 727 operating an American Airlines flight from New York to Cincinnati on the evening of 8 November 1965. The aircraft had a flight-deck crew of three, a cabin crew of three and 56 passengers. It was scheduled to leave New York at five in the afternoon and arrive at Greater Cincinnati Airport, located on the Kentucky side of the Ohio River, just under two hours later.

The Boeing took off from New York's La Guardia Airport some 20 minutes late. There were thunderstorms expected en route, but the aircraft was cleared to cruise at 35,000 feet on a west-south-west heading to Charleston in West Virginia and then west-north-west to its destination. As the weather was better than predicted, the aircraft called air traffic control when approximately 90 miles from Charleston to straighten out the dog's leg course and steer straight for the York VOR navigational beacon, and from there make straight for Cincinnati. This would save some of the time lost by their late departure and their indirect route.

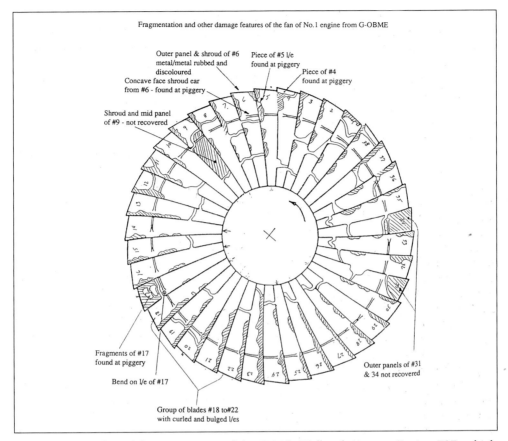

Fragmentation and other damage features of the fan of No.1 engine from G-OBME

Damage to the fan of the port engine of the British Midland Airways Boeing 737, which caused it to crash at Kegworth. (AAIB)

As they approached Cincinnati however, the weather began to worsen again, with cloud and some lightning approaching from the north-west. Nevertheless, the crew reported the airfield in sight at 6.55 pm, ten minutes short of their predicted landing time. They asked control for a visual approach, and they were cleared for a turn to the west before a final turn to port on to a southerly heading to land on runway 18, descending from their current altitude of 4,000 feet to 2,000 feet at their discretion. Three minutes later, the crew were switched from approach control to the tower controller, with the aircraft then six miles south-east of the airfield.

The crew asked the tower how close the approaching bad weather was. The tower reported it was just about overhead, though there were no signs of rain or windshear as yet. Just after 7 o'clock the controller reported 'a little rain', and as the crew were having trouble keeping the runway in clear view in the worsening visibility, the airfield lighting system was turned on to high intensity. The crew announced they would try to pick up the instrument landing system beams to guide them in on their final approach. Nothing more was heard from the aircraft.

Seconds later the 727 crashed into a wooded hillside overlooking the Ohio River, two miles from the runway threshold and a quarter of a mile from its intended final approach track. At that moment, it was flying more than 200 feet below the height of the runway. The aircraft burst into flames, and everyone on board was killed apart from one stewardess and three passengers, one of them an off-duty American Airlines pilot.

When the accident investigators inspected the wreckage, they found no sign of system failure or break-up in the air. Instead the 727 was in a normal landing configuration, with flaps set at 25 degrees and the nose pitched slightly upwards, though the landing gear was not lowered. Witnesses agreed that the aircraft's approach seemed normal, though it seemed to be unusually low when it flew over the Ohio River on its crosswind leg, before turning on to its final approach. Just before the crash the light rain which had been falling for some minutes gave way to a burst of much heavier rain.

Two witnesses had more detailed information. One clearly saw the aircraft's landing lights just before the impact, and said it was definitely flying too low to clear the sides of the deep river valley. The other was the off-duty pilot who had been travelling in the first class section of the aircraft. He thought the descent into Cincinnati seemed faster than usual, he noticed they seemed to fly into cloud just before the accident, and immediately before the impact he heard the flap setting being increased.

All of this hinted at a mistake over the aircraft's height rather than any catastrophic breakdown. The 727 carried no CVR, though the playback of the crew's communications with the tower indicated nothing out of the ordinary to account for what happened. At 6.45 pm, when they had first called Cincinnati air traffic control to report that they expected to arrive in approximately twenty minutes time, the airport passed on details of the barometric pressure on the spot.

This is done as a matter of routine to enable the pilots to set the altimeters on the flight deck, and two settings are involved. The QNH setting uses the pressure at sea level, so setting an altimeter to that reading gives the crew their height above sea level. The QFE setting uses the pressure at ground level at the airport, so an altimeter set to the QFE reading will display the aircraft's height above ground level at the destination. The difference between the two heights, which in this case was 815 feet, is equal to the airport's height above sea level. On the 727 flight deck there were three altimeters, one in front of each pilot and one in the centre of the panel. The company rules said the individual pilots' altimeters were to be set to the airport (QFE) setting, with the centre altimeter adjusted to the QNH setting.

Other information came from the aircraft's flight data recorder, which confirmed that the aircraft had been at a height of 2,000 feet when it started its downwind, northbound leg. Because of the height of the airport above sea level, this was equivalent to just over 1,100 feet above the runway. Speed was reduced to 190 knots, and when it turned on to the base (crosswind) leg over the river, it started descending again, with the speed falling back to 160 knots. As the aircraft started its last turn to port on to the runway heading for its final approach, the rate of descent started to increase from around 800 feet per minute to 2,000 fpm, then dropped back to just over 600 fpm as the aircraft descended into the river valley.

One significant clue from the FDR data was the combination of the initially high approach speed and the series of flap extensions in quick succession. This had two effects: it reduced the amount of time the crew had to complete the pre-landing checks, and it meant the engine power had to be reduced to idle to allow the speed to decay sufficiently for each additional increase in the flap settings. In addition to the extra pressure this placed upon the pilots, the sudden deterioration in visibility at a crucial moment on the approach meant they must have had little attention to spare for anything other than the runway lights ahead.

What could have misled them so fatally over their height? The runway approach lights, particularly when seen through driving rain, would have given them little idea of their height. The only other lights visible on the approach would be from houses on the banks of the river, 400 feet or more *below* the airport, which might have given them the impression they were much higher than they were. Finally, the altimeters came under suspicion for the ease with which they might have been misread. The instruments each had a single pointer which indicated hundreds of feet, and a moving drum seen through a small window in the face of the instrument which read thousands of feet.

The problem was that there was very little visual difference between an altitude of, say 800 feet above the airport, which would have been acceptable for the final approach, when the main pointer would read '8' and the drum display would show a reading of between '0' and '1'. At 200 feet below the airport, which was their actual altitude, the main pointer would still show '8' but the small window display would read a fraction below '0'. The visual difference between these two readings is very small. If both pilots were dividing their attention between the misleading signs outside the cockpit windows and the readings on their altimeters, it was all too easy for them to see what they expected to see, and not the reality that they were flying, carefully and under perfect control, into the ground.

This combination of factors produced an almost identical accident at the same spot on 20 November 1967 when a TWA Convair 880 on an intermediate stop on a flight from Los Angeles to Boston crashed short of the runway, killing 70 of the 82 people on board. On this occasion the ILS glideslope was not working, and once again weather was deteriorating rapidly. It was decided that the combination of low ground and lights on the approach, with a runway considerably higher, led the pilots to descend too low in a position from which they could not recover.

Much of the emphasis on air safety involves ensuring that nothing is omitted, and no errors are committed. In a very few cases, emergencies have occurred because pilots actually carried out actions which were strictly unnecessary, or ill-advised. On 3 November 1973 a National Airlines DC-10 was flying from Miami to San Francisco via New Orleans, Houston and Las Vegas. It was on the penultimate leg of the flight with 116 passengers and a crew of 12, cruising at a height of 39,000 feet when there was a sharp explosion and a bout of severe buffeting which shook the whole aircraft.

Something hit the window on the starboard side of the passenger cabin with a violent blow, shattering both inner and outer panes and causing a massive decompression. The passenger sitting beside that window, who had been sleeping with his seatbelt loosely fastened, was sucked through the window to his death, despite the efforts of other passengers to save him. The pilots started an emergency descent and oxygen masks were deployed for crew and passengers. In the meantime they found losses in electrical power, and there was a temporary blackout of radio communication.

Within five minutes, the flight-deck crew had been able to restore electrical power and radio communication. The flight engineer had seen an emergency light flash on the starboard engine fuel cut-off selector, but had found the lever jammed. Instead he operated the secondary shut-off selector and discharged the engine fire extinguishers. Finally they managed to call Albuquerque Approach Control, who gave them clearance to descend to 6,000 feet and then make an emergency landing at the airport, then 60 miles to the north of them.

The approach was successful, though only the port and tail engines were working, and the landing gear had to be lowered with the emergency system. The landing too was successful, though they evacuated passengers and crew within one minute using the safety slides in case of fire. When the DC-10 was inspected, it was clear that the starboard engine had burst apart in flight, but at first there seemed to be nothing to account for this. There was an unexplained fault on the FDR, although the investigators found helpful clues in the CVR playback and on the aircraft systems themselves.

It was clear from the flight-deck conversation that the captain and the flight engineer had been experimenting to determine the effect on the engines' automatic throttles, of tripping the circuit breakers which supplied the instruments which measured the rotational speed of each engine's low pressure compressor. This was strictly unauthorised, and at first appeared to cause no untoward effects. They disconnected the circuit breakers, then reduced the setting on the autothrottle system before resetting the throttles manually. Then the flight engineer reset the circuit breakers to restore the system to its original setting, when the explosion and buffeting began.

During the course of the investigation, a computer was used to predict the paths on which the engine components would have fallen from the position where the starboard engine explosion had occurred. The resulting search in the New Mexico desert found the engine cowling, the ring which held the fan blades in position and several of the missing fan blades, though the body of the missing passenger was never found. The signs of the engine damage suggested that it could only have been produced by the fan tips rubbing against the fan casing under high centrifugal forces caused by the engine running at over its designed maximum speed.

In the absence of any FDR data, the investigators were able to check the CVR background noise to determine the engine speeds through analysing the frequencies. Before the two crew members started tinkering with the circuit breakers, the engines were running at 97 per cent maximum power. They then accelerated to 100 per cent power, followed by the starboard engine oscillating between 94 and 100 per cent maximum. After the explosion the engine increased to 110 per cent of its designed maximum speed, with both other engines also overspeeding, though to a lesser extent.

It seemed clear that the tripping and resetting of the circuit breakers had disabled the system which limited the engine speed when the autothrottles were calling for more power. In just one case the acceleration and resulting forces were enough to cause the engine to fly apart, causing massive damage and the death of a passenger. Had the crew adhered strictly to the airline's operating procedures, the accident would never have happened.

Another potential catastrophe on an otherwise normal flight was encountered on 19 February 1985 by a China Airlines Boeing 747 on its way from Taipei in Taiwan to Los Angeles, with 251 passengers and a crew of 23. When they were crossing the Pacific at 41,000 feet with the autopilot in control, they encountered light clear air turbulence while approximately 300 miles north west of San Francisco. The autopilot system kept the aircraft at its set height, and operated the ailerons and spoilers to keep the aircraft on the right heading, controlled by its INS, and the speed was maintained according to pre-set limits, in spite of the turbulent conditions.

At one stage the aircraft increased its speed slightly. The autopilot system reduced the power slightly, and the aircraft slowed to just below its pre-set speed. The system then opened the throttles again to keep the speed within limits, but for some reason the starboard outer engine failed to respond. The flight engineer noticed the discrepancy, and tried moving the starboard outer throttle lever backwards and forwards by hand, but there was still no response. The engine appeared to have suffered a flame-out, and would have to be restarted.

This would involve descending to a lower altitude, and the captain told the first officer to ask for clearance for descent. He called Oakland ATC Centre, but did not tell them the reason for the request. Oakland cleared them to descend to 24,000 feet which was comfortably below the 30,000 feet peak engine height for engine restarting. The controller then called the aircraft back a total of six times, but received no reply.

In the light of what was happening, this was scarcely surprising. While the first officer was making his call to Oakland, the captain told the flight engineer to try to restart the engine at their present height. As the speed had dropped back to 240 knots, the captain disengaged the autopilot's altitude hold command so that he could push the autopilot pitch control forward to lower the nose of the 747 to maintain speed. He had forgotten, or chose to ignore, the fact that the aircraft was still being controlled by the inertial navigation system to maintain its pre-set heading.

When he partly disengaged the system, the 747 yawed to starboard because of the failed engine on the starboard side. Because the rudder was not being controlled by the autopilot, the only action it could take to try to obey the commands of the navigational system was to roll the aircraft to port. The amount of roll the autopilot could apply was less than the asymmetric forces building up on the aircraft, and it soon began to roll to starboard instead. By the time the first officer had finished his call to Oakland, the aircraft's starboard roll was noticeable, and the captain was trying to prevent the speed falling back still further. Finally, he disengaged the autopilot completely and all hell broke loose.

The yaw and roll to starboard intensified, but for some reason the captain concentrated on trying to bring the wings level instead of applying port rudder to counteract the yaw. By the time they descended into cloud at 37,000 feet, the captain was thoroughly disoriented. Although he did not know it at the time, the mighty 747 rolled right through 360 degrees, the other three engines lost power and the g-forces became so great that the pilots had difficulty moving their heads and arms. At one stage the speed dropped to an indicated 54 knots, well below the aircraft's stalling speed, and twice increased so much that it exceeded its designed maximum speed.

At last the captain and first officer managed to ease the plane out of its near-terminal dive and once they broke out into clear weather below the 11,000 foot cloud-base, they could re-orient themselves and the aircraft with reference to the horizon. The two port engines and the starboard inner started delivering power again as they continued their descent, and the flight engineer restarted the starboard outer engine soon afterwards. Only then, after two minutes of radio silence, were the shaken crew able to radio Oakland and report a flame-out, and that they were now at 9,000 feet. In view of all they had experienced, it was a classic understatement.

The flight engineer reported that the instruments showed the landing gear was down and locked, while the fluid gauge for the number 1 hydraulic system showed it was empty. They therefore diverted to San Francisco International Airport, where they landed with no injuries except for a broken foot and a strained back suffered by a passenger and a cabin crew member respectively. But the terrifying forces imposed on the aircraft left their marks on the 747.

The enormous wings of the aircraft were bent upwards between two and three inches at the tips, while the trailing edge was cracked at several points along its length, and part of the port outboard aileron was broken. Ten feet of the port tailplane, including the elevator, had separated from the main structure, and the tip of the starboard tailplane was missing. The auxiliary power unit, which provided electrical power when the engines were not running, had been shaken free of its mountings, and was lying loose in the tail cone.

So fierce were the stresses imposed on the aircraft that the extremely tough flight data recorder buckled under them. It recorded a peak g-force when pulling out of one dive of 4.8 positive g, the kind of acceleration more appropriate for a single-seat fighter than a massive passenger aircraft, and then effectively ceased to function. Computer calculations showed the aircraft later peaked at 5.1g when the pilots were fighting to regain control. Almost incredibly, the aircraft stayed in one piece during these frightening manoeuvres, and once control was regained, the subsequent flight and landing were almost routine.

To the investigators, the causes of the near-accident were clear enough. In their view the captain became obsessed with the problem of the engine and the resulting decrease in air speed. He should have disconnected the autopilot completely, and flown the aircraft manually until the situation was sorted out, the aircraft brought down to a lower altitude and the engine restarted. When they examined the starboard outer engine, they discovered the problem was not even a full flame-out but merely a power drop to an idle setting. In any case, the airline did not actually consider a single engine failure on a Boeing 747 constituted an emergency. With the proper procedures, the passengers would have ended their flight without even noticing anything was amiss.

The pilot's nightmare, where the aircraft starts to behave uncontrollably for no apparent reason, can be triggered by other unseen causes. Moreover, when this happens near the ground, without the ample margin for recovery enjoyed by the China Airlines 747, the consequences can be much more serious. On 30 May 1972, an American Airlines DC-10 and a Delta Air Lines DC-9 were both carrying out 'circuits and bumps' training over Greater Southwest International Airport near Dallas in Texas. The purpose of the succession of practice approaches and landings was to check out trainee first officers on the particular types that both were flying.

At first, the two aircraft maintained a separation of more than six miles, as the DC-10 carried out a series of 'touch and go' approaches, ending in touch-downs and immediate take-offs. The DC-9 then carried out an ILS approach and landing. The aircraft pulled to a stop before taxiing back to the threshold of runway 13 and asking for clearance for a second ILS approach. After completing this second approach, the aircraft climbed away and carried out an overshoot. The crew then asked for clearance to do an approach and a climb-out from runway 35.

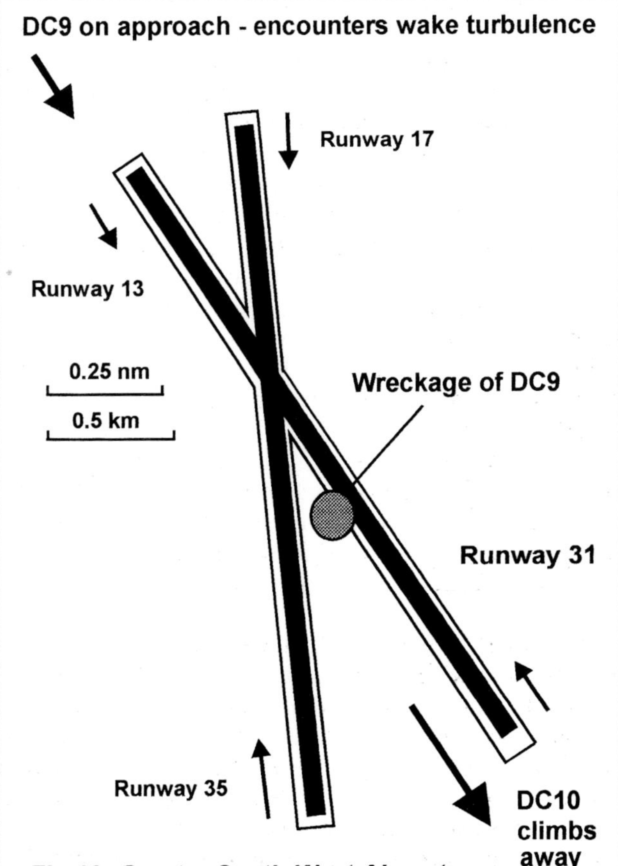

Fig 19: Greater South-West Airport

After that, the DC-9 crew asked for permission to fly a left-hand (anti-clockwise) circuit of the airfield, to approach and land on runway 17. While it was halfway round this circuit and on the downwind leg parallel to runway 17, the instructor asked for clearance to land on runway 13 instead, behind the DC-10 which was now approaching on the latest of its touch and go landings. This seemed a sensible idea to avoid the possibility of the two aircraft coming on to conflicting courses, and the controller gave permission. He added as an aside 'Caution – wake turbulence', as specified for aircraft following behind heavy jets with less than half a mile separation.

He seemed unduly cautious, as the two aircraft were approximately two miles apart. The DC-10 touched down and the DC-9 followed it, turning into line with the runway for its final approach. The bigger DC-10's wheels brushed the tarmac, and then the crew increased power to lift off and climb away for another circuit. The DC-9 was then rolling out of its turn and heading for the runway. As it lost speed and height, at about a quarter of a mile from the runway threshold, the tower controllers noticed it rolled to port, stopped, rolled back level and then over to starboard, then back to port again as it crossed the runway threshold.

With the DC-9 approximately 100 feet above the runway, the watchers were horrified to see it roll once more to starboard, this time far enough over for the wings to pass the vertical, with the starboard wingtip hitting the tarmac. This flicked the aircraft over on to its back so that it crashed upside down, wrenching off the tail and bursting into flames as it slithered down the runway. All four of those on board, which included two trainee pilots, a training captain and an FAA inspector, were killed.

When the investigators came to analyse the crash, the turbulence caused by the passing of the DC-10 down that same runway came to be a prime suspect. Measurements showed that the time separation between the two aircraft as they approached runway 13 was just under a minute. However, when they studied the weather conditions which existed over the airfield at the time, it was clear that the wake turbulence generated by the DC-10 would have had a measurable effect on the air over the runway threshold for at least twice that time.

But was that turbulence enough to cause stability problems for a relatively large passenger aircraft, which ultimately caused it to turn over and crash? An aircraft generates lift by speeding up the airflow over the upper surface of its wings compared with the airflow over its lower wing surfaces. This creates an area of high pressure air flowing beneath the wing, and low pressure air above it. As these two airstreams reach the tip of the wing, they recombine to form a quickly-rotating vortex, which trails behind the aircraft like a tornado turned on its side. At its peak, this vortex rotates far more quickly than an aircraft could be made to roll, so any aircraft flying into it would risk being thrown off balance. A series of accidents where light aircraft encountered one of the wing-tip vortices left by a large passenger aircraft helped to focus attention on the problem.

More detailed research into the airflow generated behind heavy jets showed that the most intense disturbances were caused by large aircraft flying very slowly and very close to the ground, with flaps, spoilers and landing gear extended. This was exactly the condition of the DC-10 at the time of the crash, when it was likely that the two wing vortices could have persisted over the runway for several minutes on end. The common opinion among pilots was that these might only pose a threat to a light aircraft making an approach before the vortices had decayed to a safe level. Could they really prove lethal to a competently flown airliner?

The investigators turned their attention to the FDR and CVR retrieved from the wreckage. The FDR data showed that the DC-9 experienced a sharp gust at the moment of its initial roll to port. Some five seconds later the CVR showed the training pilot told the trainees to execute an overshoot, and then called for full take-off power. This was during the correction of the initial roll to port, followed by the immediate roll to starboard, a second correction and then the second roll to port.

The CVR then showed the stall warning system was activated. The training captain took over control, the stall warning was heard again, and then the FDR showed the aircraft suddenly beginning its fast, and final, roll to starboard. Within a second there was the noise of the impact, and the recordings ceased. More precise information was needed on the behaviour and power of these turbulent wake vortices before the investigators could be sure these alone were responsible for the crash. The FAA responded by setting up a test programme.

This involved flying a DC-10 and a Tri-Star at low levels and low speeds past a tower fitted with a smoke generator and a series of velocity sensors. In each case the smoke currents showed the formation of the vortices, and the airflow speeds within them were measured by the velocity sensors. The results of the tests showed that these turbulent vortices were so intense that they exceeded the design limits of transport aircraft unfortunate enough to fly into them, and also that they persisted for several minutes after the aircraft causing them had passed by.

The investigators then fed the velocity information produced by the tests into a computer. This was used to analyse the effects of these vortices on a second aircraft at the speed and height of the DC-9 on its final approach. The simulation showed that the initial roll to port would have been caused by the DC-9 flying into the outer area of the vortex generated by the DC-10's port wingtip. This was an updraught which would have acted more strongly on the under surface of the DC-9's starboard wing, tilting the aircraft over to port. The crew then corrected this by applying a control command to the aircraft to roll to starboard.

This actually produced an over-correction so that the DC-9 then rolled its wings past the horizontal and into the start of a roll to starboard. The pilots corrected again by trying to roll the plane to port, so that another slight over-correction rolled the aircraft to port for the second time. The crew then initiated a roll to starboard to correct this second roll to port. At this very moment the DC-9's starboard wing entered the fierce downdraught at the heart of the vortex, which would have forced the starboard wing downwards, adding to the action initiated by the pilots. This flung the plane into its final and catastrophic roll to starboard. It happened so quickly that even though the pilots applied full port aileron, there was no time for this to arrest the starboard roll before the starboard wing hit the ground and the aircraft broke up.

Though a mercifully small death-toll was involved, this crash had a dramatic effect on the understanding of the dangers of running aircraft take-offs and landings too close together at increasingly busy airports. In many cases, the time separations between aircraft had been closer than those of the DC-10 and DC-9 that day. Usually, the prevailing wind would blow the vortices clear of the approach path of the second aircraft. Even so, there have been cases where airliners have been rolled violently one way or the other, and sometimes both ways in quick succession, yet have survived to allow the pilots to report what happened.

As a result of all this information, the minimum separations between heavy aircraft and any type of following traffic have been greatly increased in recent years. Not before time, since it was later found that the largest and heaviest of passenger jets, the Boeing 747, could produce powerful vortices as far as eight miles behind it!

Finally, there are those pilot-error accidents involving control movements which were clearly ill-advised at the time, yet which defy all attempts to explain or understand the reasons for them. On 18 June 1972 a British European Airways Trident 1C was departing from Heathrow Airport on a flight to Brussels, with 112 passengers and a crew of six. It was a rainy summer afternoon, with cloud-base down to a thousand feet, and the aircraft started its take-off run at 4.8 pm BST.

The take-off appeared to be entirely normal, with the Trident climbing straight ahead after leaving runway 27 Right until it reached an altitude of 700 feet. It then banked to port to begin a turn which would take it towards the Epsom non-directional navigation beacon. At 5.2 pm, the aircraft reported it was climbing as cleared, and the tower controllers passed it over to the London Air Traffic Control Centre. The aircraft crew then called London ATCC to report passing through 1,500 feet, whereupon the ATCC cleared them to climb to 6,000 feet and told them to set their transponder code to 6615. The captain replied 'up to six zero'. That was the last message received from the Trident.

Less than a minute later, the aircraft emerged from the cloud-base in a deep stall, falling out of the sky in an almost horizontal attitude, to crash in a field beside the A30 Staines by-pass, opposite the large King George VI reservoir. Everyone on board was killed in the crash, except for one passenger who survived for minutes only. The investigators examined the wreckage, which had escaped the outbreak of a post-crash fire by the fast arrival of firefighting teams. They found no evidence of any airframe or system failure which could have caused the crash, or accounted for the fact that the Trident was flying far too slowly to remain in the air.

They were fortunate in having a functioning FDR found in the wreckage. At first, though, this only deepened the mystery. It showed one inexplicable departure from the normal procedure for a take-off and climb to cruising altitude. Like most passenger aircraft, the Trident had two types of device which increased the lift generated by the wing at low speeds, such as when approaching to land, or climbing after take-off. These were trailing-edge flaps and leading-edge slats, both of which extended the curvature of the aerofoil section of the wing and enabled the aircraft to fly more slowly without stalling.

In this case, the FDR showed the slats, or 'droops' as they were known to the crew, had been retracted while the aircraft was flying at 162 knots, which was far too slow. As a result, the Trident began to stall, which activated two automatic safety systems. The stick-shaker applied a vibration to the control column to warn the pilots of the approaching stall. If they took no action, the stick-pusher forced the control column forward to begin the stall recovery action. This pushed the aircraft nose down, to increase speed at the expense of losing height. Unfortunately, the Trident had only reached a height of 1,770 feet when this happened, a paper-thin margin of safety.

Worse was to come. As the nose pitched down and the speed increased, the operation of the stick-pusher ceased, as the condition which triggered it had been removed. But the aircraft was still tail-heavy, which caused the nose to rise and the speed to fall again. So within ten seconds of its first operation, the stick-pusher forced the aircraft's nose down again, until one of the crew switched the system off. This left the aircraft free to pitch up into a worsening stall. The Trident was another high-tailed aircraft which can, if the nose rises too high in the approach to a stall, enter a 'deep stall', where the disturbed airflow from the stalled wings blankets the elevators and prevents any recovery action taken by the pilots from having any effect.

This is why the Trident, like other high-tailed aircraft, was equipped with a positive stick-pusher system to ensure it was never allowed to approach a deep stall, even if the crew did not respond to the emergency properly. In this case, by disabling the system, the crew had removed the last obstacle to the aircraft entering this terminal condition. When it hit the ground, less than half a minute later, it was still deeply stalled.

The problem for the investigators was that there was no reason why the slats should have been retracted so dangerously early in the climb. Given the effect of making that mistake why did the crew not attempt to recover? Because the engine power was reduced to the level specified for a noise-reduction take-off and climb, the pilots could have opened the engine power levers to full climb power, or re-extended the leading edge slats once the warning system was activated. If they had done either or both of these, or simply let the stick-pusher do its job, holding the control column forward to keep the aircraft's nose forward while its speed built up, the aircraft should have recovered. Yet not only had they done none of those things, they had actually taken the one action which allowed the aircraft to enter that fatal deep-stall condition.

All the investigators could do was suggest possible explanations, in the absence of any facts which would establish the true reasons for these actions. It was known from the post-mortem that the Captain, Stanley Key, was suffering from narrowed arteries, and there were signs that he had suffered an internal haemorrhage less than two hours before the crash. Since he had been involved in a sharp argument with fellow pilots over a planned pilots' strike shortly before departure, this could have triggered an attack which could have impaired his ability to fly the aircraft normally.

The other two pilots on the flight-deck (apart from a Captain Collins who was an off-duty pilot occupying the jump-seat) were two relatively inexperienced second officers, but it was thought that neither would have retracted the droops without orders from the captain. One possible explanation was that Captain Key noticed that the airspeed was dropping, and decided that the flaps should be raised to reduce the drag. This would have actually been in order, except the flaps had already been raised. The flap lever was adjacent to the droops lever on the opposite side of the engine power levers, so that it might have been possible he moved the wrong lever – though this explanation contains several assumptions. In addition, it still fails to explain the deliberate disabling of the stick-pusher system.

Perhaps a more plausible explanation might have been that Captain Key pulled the wrong lever as he was about to collapse from internal loss of blood.

If his collapse had distracted the other two pilots from what he had done with the levers, they would have been preoccupied with trying to deal with this flight-deck emergency. The operation of the stick-shaker and stick-pusher would have had no clear reason behind it. They were in cloud at the time and could not appreciate the aircraft's attitude without looking at the instruments.

When it happened for the second time, they may have assumed that a common rumour among BEA pilots at the time, that the stick-pusher system was sometimes triggered by a false alarm, had actually come true. They therefore switched the system off while they tried to help the captain, only to realise the terrible predicament they were in when it was already too late. Unfortunately the Trident was not equipped with a cockpit voice recorder, so the truth of these suppositions could never be established. But the official enquiry ended with recommendations that leading edge devices were equipped with sensors to prevent them being retracted at too low a speed, and that all British-registered airliners should be equipped with CVRs as soon as possible.

Yet the problem of even experienced and competent pilots operating the wrong controls or making the wrong adjustments still persists. As recently as 14 February 1990, and on an aircraft as modern in its equipment as the Airbus, an error by the pilots was able to turn the cleverest of aircraft systems into a recipe for disaster. An Indian Airlines Airbus A320 was approaching Bangalore in the South of India, on a domestic service from Bombay, when it descended into the ground on its final approach to the runway. A total of 92 of the 146 people on board the aircraft were killed in the crash, including both of the pilots, and most of the survivors were injured.

The flight crew had consisted of a captain being checked out on A320s and a training pilot serving as the first officer. The investigators found that the crew had selected the wrong height on the aircraft's computerised flight director by keying in an altitude which was lower than its true altitude. This told the computer to put the aircraft into what was called 'open descent' mode, where it throttled the engines back to idle power to let the aircraft descend.

As the pilots were flying a glide-path approach and trying to maintain their height, this had the effect of the aircraft's speed falling rapidly. The pilots responded by hauling the aircraft's nose up to stay on the glidepath, but this cost them still more speed. By the time the captain realised what was happening, the aircraft was approximately 130 feet above the ground, with its airspeed approximately 25 mph below what it should have been for a normal approach. He pushed the power levers forward to the take-off power position, but before the engines could spool up and deliver enough power, the aircraft continued to sink and hit the ground more than a quarter of a mile short of the runway. Once again, systems designed to make flying safer had, through the errors of those operating them, actually helped to cause a disaster.

10

Twenty-thousand bits flying in close formation

Not all the errors which contribute to aircraft accidents originate in the air, or even in the control tower. Modern investigation methods show the root cause of many disasters originates in the maintenance workshops, or even the factories where vital components and systems are made. The old RAF joke about its venerable but dependable Shackleton maritime-reconnaissance aircraft, that each one was really twenty-thousand bits flying in close formation, is at least partly true. In spite of designers' efforts to double up on crucial systems or make it impossible to operate them incorrectly, the failure of one of those twenty-thousand components in a vital place can still break up the rest of the formation, and have a deadly effect on an otherwise perfectly safe and serviceable aircraft.

On 25 February 1964, an Eastern Air Lines Douglas DC-8 was flying from Mexico City to New York, with intermediate stops at New Orleans and Atlanta. At 2 o'clock in the morning local time, it took off from New Orleans with 51 passengers and a crew of seven, on the second sector of the flight. Just five minutes later, when the aircraft was some 20 miles from the airport, it crashed into Lake Pontchartrain, killing everyone on board.

The investigators found the DC-8 had crashed in water only 20 feet deep, which meant they could retrieve some 60 per cent of the shattered wreckage from the lake bed. Unfortunately, they could not recover a working FDR, so they had to depend on retrieving as much information as possible from studying the wreckage closely.

Their first clue was revealed by the setting of the aircraft's elevator trim. The jack-screws in the trim actuator system were adjusted to a setting corresponding to both elevators being trimmed to a fully nose-down position. Had this been done by the crew, or had the system failed in some way? This setting would not normally have been selected after take-off, or while climbing to cruising height. Furthermore, in the turbulent conditions at the time of the crash, this setting could have adversely affected the longitudinal stability of the aircraft, and actually helped to cause the accident.

The investigators found two more clues in the wreckage. The chain sprocket wheel in the drive mechanism to the elevator had also failed before impact, and the engines showed that reverse thrust had been selected, also prior to impact. Finally, an analysis of the way in which the wreckage had broken up showed that the aircraft been in virtually level flight when it had hit the water.

Next, the investigators searched the aircraft's maintenance records, where they found a persistent series of problems with part of the autopilot system called the pitch trim compensator. Several autopilot problems had been caused by the inadvertent operation of this compensator system on this individual aircraft. This would cause it to adopt a nose-up attitude, and was part of a larger pattern affecting DC-8s in general.

The investigators concluded that the crash must have been initiated by another of these regular system failures. This had caused the pitch trim compensator to raise the nose of the aircraft. The crew corrected this tendency by setting the elevator trim to the full nose-down position, which had succeeded at the cost of two more severe problems. The investigators also concluded it would have had an adverse effect on the pitch stability of the DC-8, and would also have started the aircraft descending towards the lake. They were also of the opinion that the crew had tried to change the trim setting to raise the aircraft nose again, but the heavy loads by now operating on the elevators had caused the elevator drive sprocket to break. In a desperate attempt to slow down the descent, they had also selected reverse thrust on the engines. Their action was too late to affect the outcome, but they had at least managed to level it off when they ran out of height.

When the investigators checked the pitch trim compensator more fully, they found an additional problem. The airline's maintenance team had actually installed one of the bushings in the system upside down. This did not prevent the PTC from working, but it allowed the trim actuator to extend even further than usual in the full nose-down setting, which could well have increased the instability the crew had to deal with.

Another contributory factor may have been the design of the DC-8's artificial horizon, which was known to be difficult to interpret accurately at night. Not being certain as to whether they were in a climb or descent while in cloud and darkness was a great deal for the crew to contend with. There was also a suggestion that DC-8s could be unstable in the nose up or nose down mode at certain speeds, which may have played a further part in stacking the odds against them.

Another accident more than three years after the Lake Pontchartrain crash showed how long a basic design fault could go undetected in an otherwise dependable aircraft. This involved an earlier generation of aircraft on a holiday charter flight returning from Mallorca to Manchester on 4 June 1967. A Canadair C-4 Argonaut of British Midland Airways was approaching Ringway Airport Manchester from the south-east, with 79 passengers and a crew of five, on a radar-controlled ILS approach to runway 24. The Argonaut was the British name for an updated, Canadian-built version of the Douglas DC-4, originally developed as the wartime Skymaster transport, powered by four piston engines, and a vital part of the early post-war revival of passenger flying.

All was satisfactory until the final stages of the approach, when the Argonaut was approaching the ILS beam leading them to the runway. The captain called air traffic control to report he was executing an overshoot, and that he was 'having a little bit of trouble with RPM'. In fact, both starboard engines of the Argonaut had failed in quick succession. The aircraft was yawing to starboard with this total loss of power on the starboard side, and it entered a tightening turn to starboard, which eventually took it round in a full circle with the intention of approaching the runway a second time.

The Argonaut was actually within the ILS beam and almost lined up for the runway when, six minutes after the initial overshoot call, it came down five miles short of the runway threshold in the town centre of Stockport. Although 72 people died in the crash, or in the fire which broke out after the impact, it was still a remarkable escape from what could have been a much greater disaster. The captain managed to bring the aircraft down in one of the few open spaces anywhere near the town centre. He avoided blocks of flats and a large hospital, and though he survived the crash he retained no memory of what had happened to bring it about.

When the AAIB investigators examined the wreckage, they found that the starboard inner engine had been windmilling, as the crew had not been able to feather the propeller, or turn the blades sideways on to the slipstream. Having a propeller still being turned by the slipstream would have greatly increased the drag on the starboard side of the aircraft, and made it much more difficult to control. In the end, the inspectors decided it was this complete loss of power and increased drag on one side only at a low speed and low altitude, which ultimately made the aircraft uncontrollable and brought it down short of the runway.

But what had caused the engines to fail? A prime suspect was the Argonaut's fuel system, and more specifically the controls allowing the pilots to pump fuel between the different tanks during a flight. The fuel cock actuator levers were situated so that the pilots had to operate them without seeing them clearly. It was easy to select the wrong fuel cock, so that fuel was being pumped out of the wrong tank. What made the system even more dangerous however was that not being able to see the actuators properly made it just as easy to fail to close them completely, by a slight mistake in returning the lever to the 'off' position.

This meant fuel would still be consumed from a tank which the pilots believed was left as a reserve as there was nothing to alert them to the situation. If fuel had been leaking from a particular tank throughout the flight, its contents would be much less than expected. If they then selected that tank in the closing stages of the flight it could have run dry and the engines being fed from it, which in this case were the two starboard engines, would fail at almost the same moment. Had this happened at a higher altitude, there would have been time to correct the problem by switching to another tank to restart the engines. In this case, it was too low, and too late.

There was another possible consequence of the old-fashioned and inconvenient control layout on the Argonaut. The starboard outer engine failed first, and the inspectors considered it was at least possible that the captain tried to feather the starboard inner engine instead, as there were no instruments to tell him which engine had actually failed. Both propellers would have continued turning until he finished the feathering drill, so this kind of mistake was easy to make, particularly while carrying out a missed approach and an overshoot, followed by a second attempt to land.

If that *had* been the case, the captain would have realised his mistake from the aircraft's increasing yaw to starboard. It would seem he had gone on to feather the starboard outer engine, but had left the starboard inner engine windmilling before trying to restart it. Unfortunately, before he could do this, the difficulty of controlling the aircraft with all the available power on one side became too great, and a crash was inevitable. The inspectors were so critical of the old-fashioned cockpit design of the Argonaut that their report insisted the type would not have been given a Certificate of Airworthiness under current standards.

Manchester was the scene of another disaster caused by mechanical failure, in the summer of 1985. This was another charter flight, operated in this case by British Airtours between the UK and Corfu. The aircraft was a Boeing 737 and in the early morning of 22 August, it was taking off from the airport's runway 24 with 131 passengers and a crew of six. Thirty-six seconds after the start of the take-off run, the crew heard a muffled 'thump' and the captain decided to abort the take-off attempt. His first thought was that the aircraft had suffered a burst tyre, and he slowed it down with some care not to apply the brakes too harshly. Instead, he applied reverse thrust, and when the aircraft had slowed down sufficiently, he turned to starboard off the runway and on to a taxiway.

By this time the 737 was already ablaze from fuel spilling from its port wing, and the light westerly wind was fanning the flames to an inferno. Within less than half a minute, the skin of the aircraft had melted, and the rear fuselage had collapsed on to the ground. Of those aboard the aircraft, 55 were unable to escape, and one of those who did, died later in hospital. The problems with the evacuation from the crowded passenger cabin led to demands for smoke

British Airtours Boeing 737 burning on the tarmac at Manchester after the engine burst on take-off.

hoods for passengers, additional floor-level lighting to direct passengers to the nearest emergency exit, and the moving of seats to make escape routes easier to reach.

The investigators found that the thump heard by the flight crew during the take-off run had not been a tyre burst at all. Instead, it was something far more unusual, and far more serious. A jet engine works by compressing air as it enters the front of the engine, mixing it with fuel and then heating it by burning the fuel in a series of combustion chambers around the circumference of the engine. This produces a high-energy stream of very hot gases, flowing at high speed out of the engine tailpipe to drive the aircraft along.

Each combustion chamber contains an internal can, which confines the burning fuel-air mixture clear of the outside walls of the chamber. In the case of the 737's port engine, a crack in the can fitted inside chamber number 9 had been caused by thermal fatigue, or the weakening of the metal by the constant heating and cooling during the engine's working lifetime. The can had been allowed to move outwards and tilt away from its proper position, so that hot gases were able to play directly on the surface of the combustion chamber, eventually burning it through to the point of final failure.

At the moment of final collapse, the domed front section separated from the rest of the combustion chamber can, and struck the underside of the access panel to the port wing fuel tank, cracking it open. The dome itself fell out on to the runway, causing the noise heard by the crew, and allowing fuel to pour out of the tank on to the hot engine and the jet of blazing fuel escaping from the ruptured combustion chamber. The resulting blaze, fed by a full load of fuel for the flight to the eastern Mediterranean, was to consume almost the entire aircraft.

The engine in question was a Pratt & Whitney JT8D-15, and the maintenance records showed that two earlier cracks had been repaired in the same combustion chamber can. Though there was nothing to prevent this in the maker's manual, the welding had actually been below standard. It was possible that defects in the repairs had disturbed the flow of cooling air, to cause the thermal stress which led to the final and much more serious cracking. The maker's

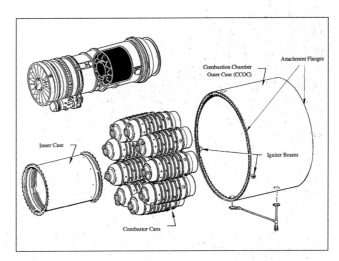

Combustion system in engines fitted to British Airtours Boeing 737. (AAIB)

The recovered remains of a combustion can from the engine of the British Airtours 737. (AAIB)

Aft Portion

Dome

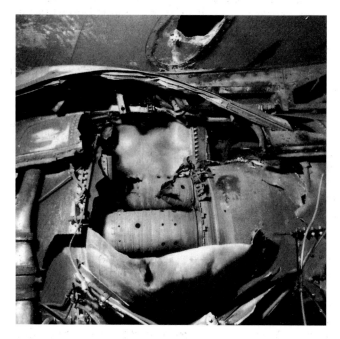

Damage to the fuel tank access panel caused by the ruptured combustion can in the port engine of the British Airtours 737. (AAIB)

records showed that this kind of combustion chamber failure only happened once in every 100 million hours operation, and in each case the domes had dropped free without damaging the wing tanks, but nonetheless there were signs which should have alerted the operators in time.

British Airtours' maintenance reports showed that the engine had been reported on 20 different occasions in 18 months of operation for accelerating more slowly than normal. This is actually one symptom of a misaligned combustion chamber can, but the manufacturers had not told the airline this. In addition, the airline had specified the installation of what were described as longer life cans, and felt its own inspection procedures were particularly strict.

Because the root of the problem was a blazing engine, the prudent actions taken by the crew did tend to make matters worse. The slow braking lengthened the time available for the blaze to take hold, as fuel from the wing tanks fed the flames. Using reverse thrust from the engines to help bring the 737 to a stop created a turbulent airflow which fanned the fire still further. Finally, turning to starboard to leave the runway placed the aircraft sideways across the prevailing breeze, with the fire upwind of the passenger cabin.

As a result of the disaster, all other Pratt & Whitney JT8D engines installed in other British-registered aircraft were inspected, while the aircraft themselves were grounded. Other engines showed similar cracks, and repairs were completed and checked before the 737s were allowed to fly again. The authorities insisted on stronger access panels in the wing fuel tanks, floor level emergency lighting and clearer access to escape routes and emergency exits within the passenger cabin. Smoke hoods were not specified as a legal requirement.

In the nature of aircraft design, the point where the intense heat from the engines comes closest to the fuel needed to keep them running is bound to be a potential weakness. This is contained as far as possible by careful engineering. An additional consequence of the Manchester crash was extra reinforcement for the structure which supported the combustion cans, for example. But experience has shown that there are other potential sources of trouble in an aircraft which have nothing to do with either the engines or the fuel system. These can still bring the aircraft down, with the deaths of all on board, unless luck takes a hand.

On the evening of 12 June 1972, an American Airlines Douglas DC-10 was flying from Los Angeles to New York's La Guardia Airport with intermediate stops at Detroit and Buffalo. During the short 175-mile sector from Detroit, the large wide-bodied aircraft was carrying a fraction of its capacity, with just 56 passengers. The take-off was normal at 7.20 pm local time, and the DC-10 began climbing to its cleared altitude of 23,000 feet. Five minutes after take-off it was crossing over the Canadian town of Windsor, Ontario at 12,000 feet when there was an explosion at the rear of the aircraft. This was followed by a rushing gust of wind through the cabin. The floor at the rear of the cabin collapsed, trapping two of the stewardesses. They had a frightening view of the interior of the lower cargo hold, and a gap where the door had been, through which they could see the clouds !

On the flightdeck, a full-scale emergency developed. After the noise of the explosive decompression, the power levers for all three engines slammed to the power shut-off position, and the rudder pedals jammed hard to port. At first the pilots thought they had collided with another aircraft, but as they checked the systems they found the centre, fin-mounted engine had failed, but the other two were still working, and hydraulic pressure seemed to be steady. The captain disengaged the autopilot and realised the aircraft was yawing to starboard, in spite of the rudder pedals still being jammed to port. He also discovered that the elevators were very reluctant to move, though he could open the throttles on the underwing engines to retain some control of the aircraft.

The captain decided to return to Detroit for an emergency landing, but this would need some very careful flying. As he had no appreciable rudder control, he had to steer the aircraft by speeding up and slowing down the two under-wing engines, enabling him to turn the DC-10 slowly and painfully back towards the airport they had left such a short time before. There was still the problem of persuading the big aircraft into a descent to reach the runway, with so little elevator control. This time he had to throttle back on both engines together, so the aircraft began to lose height at a manageable rate, aided by lowering the flaps to increase the drag.

Further down the approach path, the pilots were able to lower the landing gear, and increase the flaps to 22 degrees. But when they tried to increase the flap setting to 35, usually done for the final stage of the approach, the aircraft started to sink more rapidly. They had to wind back the flaps to 22 degrees and reconcile themselves to approaching the airfield at a higher speed and a more shallow angle than usual. When they reached ground level, it took the strength of both pilots pulling back on the controls to persuade the nose to rise into a landing flare, but the resulting landing was successful, except for a swing which they could not correct without a working rudder.

They finally brought the aircraft to a stop at least partially on the runway, by using full reverse thrust on the port engine and full power on the starboard until they could steer it on the nosewheel. When it came to rest, the emergency chutes were released, and the passengers evacuated without any casualties. The first worry about the cause of the accident was sabotage, but when the inspectors checked the structure of the aircraft they found the lower cargo door had blown open under the increasing internal pressure as the DC-10 had climbed. It had then been torn away in the fierce slipstream, and was later found in a field near Windsor.

The explosive decompression caused the floor between the passenger cabin and the lower hold to collapse. Unfortunately, the cables linking the flight-deck controls with the tail-mounted hydraulic actuators were channelled through this floor section, and when it collapsed, the cables were either stretched or severed. The effect of this was to send spurious commands to the controls, like those jamming the rudder pedals, and shutting down the centre engine. At the same time, the elevators became almost impossible to move.

Fortunately, the skill of the pilots meant that the emergency was contained, and the aircraft brought safely back to the airfield. The door which caused all the trouble could also be examined, and the cause of the problem identified. The cargo door of the DC-10 was one of the first on a pressurised jet airliner actually designed to open outwards. Most previous designs had opened inwards so in the event of them not being securely latched, the pressure difference would tend to force the door firmly closed. As this extra safety margin was not present in the DC-10 door, in the interests of easier access, great care had been taken to ensure it was properly closed and latched.

In theory, for the door to be properly closed, a series of four C-shaped latches had to be clamped over a set of matching rollers on the door jamb. They were held there by locking pins which bolted the door's electrical closing mechanism in a safe, over-centre position. The greater the pressure on the door from inside, the more tightly it would be held closed. As an extra safeguard, once these safety precautions were in place, a 'door open' warning light on the flight engineer's instrument panel would go out.

Unfortunately, all had not been well with this particular door mechanism. It was clear that the driving mechanism controlling the closure of the C-shaped latches over the matching rollers had not been locked over-centre. The result of this failure was that as the pressure difference between the hold and the outside air had increased, the stress had been carried by the bolts supporting the actuator of the door closure mechanism. When these finally tore away, the door burst open and caused the emergency.

Why had the driving mechanisms not gone all the way home, to be locked in the safe over-centre position? Tests showed that the voltage of the supply to the electrical door-closing mechanism was lower than it should have been. As a result, the mechanism had not moved through its full range of travel. The locking pins had not been able to slide into place and render the door securely closed, but had simply jammed against the latches.

The cargo handler operating the door closing system had put his full weight on the manual back-up operating lever, which actually bent the internal linkages, allowing the indicator switch to make contact, even though the pins were still not locked. This operated the circuit to extinguish the 'door open' light on the flight deck. A further safety feature, a vent on the outside of the door, gave a safe indication when the handle was pulled down. This too failed to give warning of the true state of the door locking mechanism.

The consequences of this voltage drop had already been found to be a problem by other airlines, though fortunately as a reluctance of the door to close rather than a failure in flight. The manufacturers of the aircraft had recommended

Fig 20: DC10 cargo door closing linkages

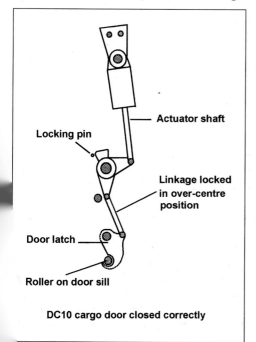

Actuator shaft
Locking pin
Linkage locked in over-centre position
Door latch
Roller on door sill

DC10 cargo door closed correctly

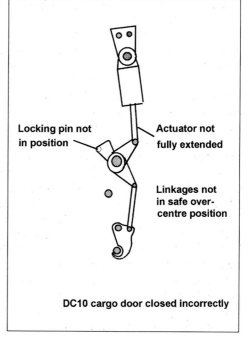

Locking pin not in position
Actuator not fully extended
Linkages not in safe over-centre position

DC10 cargo door closed incorrectly

rewiring the electrical circuit to eliminate the problem. The fact remained that if the door did not close properly using the electrical system, too much pressure on the manual handle could produce an erroneous impression that the door was safely closed.

The Federal Aviation Administration decided to publish an Airworthiness Directive, to be binding with immediate effect on all DC-10 operators. This would force them to place a small viewing window over one of the locking pins. A cargo handler working outside the aircraft could look through the window to check that the pins really were in position properly. There would also be a notice forbidding the use of excessive force in trying to close the handle. Under pressure from McDonnell Douglas, this was downgraded to a series of service bulletins, one of which required the addition of the viewing window in the lower part of the face of the door. Others demanded rewiring of the electrical actuators, and improvements to the door closing mechanism to increase its range of travel and make it more resistant to excessive force applied to the closure handle.

Unfortunately, the service bulletins did not have quite the same legal urgency as the full Airworthiness Directive. Meanwhile, the FAA's other principal recommendation, that vents should be installed in the cabin floor to allow air to escape in the event of an explosive decompression, without the floor collapsing and jeopardising the controls, was declared by the manufacturers to be 'not feasible'.

For almost two years, the problem seemed to have been solved until 3 March 1974, when a DC-10 belonging to Turkish Airlines touched down at Orly Airport in Paris on a service from Ankara to London. Because of a strike affecting British Airways flights between Paris and London, a total of 216 London-bound passengers transferred to fill the vacant seats on the widebody Douglas jet for the last short leg of its flight. This involved the loading of a large amount of extra baggage through the rear cargo door which delayed the departure of the aircraft by more than 20 minutes.

At last, at 12.24 pm, the DC-10 was given take-off clearance from runway 08. At 12.29 pm local time, the crew received airways clearance for a heading to the east of Paris, before turning to the north-west for Montdidier near Amiens. They were initially cleared to 4,000 feet and then to 6,000 feet and finally to a cruising altitude of 23,000 feet. Finally, at 12.36 pm Northern Area Control radioed the crew to turn to port on to a heading of 345 degrees to take the aircraft towards Montdidier. A minute later the crew replied, reporting they were climbing through 7,000 feet on their way to their cruising height.

At 12.40 pm, there were signs that something was very wrong with the aircraft. By now the DC-10 was almost halfway to its cruising altitude, at 9,800 feet. Air traffic control received half a minute of garbled transmission in Turkish, with a great deal of noise in the background. This included the cabin depressurisation warning, and later the overspeed alarm. At the same moment the label on the DC-10's radar echo disappeared from the controllers' radar display, and the echo itself split into two. The larger one curved to the left, on to a heading of approximately 280 degrees before it disappeared. The smaller part remained almost stationary on the radar screen, before it too vanished. There were two more radio transmissions, each shorter than the previous one and completely unintelligible. Nothing more was heard from the aircraft.

The DC-10 had crashed in a wooded area called the Forêt d'Ermenonville, near the town of Senlis, just over 20 miles north-north-east of Paris. The aircraft had plunged through the trees into a small glen called the Grove of Dammartin with fearful force. The impact speed was so high that the aircraft was torn to pieces and reduced to a trail of small pieces of wreckage over more than 300 yards in length, so that the investigators had a more difficult task than usual. It was rendered infinitely more terrible by the remains of more than 300 people on board, many of them totally unidentifiable.

The first suggestion was that the aircraft had been brought down by the explosion of a terrorist bomb. This might have accounted for its brief transition from normal flight to crashing headlong into the wood, and for the sounding of the decompression and overspeed alarms on the radio transmission. Another clue which appeared at first to hint at the same explanation was the discovery of the bodies of six of the passengers, still strapped into two triple seats, a full nine miles south of the crash. Had they been blown from the aircraft by the bomb which had brought it down?

Two searches were mounted to find the answers to these questions. At the main crash site, teams were trying to find the CVR and FDR recorders. Others were retracing the route between the spot between the crash and the spot where the seats had been found. Meanwhile, post-mortems of the passengers found strapped in the seats which must have fallen from the aircraft before the crash proper, showed their injuries resulted purely from impact with the ground, and not from any explosives. The seats showed no signs of explosive damage, which tended to discredit the bomb-on-board theory.

At last the recorders were located, and found to have invaluable information. Soon afterwards the other search teams came upon the object which must have returned that smaller, mysteriously stationary radar echo as the DC-10 carried on towards its doom. It was the battered but unmistakable port lower cargo door.

The information retrieved by the recorders told a simple but terrible tale. The investigators were able to determine from the FDR that the DC-10 had been climbing perfectly normally, controlled by the autopilot on a heading of 345 degrees and at a speed of 300 knots. At approximately 20 minutes to one, when the aircraft had passed 9,000 feet, there was the noise of a muffled detonation on the CVR, followed by the rush of escaping air, which was clear evidence of an explosive decompression. At the same time, the FDR showed the power lever for the centre engine slammed to the closed position, exactly as it had done over Windsor, Ontario in the earlier emergency.

The pressure warning began sounding, and the FDR traces showed the aircraft banking to port and beginning to lose height. As the descent steepened, the speed began to rise, and it was clear from the conversation of the flight-deck crew that none of the controls was having the slightest effect. Half a minute after the initial explosion the CVR revealed the overspeed warning was sounding, at the time when the FDR showed the DC-10 was passing its 'never exceed' speed. Almost half a minute later, the captain tried one last throw. He increased power on the two outer engines in an attempt to bring the nose up and arrest the plane's descent.

Alone of all their desperate attempts to keep the aircraft under control, this showed signs of working. The speed increased, but the DC-10 began to level out, painfully slowly and with their precious margin of height still dwindling all too quickly. For ten more seconds the uncertainty continued, until the forest rushed up ahead of the nose. The FDR confirmed the captain closed the throttles just before impact, but the effect of his action was negligible. With all the extra speed which had almost pulled the DC-10 out of its final dive, the aircraft smashed into the trees, and 346 people died.

When the investigators examined the cargo door more closely, they found the same signs as those on the door in the Windsor incident. It was clear that once again the latching mechanism had failed to lock properly, leaving the door free to blow open with the increasing pressure differential inside and outside the aircraft. An extra factor loaded the dice against the Turkish crew, compared with their American Airlines opposite numbers. The full passenger load meant pressure on the cabin floor was that much greater, so the resulting collapse caused far more damage to the basic flying controls. Damage in this case had been sufficient to hurl two triple seats and their doomed occupants out of the aircraft in the first seconds of decompression.

Meanwhile, what had become of the modifications called for in the service bulletins two years before? The investigators found that only two of them had been carried out, but the vital need for internal reinforcement had not been completed. To make matters worse, deep scratch marks on the locking pins themselves showed that the mechanism had been set up incorrectly, so the door had even less protection against partial closure than the original DC-10 design had had.

This was a case of a disaster waiting to happen. While on the tarmac at Orly Airport, the door had been closed by an Algerian-born ground handler, who could not read the English and Turkish warning signs on the door front panel. He had been warned against using too much force on the closure handle but had not been briefed on the need to look through the inspection window to check the locking pins were properly driven home. The airline's ground engineer at Orly was away on holiday, and the DC-10's flight engineer did not bother to come and check for himself the locking pins were in place. It was a mistake he would pay for with his life.

It was all too clear what had happened. An immediate result of the official report was that the FAA did what they should have done immediately after the Windsor incident, and made the recommended changes to the cargo door the subject of an Airworthiness Directive. No more cases of disasters, or even emergencies, would be caused by problems with the DC-10 cargo door. Yet there would be other cases where this apparently jinxed design would suffer failures of a totally different kind, one ending in disaster and the other in first-class piloting which turned a potential catastrophe into an epic of survival for many of those on board.

The first of these emergencies occurred just over five years after the crash of the Turkish DC-10, and on the other side of the world. Traffic was again heavy as the last weekend in May 1979 was a national holiday in the United States. Chicago's O'Hare was living up to its title as the world's busiest airport on the Friday which marked the start of the break. American Airlines flight number 19 was typical of the vast number of services scheduled to leave for destinations all over America. In this particular case it was a DC-10, loaded with 258 passengers and a crew of 13, timed to leave at three in the afternoon Central Standard Time for Los Angeles.

The flight began well enough. The weather was good, with clear skies, visibility of 15 miles and a brisk north-easterly wind. In spite of the density of traffic, the DC-10 was given clearance to taxi to the holding point for runway 32 Right with one minute still to go before its scheduled departure time. At 3.2½ pm CST, the flight was given its take-off clearance. The big jet lined up on the runway, checks were completed, and it started its take-off run.

To the watchers in O'Hare's lofty control tower, the take-off seemed routine to begin with. The DC-10 accelerated down the runway and approached its rotation speed at which the pilot would lift the nose and allow the aircraft to begin its climb. Just before that point, at about a mile into the take-off run, the witnesses noticed fragments dropping away from the neighbourhood of the port underwing engine mounting, and a trail of white smoke unravel behind the port wing. As the aircraft tilted up into the take-off attitude, they saw an almost unbelievable sight. The entire port engine with its supporting pylon, still delivering take-off power, reared upwards and pivoted about the leading edge of the wing, wrenching itself free of the aircraft.

The massive chunk of metal flew over the top of the wing and crashed back on to the tarmac. Meanwhile the DC-10 began climbing away, still under control as an initial tendency for the port wing to drop had clearly been caught and counteracted by the pilots. Apart from the fact that one of its three engines lay smoking on the runway, the take-off angle and heading seemed exactly as they should be. The nose was pitched up by around 14 degrees and the aircraft was still pointing down the extended runway centre-line. The tower controller asked the crew if they wanted to return for an emergency landing, and offered to clear traffic for any runway they chose. But no reply was received.

Things were now going very wrong indeed. Ten seconds after its take-off, the DC-10 began to bank to port again, though this time the crew seemed unable to level the wings. The horrified watchers in the tower saw the nose drop and the aircraft begin to descend as the wings first reached, then passed, the vertical. It was now side-slipping to port and within seconds the port wingtip hit the ground. The aircraft toppled nose-first into the ground, where it exploded in a huge fireball. All 271 people on board were killed. Two people on the ground, in a trailer park next to the field into which the DC-10 had plunged were killed by flying fragments of the aircraft, and two others were injured.

This was the worst airline disaster in American history, and the fact that it happened on America's busiest airfield made it especially shocking. Unlike many disasters though, it had been clear from the beginning what had actually gone wrong. In this case, the vital underlying questions were, what had caused the engine and pylon to separate from the wing at the worst possible moment? And, what had then stopped the crew, who at first seemed to be coping with the situation, from retaining control of the aircraft?

Because of the circumstances and scene of the accident, the investigators' initial task of searching for evidence was simplified in one respect, and complicated by another. The different bits and pieces of the separated engine and pylon lay on the runway for all to see. The rest of the material evidence was hidden somewhere in the burned-out wreckage of the DC-10 itself, approximately a mile beyond. There too the overall story of what had happened was clear enough, in the sense that the wingtip had left a scar in the ground. The rest of the wreckage was concentrated into a relatively small area approximately two hundred yards square. Details would be much more difficult to determine because of the severity of the impact, and the resulting explosion and fire.

Nevertheless, the severity of the accident and the seriousness with which it was viewed produced a vast effort from the NTSB, who dispatched a team of more than 100 investigators to the spot. Those who searched the main wreckage found little to indicate what had gone wrong. The landing gear was still extended, the two remaining engines had been operating at high speed, and there were no signs of hydraulic failure. Beyond that, though, the flightdeck instruments had been destroyed, and the CVR and FDR offered the only hope of finding out what had gone wrong.

Despite the difficulties, both recorders were found, and the information retrieved. The CVR proved to be of only limited usefulness, as its recording stopped abruptly due to a power failure. This must have been linked with the engine breakaway, as the aircraft was about to rotate for its take-off. However, it did allow the investigators to check that the flaps had been correctly set at ten degrees for take-off. They also learned that a combination of port rudder and starboard aileron was being used to keep the aircraft straight in the moderate crosswind blowing across the runway from left to right.

The message from the FDR was more comprehensive and revealed more of the effects of the engine separation. At the same moment that the CVR recording stopped, the FDR traces covering the port inboard elevator and aileron, the lower rudder and two of the leading-edge slats on the port wing also stopped. The remainder of the recording confirmed that the aircraft actually left the ground at six knots higher than the calculated take-off speed. It climbed away from the runway at a rate of 1,150 feet per minute, with the nose tilted up through 14 degrees, both figures being exactly as required by the book for an engine-out climb. With the starboard engine delivering full power, and the centre engine delivering slightly more than rated power, the DC-10 accelerated to a speed of 172 knots, at about 140 feet above the runway.

Then the picture began to darken. The speed began to fall off, slowly but inexorably. At 20 seconds after take-off, with the aircraft now more than 300 feet above the ground, it decayed to 159 knots, and the aircraft began to roll to port. The control settings showed the crew had responded by increasing amounts of starboard aileron and rudder, but to no avail. The yaw to port increased, the bank increased, and the nose drooped from a climb attitude to a dive into the ground. The DC-10 had been airborne for just 31 seconds.

The engine and pylon wreckage on the runway provided a different hint as to what might have gone wrong. The team searching for the evidence found a stress-induced break in the forward flange of the engine pylon's rear bulkhead. The main fracture and its associated fatigue cracking extended for five inches. At one end it reached the fastening holding the fore and aft sections of the bulkhead together, and at the other it reached a hole in the upper flange of the bulkhead. This added up to a fatal weakness in the structure which held the engine to the wing. Under take-off power the thrust delivered by the engine and the increasing lift generated by the wing between them managed to overcome the remaining strength of the pylon.

The investigators found the upper flange had failed first, and let the rear end of the pylon move downwards and forwards, as the engine pivoted around the front pylon attachments. Finally these too tore away, as engine and pylon somersaulted over the top of the wing and fell back on to the runway. The investigating team then looked at the causes of the original break. Next to the actual fracture on the upper flange of the bulkhead was a curved depression in its surface, which was the same shape and size as the wing fitting to which the rear bulkhead was fastened when the pylon was installed. It began to look as if the fracture had been caused by a misalignment when the engine and pylon were removed and replaced as part of standard line servicing on the aircraft.

When the investigators checked the airline maintenance records they found that the aircraft had had the port engine and pylon removed from the wing two months before, at the airline's workshops in Tulsa, Oklahoma. This was to replace the spherical bearings which actually fastened the pylon to the wing framework, as part of routine maintenance. The NTSB ordered the immediate grounding of all US-registered DC-10s, to check how widespread the problem was, and found to their horror that another six aircraft already showed similar fractures in their engine pylon bulkheads.

Searching for a common factor which might explain the problem, the investigators noted that two of these aircraft belonged to Continental Airlines and the remaining four to the airline involved in the Chicago disaster, American Airlines. When they checked further, they found both these airlines habitually carried out the same variation on the manufacturers' recommended maintenance routine. Where McDonnell Douglas laid down that removing an engine and its supporting pylon should be done in two stages, the airlines effectively did it in one.

Instead of using a special cradle to lower the engine on to a trolley for removal, and afterwards supporting the pylon in a sling hung from an overhead crane to complete the job, they saved time and trouble by using a fork-lift truck to support the engine cradle, and remove and replace the engine and pylon as a single unit, without separating them. In theory, this made sense as a quicker and more economical procedure, but in practice it was fraught with problems.

The main difficulty was that it was all too easy for the much heavier engine-and-pylon combination to move without warning. To make matters worse, the design of the pylon ensured that some clearances were extremely tight, and any misalignment could cause serious damage when wing and pylon were brought together. There were signs in the pylon bulkhead of the crashed DC-10 that the base of the wing fitting had come into sharp contact with the bulkhead flange, and actually initiated the crack which had led to the final failure.

This type of damage had already happened, and been reported, on two of Continental Airlines' DC-10s, though the information had not been passed to the FAA. Instead, the initial damage had been reported to the makers, McDonnell Douglas. They sent out a circular to all DC-10 operators, warning them of the problem but not explaining how it had been caused. In any case, the maintenance engineers who carried out the engine and pylon replacements at Tulsa had not seen the bulletins in question.

As far as the NTSB was concerned, stricter requirements were needed to ensure that the engines and pylons were removed and replaced separately, regardless of the extra time and effort of separating and reconnecting all the service pipes, linkages and cables. This would effectively eliminate the danger of fatigue cracking. The DC-10 should still have been capable of climbing away from the airport without the crew losing control however, even after shedding an engine so unexpectedly. What had prevented it?

There was one consequence of the aircraft not just losing power from the port engine, but having the engine separating from the airframe. The tearing away of the engine and its supporting pylon severed all the electrical and hydraulic connections routed through the engine. This deprived the pilots of crucial safety and warning systems. First of all they lost the stall warning system, and the stick-shaker which acted as a more positive back-up warning system of a stall being imminent. They lost power to the instruments on the captain's side of the flight-deck, and they lost hydraulic power and electrical connections to the leading edge slats on the outboard section of the port wing. Finally, the tearing process resulting in the pylon and engine falling away also damaged the leading edge of the wing, reducing lift and increasing drag.

In many aircraft designs, loss of hydraulic power would mean the slats could not be extended or retracted, but would simply be held in their existing position by a mechanical linkage. In the case of the DC-10, the design provided enough yaw control to cope with the loss of the extra lift generated by the slats on one wing, in normal circumstances. With an engine failing on the same side as the slats not extending, this created a much more dangerous situation. It was still survivable provided the crew carried out the correct recovery drill quickly.

Unfortunately, the engine not only failed, but broke the hydraulic connections so that the outboard slats were blown to the retracted position by the pressure of the airstream over the wings. It also cut out the warning devices which would have told the crew what action to take. With the lack of these warnings, and no additional information to tell them the systems were inoperative, the crew were fed totally false information over the position in which they found themselves. In trying to deal with the apparent emergency, they and their passengers fell victim to the very real emergency which arose so insidiously.

When the engine tore out of the port wing, the hydraulic fluid in the actuators for the port outboard leading-edge slats poured out quickly, leaving the slats free to retract. This meant the outer section of the port wing would stall at a much higher speed than the rest of the wing. The lack of any stall warning system would leave the crew unaware. Because the danger was in the outboard section of the wing, the disturbed airflow would not even cause turbulence over the tailplane, which might have alerted them to the problem. As the speed of the aircraft fell back slowly during the climb away from the runway, the outer part of the port wing stalled and caused a gentle roll to port.

With no warning of an incipient stall, the crew simply corrected the roll and carried on with the climb in the normal way. Had they realised that the wing was already on the point of a more serious stall, they could have applied the normal stall recovery technique. This would mean lowering the nose of the aircraft and increasing power. Provided they did this quickly enough to keep the speed above the 159 knots which was the effective stalling speed of the port outer wing, the DC-10 would have remained in the air. When the company's training pilots flew the DC-10 simulator with the slats retracted and the port engine out, they found they could not only complete the take-off, but they could also fly a circuit and land the aircraft without undue difficulty.

On that fatal day above Chicago, the crew of the doomed DC-10 had no such warning. They probably realised they had lost an engine, though they may not have been aware it had actually torn away from the aircraft. Because of the loss of electrical signals from the port wing, their instruments would not have shown the port outer slats had retracted, and they were unable to see the swept wing's leading edge from their seats on the flight deck. They carried on flying by the book, correcting the roll and yaw caused by the failed engine, and finally rolled the aircraft into oblivion.

Several steps were taken to make a repeat disaster impossible. Maintenance procedures were tightened up, as was the system for reporting and circulating details of problems with any of the aircraft systems. Crews were recommended to use higher climb-out speeds after any incident of engine failure on take-off. Some three years after the accident, the FAA required all DC-10s to be fitted with springs to hold the slats in position in the event of a system failure. In addition, valves were fitted to prevent fluid leakage in the slat actuators if any hydraulic lines were severed.

The temporary grounding of the DC-10s while the causes of the accident were identified echoed the initial Comet tragedy. This was the first measure of this kind to be applied to an American-made airliner for more than three decades. Nevertheless, the ban was lifted after five weeks, and the type continues in service with a large number of different operators. It was doubly ironic that another DC-10 emergency not only resulted in survival for at least some of those on board, it was also caused by a problem which overrode the safety back-ups designed into the aircraft.

It happened almost exactly ten years after the Chicago crash, and the aircraft involved was approaching the city instead of leaving it. The operator was United Airlines, and the aircraft was on a flight from Denver in Colorado, with a stopover in Chicago and an eventual destination of Pittsburgh in Pennsylvania. It had taken off from Denver at 2.10 pm Central Daylight Time on 19 July 1989, and was cruising at 37,000 feet in perfect summer weather, with 285 passengers and a crew of eleven.

An hour and five minutes into the journey, the pilots were due to carry out a gentle turn to starboard to change their course, as they flew over an airways intersection north of Storm Lake in Iowa. All this required was a change in the heading command on the aircraft's autopilot, but when the course change was almost complete there was the sound of a muffled explosion, and a shudder passed through the airframe. The flight crew first became aware that the centre, tail-mounted engine had failed and was running down, so they began carrying out the engine shut-down checks.

At that point the flight engineer noticed that the gauges showed that hydraulic pressure and fluid contents were falling rapidly on all three of the DC-10's hydraulic systems. In the meantime, the autopilot had not completed the turn with the aircraft on the new heading of 095 degrees magnetic. Instead it was continuing to turn to starboard and was starting to lose height as well. The first officer tried to readjust the autopilot to correct the heading, but nothing happened. He disconnected the autopilot and tried to correct the aircraft's attitude and heading using the main controls. Once again nothing happened, and the DC-10 continued to descend and turn to starboard.

The problem was that the autopilot had already set the controls for the shallow turn to starboard needed for the course change. Whatever had disabled the hydraulic systems had left the controls in those positions, so that if the aircraft was going to be controllable at all, the crew had to find some other way of doing it. The captain began by reducing power on the port engine, to balance the tendency to continue turning to starboard. This rolled the aircraft out of its banking attitude, and it ended up more or less stabilised on a southerly heading, very gently pitching up and down and rolling slightly first one way then the other.

The truth was that the loss of all three hydraulic systems left the pilots without any means of moving the elevators, the ailerons, or the rudder, which would normally allow them to cause the aircraft to climb or descend, or turn to port or starboard. In addition, they had no control over the trailing-edge flaps, the leading-edge slats or the spoilers, to aid in slowing the aircraft down if they survived long enough to try a landing approach. Adjusting the power settings of the two remaining engines enabled them to exert some influence over the way the aircraft headed, but this was a crude technique at best. It had no perceptible effect on damping down its continual tendency to sway up and down and from side to side. The aircraft also continued to turn to starboard and start to resume its descent every time the balance of the engine power levers was less than perfect.

Help was possible from two areas – one outside the aircraft and the other on board. The crew had reported their problems to air traffic control, and they were now in touch with the airline's maintenance experts in San Francisco for advice on how to cope with their predicament. Secondly, one of the passengers introduced himself as an off-duty training captain with the airline, and an expert on the DC-10, who could provide an extra pair of skilled hands on the flight-deck. Air traffic control first suggested a diversion to Des Moines, which lay to the south-east. However, as the DC-10 completed two wide, shallow and unsteady circuits to starboard while the three pilots fought to find a way of controlling the aircraft, it seemed more sensible to them to head for Sioux City Airport to the west. Meanwhile, as the descent continued, they dumped excess fuel to reduce weight and the risk of fire on landing.

Unfortunately, two factors meant they would have to land the aircraft at a much higher speed than normal. The first was the lack of flaps, slats and spoilers. The second was that the engine power settings needed to keep the aircraft straight and level were higher than they would be for a normal approach. The crew managed to lower the landing gear in spite of the lack of hydraulic power, and this would have some effect on slowing the aircraft down, but the continuing tendency to swing to starboard would be a major problem.

By an almost superhuman effort, the pilots managed to use the engines to force the DC-10 into a clumsy, hesitant turn to port on to an approximately south-western heading, for Sioux City Airport. Any complex turns to land on one of the two operational runways would be impossible. All they could do was keep heading on as accurate a course for the airport as they could, for a straight-in approach on the old runway 22, now officially closed but at least clear of obstructions. Even

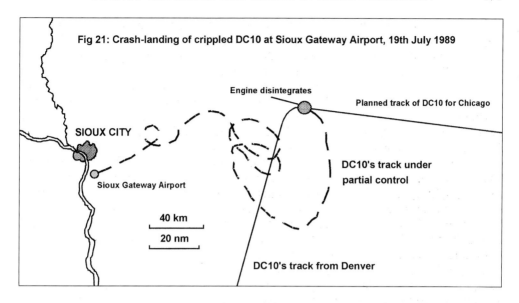

Fig 21: Crash-landing of crippled DC10 at Sioux Gateway Airport, 19th July 1989

Engine disintegrates

Planned track of DC10 for Chicago

SIOUX CITY

Sioux Gateway Airport

DC10's track under partial control

40 km

20 nm

DC10's track from Denver

then, they could not stop the DC-10 from carrying out another full 360 degree turn to starboard on the way.

At last the runway appeared in sight, and gave the pilots something definite to aim for. At more than 200 knots and losing height at a fast rate of 1,600 feet per minute, the airliner was committed to a landing, but one problem still remained. When the crew shut off power for the touch-down, it would once again try to descend and turn to starboard, which could turn the landing into a full-scale crash. It was a desperately difficult dilemma, with no apparent solution.

The United DC-10 on final approach to Sioux Gateway Airport with all major control systems unserviceable. The small tear in the leading edge of the starboard tailplane is the only sign visible from the ground of the disintegration of the centre engine fan disc which did the damage. (National Transportation Safety Board)

The captain ordered the power to be shut off as the DC-10 sank over the runway threshold with a hundred feet to go to touch down. When the engines were throttled back the starboard wing started to drop, and though the throttles were opened again immediately, it was too late. The starboard wingtip hit the ground, and a moment later the starboard main landing gear struck the runway edge very heavily, and then collapsed. The starboard wing took the whole weight of the aircraft and collapsed as the DC-10 continued to roll over it. It turned right over on its back and broke into three main sections before finally coming to rest more than half a mile down the runway, in an adjacent field of corn.

Fire broke out in the main section of fuselage, but the arrival of the emergency services within seconds prevented a major blaze. A total of 110 passengers and a member of the cabin crew died in the impact and the effects of the fire, and another passenger died later from injuries sustained in the impact. But an amazing 184 of those on board the stricken jet escaped with their lives, with only 46 of those suffering serious injuries. It was a tribute to the skill and courage of the pilots, who succeeded in coping with an appalling situation with the minimum of warning.

What had caused the catastrophic loss of control in such a routine manoeuvre, in perfect flying weather? During the long and careful approach to Sioux City, a member of the cabin crew had noticed damage to the aircraft's tailplane, and photographs taken by an eyewitness on the ground as the DC-10 made its final approach also showed holes in the leading edge of the starboard tailplane. Might these be linked to whatever had caused the tail-mounted engine to fail, at the start of the emergency?

When the investigators searched the wreckage, they found that all the aircraft systems seemed to have been working properly, apart from the central engine and the parts of the aircraft operated by the three hydraulic systems. There were some unexplained holes in the tail which appeared to have been caused before impact. They also found blades from the number two engine embedded in the tail, and this hinted at a break-up of the engine in flight as the primary cause of the crash. If the break-up had been sufficiently violent, fragments of the engine could have severed the hydraulic lines in all three systems, and deprived the crew of most of their control functions.

What could have caused the engine to fly apart? Jet engines are considerably more reliable than piston engines, and in most cases a failure results in damage being contained within the engine itself. Slowly and painstakingly the investigators collected the fragments of the centre engine, to reassemble it in a nearby hangar. The task was complicated by the fact that the shock of impact had torn the engine free of its mountings and sent it somersaulting down the runway. Nevertheless, it soon became clear that the engine was complete except for the absence of one major part. The engine's fan disk and its array of blades, apart from those broken off and found in the tail, were missing. If this had flown apart while the engine was running, centrifugal forces could have hurled fragments through the tail and broken the hydraulic lines.

Some of the missing engine components were found by farmers in the area immediately beneath the DC-10's position when the emergency had occurred. Only when the Iowa corn crop had been harvested, were the two large frag ments into which the disk had split finally revealed, however. When these were placed together, it was clear that a massive double fracture had been responsible for the disk flying apart, and when the broken surfaces were examined closely, they suggested the origin of the problem had been a long-standing fatigue crack inside the material of the disk itself.

When the fracture was analysed in the laboratory, it emerged that it had originated in a small defect in the titanium alloy ingot from which a batch of disks had been forged, possibly due to a reaction with atmospheric gases while the metal was cooling. When the ingot was sliced up into billets to make the disks, either the machining operations or the shot-peening treatment designed to harden the surface of the forging could have created an internal cavity. This would have led to cracks being opened up beneath the surface. When the disk was fitted into an engine, then operating loads would enlarge the cracks, to the point of the final and catastrophic failure. More worrying was the fact that none of the stringent and sophisticated checks during production, or during the operating life of the engine, had revealed the fault.

Three steps were taken to guard against the possibility of another accident like this being caused by a similar engine problem. The other engines which had disks manufactured from the same original ingot as the one which blew apart over the cornfields of Iowa were traced and checked, and the disks taken out of service. McDonnell Douglas introduced modifications to the DC-10 hydraulic systems including new sensors, valves and warning lights to ensure some hydraulic power would remain for the basic flight controls even if all the lines were severed by a similar engine break-up. Finally, the FAA called for new methods of inspection which could spot this type of weakness when the ingot was cast, or as the engine was put together.

Part of the shattered fan disc from the DC-10's centre engine which was later retrieved from an Iowa cornfield. (National Transportation Safety Board)

11

The threat in the hold

Over the years, one of the most difficult factors to eliminate in the interests of greater flying safety has been the action of the terrorist or saboteur. This remains a specially difficult crime to detect or to prevent, though security measures have improved out of all recognition during the three and a half decades since the first known successful sabotage of a commercial jet. This occurred on 22 May 1962, when a Continental Air Lines Boeing 707 was flying from Chicago to Kansas City on the first sector of a late evening service to Los Angeles, carrying 37 passengers and a total crew of eight. The aircraft was just over halfway on this sector, cruising at 37,000 feet over the prairies, and all seemed well after a series of course changes to keep clear of thunderstorm cells. Then the 707 disappeared, and all communications with the aircraft ceased.

The next morning, wreckage was found in a field five miles north-north-west of the town of Unionville in Missouri. All those on board had been killed, save one survivor who survived some 90 minutes after being found by rescuers. When the investigation team examined the wreckage, they found large parts of the aircraft were missing. Widening the search turned up a trail of fragments for 40 miles along the aircraft's track, with some smaller and lighter pieces as distant as 120 miles from the crash site.

Closer scrutiny revealed traces of explosive damage in panels next to a used-towels storage bin. This was located underneath the washbasin in the rear lavatory on the starboard side of the aircraft. The detonation of this bomb had not produced instant disaster though, as the flight crew were wearing oxygen masks. After the violent decompression the bomb must have caused, they had tried to bring the aircraft down to a lower altitude. The main landing gear was lowered, but in the end their actions had little effect.

The weakness in the rear fuselage structure caused by the bomb resulted in a large part of it, some 38 feet in length, separating from the rest of the aircraft at a high altitude. Deprived of the stabilising effect of the tail, the 707's nose had pitched downwards sharply. This caused stresses which tore away all four engines, the outer part of the starboard wing and most of the port wing in quick succession, leaving the remainder of the fuselage to plunge to earth with no control at all. No terrorist group claimed responsibility, and it was believed the bomb had actually been carried aboard by a passenger involved, deliberately or unwittingly, in an insurance fraud.

At least the wreckage had yielded up a wealth of evidence which enabled the investigators to determine what had happened. When a BEA Comet vanished into the sea off the Turkish coast in the early morning of 12 October 1967, there was almost no evidence at all. The aircraft was on a flight from London via Athens to Nicosia in Cyprus, and had been cruising normally at 29,000 feet. The weather was calm and clear, and the Comet had belied its tragic history to become a popular and reliable workhorse of the airline.

The aircraft had left Heathrow the previous evening with 38 passengers, three on the flight deck and four cabin crew. The flight had been straightforward, and the aircraft landed in Athens at 1.11 on the morning of the 12th. There six passengers left the aircraft, and another 27 new passengers joined the flight, making a total of 59 for the second sector to Nicosia. As the Comet took on more fuel, the baggage belonging to the passengers who had just joined the flight was loaded. It was placed with freight taken on board at Athens in holds 1 and 2, while the baggage and freight from London was still in holds 4 and 5.

The aircraft took off at just after 2.30 am. Later, a message from the Comet told air traffic control it had passed R19B, a reporting point on the route from Athens to Cyprus, at a height of 29,000 feet. At 2.58 am a northbound BEA Comet passed a thousand feet below it, and the crew of each aircraft saw the other clearly in the good visibility. Twenty minutes later, air traffic control at Nicosia received a message which gave the Comet's registration (G-ARCO) as its call sign. The message ran 'Bealine Golf Alpha Romeo Charlie Osc....' The message broke off abruptly, and nothing further was heard.

After the Comet was reported missing, the RAF base at Akrotiri on the southern coast of Cyprus sent up a search and rescue aircraft at 4.40 am, to patrol the area from which the last message had been received. The aircraft was flying at 1,000 feet above the sea when, at approximately 6.10 am, the crew spotted a 'kidney-shaped' fuel slick with floating bodies and two distinct areas of floating debris between a mile and a mile and a half apart. The smaller one was to the north, and the debris included blankets, inflated life jackets and floating seat cushions.

Ships were sent to the area to pick up bodies and any floating wreckage. It was already clear that the main wreckage on which the investigators would normally rely to explain how the crash had been caused was at the bottom of the sea. The seabed was more than a mile below the surface and far beyond the reach of any existing salvage gear. All that could be found were small items of floating debris, which seemed unlikely to reveal anything very significant.

Nevertheless, some clues began to emerge from the sparse evidence. One of the rescue vessels picked up six bodies from the southern sector of wreckage. A crew member noticed that they had all been soaked in aircraft fuel, even though there was no sign of burning. When the investigators examined the bodies from the northern area wreckage, there was no sign of fuel contamination at all. The later post-mortems showed that bodies differed in another important respect too. Those bodies which were contaminated by fuel were severely damaged, while the uncontaminated bodies were mainly intact. In neither case, the pathologists were surprised to find, were there any symptoms of explosive decompression injuries.

The investigators then started comparing the types of wreckage found in the two areas. In the northern area, less contaminated by fuel, they had found parts from the aircraft's forward toilet, a fire extinguisher bottle normally held in the centre section of the wing, and life-jackets stowed in the forward part of the cabin. In the southern area, they found mainly seat cushions, parts from the carpets and the galley and from other cabin furnishings. These were mixed together with personal belongings, handbags, life-jackets and three inflated life-cots of the type provided for small children.

The investigation team then turned for information to Athens airport, and two groups of people connected with the flight. The cabin crew who had been relieved for the final sector of the flight were asked about the seat positions of the passengers from London who had remained on board. The ground personnel who had allocated seats to the passengers that had joined at Athens were asked about which seats had been assigned to particular individuals.

The items of floating wreckage retrieved from the sea were sent back to Farnborough. There, they were laid out in the correct position on a full-scale floor plan of the aircraft, where investigators then made another significant discovery. All those items which had been in the forward section of the fuselage, ahead of the leading edge of the wing, were clean and uncontaminated by fuel. All those items which had been to the rear of the leading edge of the wing, were heavily contaminated.

This suggested that the forward part of the fuselage, which had not been contaminated by fuel, must have crashed where the northern part of the wreckage had been found. The rest of the aircraft structure, with the wings and fuel tanks, had probably hit the sea where the southern part of the wreckage remained on the surface. The second conclusion was that the aircraft must have split in two, at a point close to where the leading edge of the wing met the fuselage, well before it hit the sea. This was confirmed by the designers of the aircraft as the most likely point of failure, if the aircraft had been subjected to loads too strong for the structure to withstand.

The investigators then turned their attention to the distance separating the two groups of wreckage. This was too short for the break-up between the front and rear parts of the aircraft to have taken place at its cruising height of 29,000 feet. Instead, the separation must have occurred at around 15,000 feet, which implied that whatever had made the aircraft descend from its initial altitude had not caused it to break up immediately. This would certainly account for the pathologists' reports of the absence of any injuries to the victims indicating explosive decompression. If the break-up had happened at 29,000 feet, the signs on the bodies would have been unmistakable.

Even the fire-extinguisher bottle found in the northern area of wreckage had a small story to tell. It was discharged, and had probably been triggered by a system called the crash inertia switch. This must have happened before the Comet struck the sea, and could only have been caused by a violent shock to the aircraft.

The nature of that shock was revealed by some of the floating seat cushions. One of the cushions from the port side of the aircraft showed signs of explosive damage from below, while the seat had still been occupied. Postmortem examinations of the bodies revealed that one of the passengers had suffered injuries from the fragments of the bomb casing and also that this person had been sitting in the row behind the explosion, and in the centre seat of the row of three. This was the only body found to have explosive injuries. But seven bodies were never recovered, and one of those could well have been the occupant of the seat below which the bomb was detonated although the investigating team could not be precise about the individual seat where the explosive had been placed. The passenger whose body showed they had been close to the explosion had boarded the aircraft at Athens as part of a block booking, so they could have been sitting in one of five rows.

After checking the whereabouts of all known passengers on the seating plan, and the location of the passengers whose bodies had never been recovered,

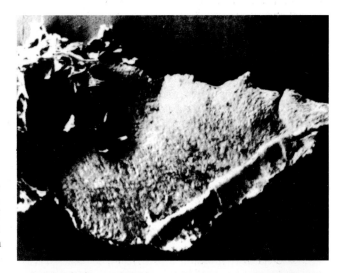

Comet seat fragment with damage to the foam upholstery showing that it had been exposed to explosives. (Reproduced by permission of ICAO)

'Gas wash effect', a characteristic sign of explosive damage, on a fragment from the Comet blown up over the Eastern Mediterranean. (Reproduced by permission of ICAO)

the investigators were able to narrow the site of the explosion down to seat 4A, 5A or 8A. Had it been seat 8A, this would have placed the explosive directly over fuel tanks which, at that stage of the flight, would have been full of highly inflammable vapour. This would probably have blown the plane apart at its cruising altitude. It was therefore almost certain that the explosive had been placed under seat 4A or 5A.

Because the watches worn by the passengers had stopped when they hit the sea, an average of the readings gave a time of the impact, which could then be compared with the time of the interrupted radio message received by Nicosia Air Traffic Control. The difference was almost seven minutes. This confirmed that the aircraft had remained mainly intact after the explosion, but had descended rapidly from its cruising altitude, probably out of control. At the time when its plunge reached 15,000 feet the denser air and the increasing loads on the airframe caused it to break apart into two main sections, which then plunged separately into the sea.

It was an almost incredible piece of deduction, from the sparsest of evidence. The only thing the investigators were unable to determine was who had placed the bomb, and why. A rumour that 'General' George Grivas, one-time leader of the EOKA terrorists on Cyprus, was due to board the flight might have been reason enough for his opponents to place the explosives on board. On the other hand, two of the doomed passengers had been found to carry unusually high insurance cover. In one case, this had been arranged just before the flight, so that fraud was another strong possibility.

But the most tragic terrorist action of all remains the placing of the bomb on the Pan American Boeing 747 bound from London Heathrow to New York JFK on the night of 21 December 1988. This was the second sector of a flight which had actually started in Frankfurt, though the first sector had been flown by a PanAm Boeing 727, which brought 109 passengers into London. A total of 49 of those were joining the exodus to spend Christmas in the USA, and so they were transferred to the 747 standing at the next pier, together with another 194 passengers starting their flight from London. The baggage of the Frankfurt to New York passengers was transferred from the 727, to join that already loaded for the passengers departing from London.

The 747 was cleared for departure at 6.4 pm, but air traffic delays meant it finally took off from runway 27 Right at 6.25 pm. It was cleared in stages to its final cruising height of 31,000 feet which it reached at 6.56 pm. Two minutes later, the first officer called Shanwick Oceanic Area Control for clearance for its transatlantic route to New York. At almost 7.3 pm, Shanwick called the 747 with details of its clearance, but there was no reply from the aircraft. At approximately the same time, its radar echo disappeared, to give way to multiple smaller echoes fanning out in a downwind direction.

Apart from those on board the 747, or watching its echo on ATC radar screens, the first people to be aware that something was wrong were the inhabitants of the small Scottish town of Lockerbie in the border county of Dumfries. Witnesses were appalled to see a blazing mass emitting a thunderous roar had embedded itself in the ground, creating a crater 15 feet deep in the north-eastern part of the town. This was the starboard inner engine of the 747. On the southern edge of the town, the main wing structure of the airliner produced an even bigger crater, before the vast amount of fuel in the wing tanks exploded in an immense fireball, spreading fires and rupturing gas mains over an area a quarter of a mile wide. Two houses were completely destroyed and tons of debris was blown across the main road linking Scotland with England, which runs just to the west of the town. So enormous was the impact of the crash that it registered 1.6 on the Richter scale, used to monitor earthquake shocks.

These were just the opening salvoes in a cannonade of wreckage to hit the area in quick succession. The other three engines of the 747 fell within Lockerbie's boundaries, while the rear section of fuselage fell on to a council estate just over a third of a mile from the initial impacts. This wreckage, together with the port engines and the starboard outer engine, formed the beginning of one of two wreckage trails stretching back to the east. It included more fragments from the rear fuselage, the wings and the tail of the aircraft.

Two and a half miles east of the town, searchers found the flight deck, still with the bodies of the crew strapped into their seats, and the front section of fuselage. This marked the start of a second southerly wreckage trail, which extended in a swathe right across northern Britain to the verge of the North Sea coast. All over the area of Lockerbie, smaller pieces of wreckage including baggage and letters from the mail containers carried on board the aircraft, together with bodies and fragments of bodies, made a terrible spectacle. In addition to the 259 people killed on board the aircraft, 11 local residents were killed in the rain of falling wreckage or the resulting explosions. Five more were injured. Twenty-one local homes had to be demolished, and many more needed major repairs.

The flight-deck of PanAm Boeing 747 blown up over Lockerbie. (Associated Press)

The team of investigators from the AAIB arrived the next day, aboard a special PanAm Boeing 727 which flew into Carlisle Airport. Their first target was the remains of the flight deck. It was clear that the damage to the aircraft structure showed no sign of corrosion or fatigue on a scale which could have caused the 747 to break up so catastrophically. When they checked the flight-deck controls, the settings were those for normal flight. There was no sign of the crew having taken any emergency action before death overcame them. Yet postmortems on the first of the passengers' bodies revealed lung damage which showed the aircraft must have broken apart at high altitude, confirming the length of both wreckage trails. As yet, though, there was no evidence at all of any injuries from explosives, on either the victims or the fragments of the aircraft structure.

Lockerbie two-dimensional crash reconstruction in Carlisle. (Reproduced courtesy of AAIB Crown copyright)

A model of the Boeing 747 blown up over Lockerbie showing the whereabouts of main groups of wreckage. (Reproduced courtesy of AAIB Crown copyright)

The next step was to collect as much as possible of the wreckage, and to try to piece it together to arrive at an explanation of how the 747 had broken up. The sheer magnitude of this task can be appreciated, as it involved more than four million fragments of debris, spread over an area of almost a thousand square miles of northern Britain. The pieces were taken to a reassembly site at an army ammunition depot near Carlisle. By the end of the investigation almost 90 per cent of the aircraft's structure had been collected and laid out in a two-dimensional reconstruction. Even as the evidence was being collected, some significant facts were emerging. For example, pieces from the rear cargo hold were scattered within the boundaries of the town, but their equivalents from the forward hold were spread for miles over the more southerly of the two trails of wreckage.

As the assembly took place, it became clear that the forward hold had held two cargo containers, one made of metal and the other of fibreglass, which did show damage by explosives. Closer study revealed that a bomb must have been detonated inside the metal container, and particles were blasted into the walls of the fibreglass container and into the adjacent skin panelling of the aircraft. One investigator even found a tiny portion of printed circuit board which had been forced into a wrinkle of the container panelling, which was traced to a Toshiba radio/tape cassette player. This must have contained the explosive, which was revealed to be the terrorists' favoured Semtex. It had been hidden in turn inside a brown suitcase loaded into the outboard portion of the container, next to the skin of the 747.

To discover what linked the detonation of the bomb to the break-up of the aircraft, the investigators decided to transport all the fragments from the part of the fuselage where the explosion had occurred down to the Royal Aircraft Establishment at Farnborough. There, a full three-dimensional reconstruction

The seat of the explosion – the bottom of the baggage container which contained the bomb on the Lockerbie Boeing 747. (Reproduced courtesy of AAIB Crown copyright)

The adjacent baggage container recovered from wreckage of the Lockerbie Boeing 747. (Reproduced courtesy of AAIB Crown copyright)

could be carried out, so they could determine the sequence by which the initial explosive damage had led to the 747 breaking apart. In the meantime, the CVR and FDR were retrieved and examined, as were the four engines from the airliner.

The three dimensional reconstruction of part of the Lockerbie Boeing 747 fuselage in the vicinity of the site of the explosion. (Reproduced courtesy of AAIB Crown copyright)

The recorder evidence was negative, in the sense that it showed the crew and the aircraft operating perfectly normally, except that the CVR revealed a loud noise just before the interruption of power stopped both recorders. This was almost certainly the sound of the bomb detonating in the port side forward baggage hold. The engines revealed more significant clues. The port inner engine, closest to the site of the explosion, had damaged fan blades. These were almost certainly distorted by the effect of blast from the explosion while the engine was delivering power.

Inside the engine air intake they found scratches and paint marks which were caused by cables which carried the curtains closing off the hold baggage containers. Nor was this all. The four engines all showed another kind of damage in common. This was caused by the blades rubbing against the fan cases, because of changes in direction of the airflow through the engines. The site and type of damage indicated the aircraft must have dropped its nose into a dive and rolled sharply to port soon after the explosion.

The reconstruction provided additional information on what had happened. It was clear from examining the patterns of breakages between different parts of the fuselage structure that the initial explosion had blown a small hole in the fuselage of the 747 low down on the port side, ahead of the leading edge of the wing. This had twisted the edges of the fuselage, which were then pulled back by the force of the slipstream with the aircraft travelling at more than 430 knots. This enlarged the hole, and started secondary cracks, which began lengthening to weaken the structure further.

In the meantime, though, part of the blast of the explosion was reflected back into the fuselage to cause secondary damage to other parts of the structure. All this led to a trail of debris falling away from the aircraft to form the longer, southernmost trail of wreckage across the countryside. Within seconds of the blast, the integrity of the forward fuselage had collapsed to the point where the fuselage was beginning to twist under the stresses of flight, applying loads to the control cables and causing the aircraft to fall into a dive and the roll to port revealed by the engine damage.

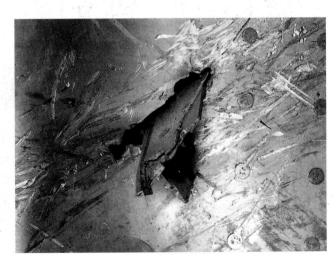

Part of the 747 fuselage panel close to the explosion site, with a fragment of wingtip embedded in it, showing it must have impacted against the wingtip as the forward fuselage broke up. (Reproduced courtesy of AAIB Crown copyright)

This turn was enough to tear away the nose section of the aircraft, which collided with the starboard inner engine, violently enough to cause that to separate from the aircraft too. The dive steepened until by the time the 747 had fallen through 12,000 feet it was plummeting vertically, and shedding more of its structure all the time. As it fell another 10,000 feet it progressively fell apart, creating the more compact northern trail of wreckage. The fin and rudder were torn away, which allowed the remaining part of the aircraft to yaw far enough to tear away the three remaining engines. The rear fuselage then fell away with the main landing gear, leaving the wing to crash on the town and cause the huge fireball. In just over a minute and a half, a one-kilo-gram charge of Semtex had destroyed a 300-ton airliner and killed 270 people.

Because this was a terrorist outrage rather than a failure of the aircraft or the air traffic control system, there was little more the air accident investigators could do. The responsibility for unravelling the full story fell on to their oppo-site numbers at the Royal Armament Research and Development Establishment, based near Sevenoaks in Kent. They assembled a series of Semtex charges in similar Toshiba cassette radios. These were packed in clothes in identical suitcases, and then detonated in identical luggage pallets to the one which had carried the fatal load on board the PanAm 747.

They then matched the damage to the pallet to that shown in the wreckage. This indicated that the case must have been loaded above the bottom layer of baggage in the pallet. This in turn meant it must have travelled to London from Frankfurt on board the Boeing 727, and then been transferred with the rest of the New York-bound bags.

The forensic specialists also managed to identify clothing fibres found in the fragments of the case which had held the explosive cassette radio. These were traced to articles which had been bought in Malta and flown to Frankfurt on the day of the flight, though no passenger on the London-bound 727 had been identified as coming from Malta. Police investigations later traced the purchase of the clothes to an unnamed Libyan. The inference was that the blowing up of an American airliner four days before Christmas was an act of revenge. A US Navy cruiser, the *Vincennes*, had shot down an Iran Air Airbus and its cargo of pilgrims over the Gulf four days before the Muslim festival of Id Al-Adha earlier that year.

The air safety organisations could do little to prevent a recurrence of this type of catastrophe. They recommended stricter checks on baggage loaded on to aircraft, and more stringent matching-up procedures between passengers and luggage, especially where transfers between flights were involved. More recently, new types of protection inside the aircraft to limit the damage caused by explosions have shown promising results. If these are widely adopted though, there is always the danger of terrorists switching to heavier explosive charges to do their deadly work. On the other hand, the larger the charge, the more likely it is to be detected by sophisticated devices like thermal neutron analysis detectors, and another 'Lockerbie' averted by greater vigilance.

12

Towards a
safer future

The first flight in a heavier-than-air machine took place almost a century ago. Over most of that time, aviation has made an enormous difference to the world, from the horror of war to the ideal of cheap, fast, long-distance and above all *safe* travel for people who, had they been born in earlier times, may never have journeyed beyond the boundaries of their homelands. But at the end of flight's first century, how safe has it become? And how much safer can it be made?

The story told is one of unceasing effort to build barriers against the workings of chance or carelessness, so that passengers and crews can take off, fly and land again without any of the systems on which they have to rely letting them down, with terrible consequences. From the design of the aircraft to the organisation of the ways in which they are built, tested, maintained and operated, from the manner in which they are controlled to the way in which accidents are investigated, explained and analysed, this work has one overriding objective. To make disasters less likely, less possible, less lethal with the passing of time. How successful has it been?

There is little doubt that the old dangers of flying have been virtually eliminated. As a given type of aircraft or engine continues in service, airlines gather a vast amount of data on the operating life of particular assemblies or components. Every mechanical and electronic factor involved in a modern aircraft is recorded on every flight, and downloaded into a computer on landing, or by radio while the flight is in progress. This enables maintenance engineers to spot a set of symptoms which, while innocuous in themselves, will show a pattern which may develop into a possible component failure in time. To prevent any danger of this happening, an apparently perfectly healthy engine may be changed on an aircraft on the other side of the world from its home base. Large aircraft like the 747 can carry a fifth engine beneath the wings to transport replacements to distant destinations, or to bring home power units for more complex repairs to be carried out.

Weather, too, is far less of a problem than it once was. Better weather radar systems, on the ground and on the flight-deck, give more precise warnings of thunderstorm cells and their associated windshear. Clear air-turbulence is better understood, so that aircraft can avoid it altogether, or fly through it with greater safety. Even windshear near the ground is less of a problem, since crews continually practise the most dangerous combinations of head-winds, tail-winds and downdraughts on take-off or final approach in the safety of the simulator.

Of all safety aids, the simulator has become one of the most important. Because of the increased accuracy with which simulators reproduce various emergencies, they can help crews practise coping with the losses of control systems, hydraulics or engines. Part of this accuracy extends to the background effects of the emergency. For example, today's simulators can reproduce the noise and vibration of an engine failure on take-off so pilots who have practised the correct recovery action have no problem in recognising the condition, and dealing with it, should it happen in reality.

Another progressively more effective safety aid is the autopilot system which, on the latest generation of airliners, can actually recognise the symptoms of windshear associated with microburst activity much faster than the most alert and experienced pilot. They can also carry out the right recovery action more quickly and more effectively, because they need no 'thinking time' to reverse the automatic actions of a flying lifetime, when dealing with these highly unusual meteorological challenges.

Increasingly crowded skies in the vicinity of airport terminal areas and at the intersections of busy air routes place higher pressure on controllers and pilots alike. New ATC equipment can detect potential conflicts early enough for remedial action to be taken. More airliners have been fitted with TCAS collision avoidance systems, to give their crews positive warning of another aircraft approaching dangerously close. TCAS reacts to the presence of any aircraft with an operating transponder. In the collisions covered in the book, it would almost certainly have provided the few moments' warning to enable the crews to take successful avoiding action, quite independently of the actions or the omissions of the air traffic control system.

Where pilot-error has been identified as one of the causal factors in an accident, particularly where the crews involved have been both skilled and experienced, a possible cause for concern in the past has been over-familiarity with the job. As more and more of a pilot's duties are taken over by computers, there is an increasing risk of boredom. On long-distance over-water routes, compulsory reporting points have been introduced to ensure a positive role for pilots in monitoring even the smoothest and most unruffled of flights.

The other positive measure is the additional training given to all pilots by the major airlines in what has become known as Cockpit Resource Management. This lays down a precise division of roles and responsibilities between the two pilots, depending on who is actually flying a particular sector. The objective is to eliminate the danger of both pilots making the false assumption that the other one is checking a vital detail of the procedure, and as a result leaving a potentially dangerous loophole.

In the meantime, increasingly computerised flight-decks call for even greater care and vigilance from the pilots. Where a computer can display checklists and monitor human commands, display important information on a VDU without needing to be asked for it, and take over the once time-consuming chore of navigation, it does call for a high level of precision in the information fed to it. In one case, entering the wrong descent information caused the computer to throttle back the engines at a critical stage of the approach. In another, the investigation

The glass cockpit of an Airbus A340 showing computer VDU displays. (Mark Wagner)

showed the crew might have entered descent information in the wrong units, producing a much faster descent rate, causing the aircraft to crash short of the runway.

For all the sophistication of present-day aircraft design, testing, maintenance and operation, three insidious threats still cause concern. The so-called geriatric jet problem involves older jets continuing in service beyond what was thought possible at the time of their introduction. In theory, there is no definite upper limit from a safety point of view, with regular safety checks to monitor any growth in corrosion or fatigue, and provided parts are replaced before failure. The RAF has recently upgraded its maritime reconnaissance aircraft, based on modified Comet fuselages dating back more than thirty years, and which have to cope with the much higher stresses and tighter operating margins of military flying!

However, as aircraft age, they need more and more spare parts to keep them going, and one of the most sinister developments in recent years has been the growth of the counterfeit parts trade. Particularly widespread in America, this is a business that relies on parts retrieved from damaged or crashed aircraft, or cheaper substitutes for proper parts, produced in backyard workshops and indistinguishable to the naked eye.

The *Sunday Times* cited a case where an American Airlines Boeing 757 crashed into a mountain in Columbia in December 1995. Before the wreckage could be analysed to determine the causes of the accident, parts were stolen and resold to unsuspecting aircraft operators. They included a total of 523 parts from the doomed airliner, from its engines to its landing gear, from its toilets to its Flight Data Recorder. In the case of parts which were not even genuine to begin with, the potential profits are enormous – a substitute bolt to help hold the engine pylon of the DC10 to the wing might cost 75 dollars, when the genuine article costs more than twenty times as much.

The main existing defence is the paperwork. Yet criminals have counterfeited the authorisation and inspection tags accompanying genuine parts. In 1989 a Danish Convair 580 broke up and crashed in the sea. The wreckage showed the fin had developed a fierce vibration causing the rudder to jam and the tail to collapse. The vibration had started because counterfeit bolts holding the fin to the fuselage structure had worn much faster than genuine bolts would have done. Those components had been bought through the normal market, with full documentation.

In the end, the only sure remedy is to subject replacement parts to the same strict checking as the aircraft themselves. Which brings the story full circle, back to the original problem identified with the Comets of the 1950s and still defying elimination today – fatigue. This needs constant attention, as so many aircraft manufacturing techniques can actually introduce fatigue. These include heat treatment and work hardening, drilling and riveting and fastening components together, quite apart from age-induced hardening. So no aircraft ever built will be completely free of all fatigue cracking. But identifying local areas of corrosion and fatigue cracks, and monitoring how quickly they grow, enable parts to be replaced or repaired in perfect safety.

One way of avoiding fatigue is to use more composite materials, with the ultimate goal of the plastic aeroplane. Because composites do not need drilling and riveting to fasten them together, they remove one common cause of fatigue cracking. Unfortunately they tend to absorb moisture into their structure as the aircraft climbs and descends through damp layers of air. This moisture freezes when the temperature drops and thaws again as conditions warm up, progressively weakening the material structure to failure point, as happened with part of Concorde's rudder assembly.

Here too the solution is to replace vital components before they become vulnerable. The RAF carry out local repairs to composite components like Harrier wings, where once they would have been thrown away. British Airways apply artificial intelligence to analysing data on these composite structures and, for example, the performance of the Concorde's engines and the RB211 power units of the 747–400. By developing neural networks to analyse complex patterns of behaviour, they can predict a problem and replace the components before an incident actually occurs.

Aircraft engineers can now use remote visual aids involving miniature digitised cameras and oil-filled fibre optics to scan the inside of engines without dismantling them, in a mechanical equivalent of non-invasive exploratory surgery. New optical methods can scan large surfaces and by accurate comparisons with previous scans, engineers can spot tell-tale signs of 'pillowing', where the surface swells because of hidden corrosion which can provide another source of fatigue. Computer-controlled lasers can target an individual bolt at long distance and show the pattern of stresses it carries when loaded.

As aircraft become more computer-controlled, more and more of that computer power will become available for monitoring aircraft systems and flagging up potential faults before they develop into failures. Information can be relayed from the aircraft to ground-based support services to give tomorrow's pilots the kind of back-up enjoyed by astronauts, with an open line to the experts at Mission Control.

If all this seems like a technological sledgehammer to crack a safety nut, then it's worth recalling that so many accidents, and causes of potential accidents, have been eliminated by the careful work of the accident investigators and the way in which their findings have been fed back into the system.

Yet the sad truth remains that in overlooking an apparently completely trivial item, these sophisticated defences may be rendered useless. For all its high technology and awesome performance, Concorde had the most enviable of safety records, until one terrible tragedy befell an Air France aircraft on the outskirts of Paris in July 2000.

Laden with passengers and fuel, the aircraft was accelerating down the runway at full take-off power when the heavily laden undercarriage ran over a piece of metallic debris which had dropped from an earlier aircraft using the same runway. It is clear that one of the tyres burst and was a major contributory factor in the disaster that followed. By the time the airliner lifted off the ground, flames were pouring from the two port engines, and there was little the pilot could do to save the situation. Lacking the time to turn round and land at Charles de Gaulle airport, he declared an emergency and was given clearance to try to reach the old Paris airfield of Le Bourget, a few miles away to the left of his heading.

Unfortunately the flames were too fierce, and time too short. Subsequent events including the fire caused the aircraft to be lost. The Concorde crashed into an airport hotel, killing all 109 people on board and another four on the ground. Air France's five remaining Concordes, and later the seven British Airways aircraft, were taken out of service, pending the investigation. As details of the cause of the disaster emerged, two measures were introduced. The simpler and more immediate was to keep closer watch on runway debris, with more frequent sweeps of the surface.

The more complex task was to ensure that even if runway debris did cause a tyre to burst, this catastrophe could not occur again. Modifications were made to the Concorde fuel tanks to protect them against flying fragments, and a new type of radial tyre was developed with a high-tech lining. This would be more resistant to foreign object damage and, in case of a burst, would break up into smaller and less deadly particles. A modified Concorde was subjected to ground and wind tunnel tests, and additional research to determine the effects of fuel system leaks on engine performance, particularly vital in the take-off phase, was conducted at the UK's Defence Evaluation and Research Agency (DERA) facility at Shoeburyness in Essex.

With these comprehensive and expensive modifications, Concorde is returned to passenger service in the autumn of 2001, but other areas of concern are still being explored at the time of writing. While the crash remains a tragedy, like all air accidents, the ensuing measures show the aviation system at its careful and painstaking best. A careful, detailed and impartial enquiry is followed by action to ensure that a particular type of accident cannot occur again for the same reasons. More than two hundred years ago, John Philpot Curran said 'the condition on which God has given liberty to man is eternal vigilance'. Safety, especially in flying, comes with the same price-tag.

Bibliography

Air Crash Detective,
Stephen Barlay, Hamish Hamilton, 1969.

Air Crash: the clues in the wreckage,
Fred Jones, W. H. Allen/Virgin Publishing, 1986.

Air Disaster (Volumes 1 and 2),
Macarthur Job, Aerospace Publications Pty Ltd (Australia)
1994 and 1996, distributed by Airlife Publishing.

Air Disasters,
Stanley Stewart, Ian Allan, 1986.

Air Travel how safe is it?
Laurie Taylor (editor), Blackwell Science, 1997.

Aviation Disasters,
David Gero, Patrick Stephens Limited, 1993.

Black Box: Why air safety is no accident,
Nicholas Faith, Boxtree, 1997.

Disaster in the Air,
Andrew Brookes, Ian Allan, 1992.

Flights to Disaster,
Andrew Brookes, Ian Allan, 1996.

Flying into Danger: The hidden facts about air safety,
Patrick Forman, Mandarin, 1991.

The Human Factor in Aircraft Accidents,
David Beaty, Secker and Warburg, 1969.

How safe is UK Airspace?
David Ogilvy, Haynes, 1989.

The ICAO Manual of Air Accident Investigation,
ICAO (Montreal), various editions.

I learned about flying from that,
Squadron Leader John Chapman and Lindsay Peacock,
RAF Benevolent Fund Enterprises Publishing, 1996.

It doesn't matter where you sit,
Fred McClement, Cassell, 1970.

Lockerbie,
David Johnston, Bloomsbury, 1989.

Unsafe at Any Height, John Godson,
Anthony Blond, 1970.

Various reports published on individual accidents by the AAIB in the UK
and by the NTSB in the USA.

Index

Figures in bold italics refer t illustrations.